W9-BPR-367

FORTUNE'S
FAVORITES

FORTUNE'S FAVORITES

PORTRAITS OF SOME
AMERICAN CORPORATIONS
AN ANTHOLOGY FROM
FORTUNE MAGAZINE

HD 2785
F74

Essay Index Reprint Series

ESSAY INDEX

90309

BOOKS FOR LIBRARIES PRESS
FREEPORT, NEW YORK

First Published 1931
Reprinted 1968

LIBRARY OF CONGRESS CATALOG CARD NUMBER:

68-20300

PRINTED IN THE UNITED STATES OF AMERICA

CONTENTS

WORLD'S BIGGEST CORPORATION

A Study of A. T. & T. Common Stock
The Central Fact is a Social Philosophy
Which One Type of Financial Mind is
Congenitally Unable to Grasp

AMERICAN TELEPHONE
AND
TELEGRAPH COMPANY

ᏳᏩᎧᏱ

ONE of America's dozen greatest industrialists was asked what stocks he would buy if he had $500,000 and no more to invest in common stocks.

"I would put," said he, "$200,000 in American Telephone & Telegraph. . . ."

It is such statements as this, repeated in modified form dozens of times daily, that justify the characterization of A. T. & T. as the premier stock of the entire U. S. If a small investor insists upon buying common stock, he is likely to be told: "A. T. & T." If a great capitalist finds himself with several hundred thousand to put away, he is likely to think, "Well, in the long run, I can't do better than A. T. & T." In short, it would seem that there is almost no investor in a great nation of investors for whom A. T. & T. is not appropriate.

This inquiry will concern itself with the almost universal favor in which the Telephone stock is held. For this favor presents an extraordinary paradox.

Let it be immediately insisted upon that the proper approach for a study of the Telephone company involves Telephone securities rather than Telephone telephones.

The telephones are there, of course—15,700,000 of them—and the owner of a share of Telephone stock is, from one standpoint, the owner of a fraction less than one telephone and its accessory plant. Neither have we the slightest intention of writing an A. T. & T. market letter and discussing at what figure one should make one's commitments and at what figure one should unmake them. It is the paradox, a financial curiosity and a sociological fundamental, with which we are concerned. Put in its simplest terms, the paradox is this: Wall Street likes the stock for a particular reason which the company says is absolutely invalid. Wall Street says that earnings of A. T. & T. would permit a higher dividend or that, at any rate, future earnings will ultimately necessitate a larger return to stockholders. The company says this simply is not so.

There can be no question of the sincerity of the company. It is committed to a policy of distributing excess profits not to stockholders in cash but to its public in service—a policy expressed time and again, most officially by President Walter Sherman Gifford, who said in 1927 at Dallas, Texas:

> It . . . would be contrary to sound policy for the management to earn speculative or large profits for distribution as "melons" or extra dividends. On the other hand, payments to stockholders limited to reasonable regular dividends with their right, as the business requires new money from time to time, to make further investments on favorable terms, are to the interest both of the telephone users and of the stockholders.
>
> Earnings must be sufficient to assure the best possible telephone service at all times and to assure the continued financial integrity of the business. . . . Earnings in excess of these requirements must either be spent for the enlargement and improvement of the service furnished or the rates charged for

the service must be reduced. This is fundamental in the policy of the management.

Note well the word "earnings." Mr. Gifford is dealing with fundamentals, not details. He pledges his company not to increase its earnings beyond the point of fair returns to stockholders, which point he considers already reached. Beyond a "fair return" Mr. Gifford pledges all profits to the public, *not* to the stockholders. In March, 1928, Mr. Gifford wrote his 1927 report to stockholders and repeated, almost in the same words, the gist of his Dallas message. And an official of the company, speaking at a Bell System conference in October, 1928, followed Mr. Gifford's platform through to its logical implication with the statement that:

> The emphasis we place is not upon giving the last possible cent to the stockholder as soon as we can get it to him. . . . A lawyer once phrased it that in the Bell System the public was the residuary legatee of all benefits, whereas in most businesses the stockholder was the residuary legatee of all benefits. That is an accurate description of our motives.

Now it is true that nearly all corporations—and particularly large corporations—are likely to mention their duties to their public, and it is especially true that a utility—and a very monopolistic utility—would be more than likely to make pronouncements concerning its social responsibility. But the flat statement that the public and not the stockholder is the "residuary legatee of all benefits" attacks the theory of private management in that theory's most tender portion. What is the function of a company's management, if it is not to make as much money as possible (and as soon as possible) for the stockholders? Who owns the company, including its excess profits, if not the stockholders? Wall Street values a stock in terms of earnings per share, more or less regardless of dividends per share. Wall Street always considers undistributed earnings as a barrel that will some day be tapped for the benefit of the corporate family. How, then, can the securities of a company which runs flatly counter to this investing tradition be more popular than the securities of companies which exhibit a whole-hearted devotion to split stock and extra dividends? According to the policy of the Telephone management, A. T. & T. common is essentially to be regarded not as a common stock, but as a bond with a high yield or as a preferred stock with a good yield. Yet during a period in which the investing public was extraordinarily common-stock minded (and with a strong bias toward common stocks in their more speculative aspects) Telephone stock rode buoyantly along on the wave of market inflation and was purchased by many an investor at prices which left him a return on his investment of approximately 3 per cent. Here, then, is a double contradiction. A privately owned corporation announces that its primary allegiance belongs to the people who buy its service instead of to the people who buy its stock. And after making—and reiterating—this announcement, it easily retains its position as the corporation with the most widely distributed securities in the world, its stockholders numbering more than 567,000, including a large portion of the investment trusts and capitalists of the U. S.

But before looking more closely into this apparently anomalous situation it is advisable to explain, briefly, what the American Telephone & Telegraph Co. is. No man has ever made more than a brief explanation. For one thing, a complete statement (besides defining electricity) would have to account for the 400,000 workers who spend their days and nights in Bell telephone service. Briefly, the Telephone company is a corporation lodged in its own conservatively impressive building on Broadway at Fulton. Just to the north, across Fulton Street, is St. Paul's Chapel, with its little cemetery which callous custom and obvious convenience have turned into a public park. If you are a Telephone man, your eyes are likely to travel farther afield and look toward West Street, where the ponderous tower of the New York Telephone Co. bulks up across a stretch of low buildings from which it rises like a medieval castle against the mean roofs of a village. Then you may realize that this building is only one example among thousands of telephone buildings throughout the country and that in this building and its companions more than 155,000 girls sit before switchboards and say "Thank you" over 65,000,000 times a day. Because only a fragment of the Telephone plant can be seen on any given occasion, it is difficult to visualize that plant as a unit. Yet if everything that the Telephone company calls *assets* were suddenly changed into gold, there would be three times as much of the precious metal as would result if everything that General Motors calls *assets* underwent the same Midas-like transformation. The Telephone business is the biggest business in the world. Almost the only comparison to it is that other and even more complete utility monopoly operated by the federal government and known as the U. S. Post Office.

In addition to being a giant, the Telephone company is an independent giant. It began life as a patent monopoly, like the Aluminum Co., and—also like the Aluminum Co. —might very well have come under the domination of one or another of its early backers. But there were no Mellons among the Bostonians who furnished its early capital, and except for an otherwise surprisingly large New England representation on its directorate, it has long outgrown its founders. Nor has any banking Jack climbed any financing bean-stalk to hew the giant down. The company has amicable relations with many bankers, including the House of Morgan, but no one has ever underwritten any of its stock issues and it sits under no golden thumb. In its formative stage in 1876 it tried to sell itself to Western Union, but the telegraph company (in what now appears as one of the major stupidities of modern economic history) did not think telephones worth $100,000 and so failed to make an investment which has now grown to be 42,000 times that. Even since that early day the Telephone company has stood on its own feet, and it has always grown bigger. Today with over 567,000 stockholders averaging about thirty-two shares each and not one holding more than seven-tenths of 1 per cent of the stock, the management of the company is responsible only to its board of directors, which is dominated by no bank, no *interest*, no controlling clique. It is important to remember this point in view of Mr. Gifford's resultant ability to practice what he preaches in the way of a fair return on invested funds.

And, finally, the Telephone company is nearly a monopoly. There are three major divisions in the telephone business. One is A. T. & T. One is the Bell System. One is Western Electric, Inc. To confuse them is possible but not excusable. A. T. & T. is partly a holding company, partly an operating company, partly an organization for research and for service. As an operating company, it operates the long lines. As a holding company, it owns approximately 93 per cent of the common stock of twenty-one operating telephone companies of the Bell System in the U. S. These companies are:

New England Telephone and Telegraph Company
Southern New England Telephone Company
New York Telephone Company
New Jersey Bell Telephone Company
Bell Telephone Company of Pennsylvania
Diamond State Telephone Company
Chesapeake and Potomac Telephone Company
Chesapeake and Potomac Telephone Co. of Baltimore City
Chesapeake and Potomac Telephone Co. of Virginia
Chesapeake and Potomac Telephone Co. of West Virginia
Southern Bell Telephone and Telegraph Company
Ohio Bell Telephone Company
Cincinnati and Suburban Bell Telephone Company
Michigan Bell Telephone Company
Indiana Bell Telephone Company
Wisconsin Telephone Company
Illinois Bell Telephone Company
Northwestern Bell Telephone Company
Southwestern Bell Telephone Company
Mountain States Telephone and Telegraph Company
Pacific Telephone and Telegraph Company

It owns a little over one fourth interest in the Bell Telephone Company of Canada and a half interest in the company owning the telephone cable from Key West to Cuba. The A. T. & T. also owns 98.3 per cent of the Western Electric Company, the manufacturing end of the Bell System, and the A. T. & T. and the Western Electric jointly own the Bell Telephone Laboratories, the research end of the Bell System.

The people of the U. S. do their telephoning on 20,200,-000 telephones. Of these instruments, 15,700,000 belong to the Bell System and are called Bell System telephones. There are 4,400,000 telephones belonging to *connecting* companies. A connecting company is a company which does not belong financially to the Bell System, but whose lines are connected to the Bell lines and whose subscribers depend upon Bell facilities for long-distance telephoning. The remaining 100,000 telephones belong to *competing* companies in which the Bell System has no financial interest and with which it has no physical connections. The Bell System therefore controls more than 75 per cent of U. S. telephones. Its percentage of the telephone business, however, is much higher. In the first place, it has most of the telephoning in the larger cities. In the second place, it has most of the long-distance (also of transoceanic) telephoning. The Bell System within the area it serves is essentially a monopoly and makes no bones about its position as such. On the other hand, it is not an unregulated monopoly. There are forty-five state public service commissions (all states except Texas, Delaware, and Iowa) and the Interstate Commerce Commission, all with jurisdiction over telephone rates. The rates charged by the various telephone companies are subject to the approval of these commissions except that should any commission impose a rate which the Telephone company should consider confiscatory, the Telephone company has the right to bring its case to the U. S. Supreme Court and there argue it on the confiscation basis. Because American industry is operated primarily on the theory that reasonable prices are guaranteed as the result of free competition between relative equals, an industry (such as the telephone industry) which is a natural monopoly and in which regulation must substitute for competition is inescapably regarded with a certain suspicion. The Telephone company on the whole enjoys a better popular reputation than the light and power utilities and a good deal better reputation than most of the transportation utilities. Yet the regulated position in which Mr. Gifford finds himself must always be kept in mind as one of the factors which contribute to his profit-making restraint.

Belonging 98.3 per cent to A. T. & T., but sponsoring no telephone conversations, is Western Electric, Inc., which attends to the manufacturing end of the telephone industry. It is obviously necessary that someone should make the telephones with which the nation's telephoning is done, and it is obviously advantageous for the company which uses the telephones to control the company which makes them. Because the Western Electric statements are not included in the consolidated reports of the Bell System, because Western Electric is a manufacturing company (and therefore not subject to utility commissions), and because Western Electric (through Electrical Research Products, a wholly owned subsidiary) carries on a non-telephone business—chiefly the distribution of talking motion-picture mechanisms—there is a strong tendency to regard Western Electric as the rabbit in the Telephone company's hat. Into this Western Electric *mystery* we shall inquire below; meanwhile it should be remembered that although Western Electric is certainly a very large company (probably few people realize that its annual sales are about the same as those of General Electric), the bulk of its business does lie in the manufacture of telephone equipment and about 90 per cent of its business is done with Bell companies. Operating telephone companies are not compelled to buy their instruments from Western Electric, but they do buy such instruments as a matter of usual practice. So do many of the connecting companies. If, therefore, Western Electric is regarded not as a side show or as a bypath, but as the vital and intimate manufacturing end of the telephone business, such an outlook cannot be accused of much astigmatism.

We have, then, the A. T. & T. as parent company, service and research organization, and financial headquarters of the telephone industry. We have the twenty-one operating companies and the A. T. & T. in its operating function (the long-distance lines) as the operating division of the Bell System. And we have Western Electric as its manufacturing division. Such, in very broad outline, is the organization of what has already been noted as the world's greatest business.

Now since the purchaser of A. T. & T. stock has, for all practical purposes, purchased an interest in the Bell System as well, including Western Electric, he has unquestionably identified himself with the No. 1 corporation of the universe and is entitled to whatever sentimental overtones such an association may bring him. Remembering, however, the Telephone platform of *no extras*, let us become momentarily mathematical and see what the Telephone investor's return may be in actual dollars and cents. Suppose that the investor bought 100 shares of Telephone stock in February 1931, and paid for it $200 a share. The regular dividend of the Telephone company is $9.00 a share. That dividend stood at $8.00 from 1906 until 1921. In the second quarter of 1921, when Telephone stock was having some difficulty in maintaining its par of $100, the dividend was raised to $9.00. Since the stock's 1930 low of 170 was 70 points above par, the par problem appears definitely to have disappeared, and with it the necessity for raising the $9.00 dividend. Simple arithmetic demonstrates that $9.00 on $200 amounts to $4\frac{1}{2}$ per cent.

But, of course, Telephone stock is not a $4\frac{1}{2}$ per cent investment. Nearly all corporations from time to time offer to their stockholders opportunities to purchase new stock at a price considerably below the market. With the Telephone company such opportunities are a basic financing method and can be counted upon to recur at frequent intervals. In 1922, 1924, 1926, 1928, and 1930 holders of Telephone stock were offered additional stock at the par value of $100, which was anywhere from 25 to 100 points below market. The first two of these offerings were made on the basis that the stockholder could purchase one new share for each five shares already held, and the last three were made on the basis of one new share for each six shares already held. From an official A. T. & T. standpoint these subscription offerings were not at all in the nature of gifts, but they were very much in the nature of assessments, because, from this same standpoint, a share of A. T. & T. stock is always dealt in at its par value and the stockholders were simply being requested to make a further monetary contribution to their corporation. From the investor's standpoint, however, the fact that Wall Street values A. T. & T. stock not at $100 but at $200 of course means that the A. T. & T. stockholder is given the privilege of adding to his holdings at a price very much below the market and that with the exercise of every such privilege his return on his investment is increasing over its original $4\frac{1}{2}$ per cent.

The question of how much more than $4\frac{1}{2}$ per cent the Telephone investor gets by reason of his frequent opportunities to make an additional purchase at 9 per cent is somewhat obscured by the fact that what might be termed the speculative position on A. T. & T. is a good deal more concerned with Telephone earnings than with telephone stock subscriptions. On the other hand, inasmuch as the exercise of these opportunities to buy stock at par is a very important item in the return which the telephone investors secure, it is advisable to consider, very briefly, how much the investor should value the subscription feature of his stock.

Suppose that the investor with 100 shares exercises his subscription rights at a one to six ratio and therefore (in even numbers) buys seventeen new shares at $100. When another one to six offering happens along, he now has 117 shares and so gets not seventeen but nineteen additional shares. If he gets a chance to keep on compounding his holdings every other year, and at the same ratio, in ten years (or five offerings) he will have bought 117 new shares at $100 and will have paid $11,700 for them. Adding his new shares to his original 100 shares (which he bought at $200 and which cost him $20,000) he will have a total of 217 shares on which he will get $9.00 a share dividends. His return will be $1,953, which is slightly over 6 per cent on his total investment ($31,700). At the end of five offerings (ten years), therefore, the investor has a 6 per cent investment and has more than doubled his holdings. And in subsequent years both the return and the shares increase, the ratio of income to investment slowly approaching a 9 per cent millennium, which, however, it cannot quite reach even at infinity.

It should be parenthetically noted, however, that the investor with rights to buy additional shares at par can sell his right to buy new shares while retaining his old, and that this possibility opens up several more or less speculative methods of juggling rights to get the largest immediate return. Assume that the subscription privilege is usually set as to make the rights worth $20, the man with 100 shares can sell his rights for $2,000, add this to his $900 dividends and show for his $20,000 investment a return of $2,900 or $14\frac{1}{2}$ per cent. But, of course, he will always have only his original 100 shares and on years in which no rights are offered he will never make more than $4\frac{1}{2}$ per cent. Should rights worth $20 be offered every other year, and should he always sell them and bank the money, his investment would net him an average of $9\frac{1}{2}$ per cent per annum. But his number of shares does not increase, his percentage of ownership of the company decreases, and a slump in the market of course reduces the selling price of his rights. It is also possible to sell rights and to buy additional shares with the money so obtained. This system has the advantage of increasing the number of shares without increasing the capital investment; on the other hand the shares increase slowly and the speculative element of the market price again becomes prominent. On the whole, the investor who continually exercises his rights builds up his holdings so much more rapidly than by any other method that his system is not only the safest but, in the long run, probably the most profitable. And it is certainly the system recommended by the Telephone company and practiced by the majority of telephone stockholders.

It is probable, however, that a good many purchasers of Telephone stock and an even larger percentage of those who advise others to purchase Telephone stock have their eyes fixed mainly on the earnings-per-share of the Telephone company. A. T. & T. itself (as distinct from the Bell System) reported 1930 earnings of $10.44 a share. But the per share earnings of the Bell System itself were somewhat larger, since most of the subsidiary companies in addition to paying A. T. & T. a dividend retained some of their earnings to put into their own surplus. If, for instance, a wholly owned subsidiary made $10,000,000 and paid $9,-000,000 in dividends, there would remain $1,000,000 which would not show in the earnings-per-share of A. T. & T. With twenty-odd companies each annually earning a surplus in excess of dividends, it is obvious that the combined surplus of the entire System would, over a period of years, run into very large figures and also that these figures would not appear in the A. T. & T. report. From this situation has arisen the theory that the Telephone company is "really" making "a lot more money" than it "shows," and the inference that in buying A. T. & T. stock one is buying a share in a great profit reservoir which will some day burst its confines and rush out in a golden flood. "The Telephone company reports $10.44," says the knowing investor, "but it actually makes at least $13, and while perhaps it could not pay more than $9.00 on $10.44, it can certainly pay more than $9.00 on $13. And the longer they keep on paying only $9.00, in dividends, the bigger the melon that we, the stockholders, will some day cut."

It is, of course, true that the $10.44 reported by the Telephone company does not represent the System's earnings per share. But this theory, popular in Wall Street in 1929, that earnings, if completely consolidated, would substantially increase the reported per share figure was knocked somewhat askew when the 1930 report gave—for the first time—these figures. Telephone's share of undistributed earnings of subsidiaries, it announced, amounted to about $10,000,000. This was 63 cents a share. Moreover, the idea that the Telephone company is running up a big hidden surplus in Western Electric conflicts violently with the fact that Western Electric last year paid $23,500,000 in dividends against reported earnings of only $15,625,000, thereby reducing its surplus to a negligible $7,000,000.

Furthermore—and this is the most vital point—the Telephone company, cheerfully conceding earnings over a period of years to be considerably in excess of dividend payments (it averages about $2.80 per share reported over the past five years), says that it needs the difference in its surplus, that it cannot and will not pay out a nickel more in dividends, and that *anybody who thinks he could run the telephone company and pay more than $9.00 without injuring the value of the investment does not know what he is talking about.* It says that it considers that its stockholders are *at present* getting a very equitable return on their investment, and the fact that these stockholders are being well treated is conclusively shown by the fact that the Telephone company has not the slightest difficulty in raising funds by selling stock. The Telephone company did not (and could not) say that it would never pay more than $9.00 for its regular dividend, but it certainly left the strongest of inferences that since, under the present conditions, it continues to attract additional capital sufficient for its growth, it has not the least intention of giving its stockholders more than they *at present* are receiving. If, then, it is pointed out that a security with virtually a fixed yield is essentially a bond or a preferred stock, whether it is called a common stock or not, the Telephone company enthusiastically agrees with this analysis and says it is more than happy to have its common stock regarded as primarily a high-grade bond. The arithmetic of $59 earned in the 1925–1930 period minus $45 paid out equals $14 melon may be very compelling to the investor. But the Telephone company says it needs the surplus represented by the $14 difference, and so there is no melon, and, most fundamental of all, *even if there were a melon, the only cutting would be a cutting of telephone rates or an improvement in service.* Of course, if this $14 retained by the company earns at the rate of 7 per cent, and the amount retained averages $2.80 per share over a period of years, eventually the return to the stockholder is bound to increase. But that eventuality is some years off.

There remains one last refuge for the bull speculator in Telephone stock. He may argue that, narrow-minded as the Telephone company may be with reference to its *utility* earnings, it might at least be a bit more liberal with its *non-utility* earnings. The Telephone company has in Electrical Research Products, Inc. (a wholly owned subsidiary of Western Electric), a corporation engaged in activities which do not apply to the telephone and are a strictly private manufacturing enterprise. Most obvious of these activities is the talking-picture machinery, handling of which Electrical Research has taken over from Western Electric. Most discussed of these activities is television (developed jointly with Bell Telephone Laboratories, Inc.), which has provoked many rosy prophecies and has also frightened the cinema people. Least heard of, but perhaps most immediately practical, is a sort of wired-wireless device for telephone broadcasting, by which, roughly speaking, the telephone owner could get a radio program over his telephone. Now what, says the speculator, would prevent the Telephone company from segregating these non-telephone businesses, either under Electrical Research or some new company, and getting out a big stock offering in which holders of Telephone stock would probably get a preferential treatment and from which they could draw dividends diluted by no complex of social responsibility?

To all of which the Telephone company replies that it considers itself in the telephone business, that it considers the profits derived from any non-telephone business as a part of what goes into the Telephone pot, and that any such profits, no matter how large, will be distributed on the same basis as if they were a result of telephone operation. In 1925, for example, Western Electric sold its foreign properties and in 1927 paid to A. T. & T. an extra dividend of $47,000,000. Here was a non-recurring, non-telephone profit, exactly the type of profit that could most readily be regarded as a bonus and distributed as such. But there was no distribution. The Telephone company in 1927 paid its regular $9.00 dividend, put the $47,000,000 into its surplus, and used it to run the telephone business. And in its 1929 report, the Telephone company went out of its way to

Age.—June 2, 1875, the first telephone conversation over electric wire took place between Alexander Graham Bell and Thomas A. Watson. In 1877 Somerville and Boston were connected by one telephone wire.

Most critical age.—Not until litigation with Western Union, culminating in the famous settlement of 1879, was the patent protection of the Bell System assured. This made it possible for the American telephone system to develop monopolistically.

Present fortune.—Assets—$5,000,000,000; debts—$1,115,-000,000; reserves—$823,000,000; net worth—$2,856,000,000.

Present income.—Receipts $1,151,000,000
             Expenses   883,000,000
             Interest   66,000,000
             Profit   202,000,000

Source of income.—15,700,000 phones owned; 4,400,000 phones connecting in this country. Dividends from Western Electric and investments in Canada and in certain connecting companies.

Offspring.—(1) Western Electric Company with total sales of $361,000,000 in 1930, profits on these sales of $15,600,000.

(2) International Western Electric, to the loss of which the parent Western Electric was reconciled in 1925 through a payment of some $30,000,000 by its near cousin, International Telephone and Telegraph.

(3) Electrical Research Products organized in 1926 for participation in sound and radio developments.

(4) Graybar Electric Company, wholly owned subsidiary of Western Electric Company, largely non-telephone equipment, sold in 1928 to its employees.

Annoyance.—Rumors of stock split-ups, distribution of Western Electric and Electrical Research Products stock to its own stockholders.

Mature philosophy.—The public is the residuary legatee of of all profits above a fair return to stockholders.

discourage bullish interpretations of non-telephone activities by stating that although the business of Electrical Research was important in its own field, "its earnings obviously cannot be a material factor in an enterprise of the size of the Bell System." It is the policy of the company that all income is telephone income and, as such, subject to distributive restraint.

The persistence with which the Telephone company is regarded as holding back money which it will ultimately divide among its shareholders is simply an inability to grasp its way of looking at its business. Certainly such an inability emphatically exists in Wall Street. Explain to almost any professional investor the Telephone philosophy concerning the public as residuary legatee, and he will look at you with blank disbelief. Indeed, he feels sorry for anyone who can be so easily taken in. That a company can exist on any other basis than the making of the greatest and most immediate profit is a proposition which the speculative mind is congenitally unable to grasp.

Yet, from a broader standpoint than the excited individualism of a bull market, it is not so strange a proposition. As large corporations reach the point at which their management becomes virtually independent of their stockholders, it becomes possible for that management to take thought of itself in its institutional aspects. It is particularly true that a great and monopolistic utility such as the Telephone company may consider public opinion at least as important as stockholders' opinion. Mr. Gifford and his associates have been in the utility business for a long time. They have also been, for a long time, prosperous and powerful. If they give an investment return which is not sensational, they give also a return which is steady and sure. They have had the leisure to wipe the corporate sweat from their brows and consider themselves as a public institution as well as private enterprise. They can take a Main Street rather than a Wall Street attitude. It is possible for private capital to become social minded. The Bank of England, for example, is privately owned, yet the Governor of the Bank of England probably thinks more often of public welfare than of private profit. The Telephone company has not been a public institution for as long as the Bank of England. It is, however, one of the most seasoned of American utilities and certainly the greatest. There is no other company that could more appropriately regard the public as the residuary legatee of its benefits, and no other company that has acted on the belief that giving this consideration to the public is the best service for its stockholders in the long run. That the Telephone company does so regard its public is a statement which no one is compelled to believe. It is also a statement which it would be presumptuous for anyone to deny.

A. T. & T.'S
BOARD OF DIRECTORS

The outstanding characteristic of a director is that he does not direct. He represents. He may represent, individually, stock ownership or financial backing or management or general respectability or what not. But taking him and his fellows together as a unit—as a board—he represents the character of his corporation. He is partly a mirror in which the corporate character may be reflected to the general eye. But like the sundial that numbers only happy hours, he must also be a mirror that reflects only a true picture. He must guarantee as well as illustrate the integrity of his corporation. The standing of any business can be only as high as the calibre of its directorate. The presence of a Kuhn, Loeb partner on the board of Paramount, for instance, is as indicative as the absence of a great financial name on the board of the old Fox Films. A company is known by the directorate it keeps.

And the directorate of the Telephone company does excellently hold up the mirror to the Telephone nature. It includes a strong representation from the New England group by whom the company was originally founded. It includes an excellent selection from our more notable financial intelligences. And—as a great utility should—it includes a very marked percentage of public service coupled with a noticeable leaning toward what might be termed an aristocratic liberalism. These qualities are, of course, not mutually exclusive, and the Telephone directors are not to be labeled in precise and water-tight compartments. As a group, however, they do suggest the mingling of three major traditions—a New England tradition of family, a Wall Street tradition of finance, and a public service tradition compounded partly of war-time service and partly of Wilsonian democracy.

Among the New Englanders, William Cameron Forbes, who was director until August, 1930, is perhaps most typical. His father was Colonel William Hathaway Forbes, president of the National Bell Telephone Co., A. T. & T. predecessor. His mother was Edith Emerson, daughter of

Ralph Waldo Emerson. Among his Harvard classmates (1892) were Thomas Lamont, Morgan partner; Arthur Woods, one-time N. Y. Police Commissioner; Jeremiah Smith Jr., fellow Telephone director and one-time financial savior of Hungary. Among his friends are Edwin Sibley Webster, of Stone & Webster; Fred Rice, of Rice & Hutchins (shoes); Harold Keith, of Walkover (shoes); H. Wendell Endicott, of Endicott-Johnson (shoes); Bradley Palmer, of United Fruit. At Naushon, off the Massachusetts coast, he has an island empire. He served in the Philippines under William Howard Taft, was Governor-General of the islands from 1909 to 1913, and here represents no liberal tradition. As Philippine mementos, however, he cherishes a dagger presented him by Aguinaldo and a sort of plaque (also a presentation) constituting a map of the Philippine region in which the ocean is made of silver, the islands are made of gold, and the civic improvements of his administration are picked out in glittering jewels. Over sixty, Mr. Forbes is active at yachting, at shooting, and at polo (he has a private field on his Westwood, Massachusetts, estate). In 1930, however, he again traveled far to the East on his country's business, for President Hoover appointed him Ambassador to Japan, and he resigned his directorate.

Another director partly by inheritance is Philip Stockton, whose father, Howard S. Stockton, was Bell president from 1887 to 1889. Yet Mr. Stockton's position could not be considered purely dynastic. In his own right he is one of New England's two or three most able bankers, was for many years president of the Old Colony Trust Company. When Old Colony and First National (directed by Daniel

Gould Wing, New England's outstanding banker) were combined, Mr. Stockton became president (Mr. Wing remaining chairman of the board) of the united institution. He is reputed to belong to more clubs than any other Bostonian, and probably to more directorates, including the boards of Gillette Safety Razor, Campbell Soup, General Electric, American Sugar Refining, and International Paper & Power.

Other Telephone New Englanders include Arthur Lyman, one-time mayor of Waltham and long a financial pillar for the Massachusetts Democratic Party (he was state treasurer in the 1928 campaign that carried Massachusetts for Alfred Emanuel Smith). Mr. Lyman married a Cabot, and his father married a Lowell. On his Waltham estate camellias blossom in February (here was built one of the first U. S. greenhouses), plows are still drawn by oxen, and there is an ancestral manor in which Washington and Lafayette are reputed to have slept.

There is also George Peabody Gardner, perhaps wealthiest of the Boston contingent. Mr. Gardner gave Boston its aquarium, and a boulevard in South Boston is named in his honor. He is past seventy-five, owned Telephone stock even before the company moved to Manhattan, and still comes regularly to Telephone meetings. And not to be forgotten are Henry Saltonstall Howe, who is an octogenarian and whose family was among the earliest Telephone investors, or Eugene V. R. Thayer, who was once president of the Chase Bank and is now chairman of the executive committee of the (Dawes) Central Trust Company of Illinois. It is a long time since the New England group who furnished the early capital for the Yankee toy that Alexander Graham Bell invented at Boston, Massachusetts, have controlled the Telephone company, but many an able son of an able father has continued its influence.

The difficulty of drawing hard and fast Telephone classifications is illustrated by the fact that two of its most distinguished public servants are also New Englanders of the rockiest rib. They are Thomas Nelson Perkins and Jeremiah (Jere) Smith Jr. Mr. Perkins was counsel for the War Industries Board (of which Daniel Willard was chairman), later accompanied Colonel House to Europe, and served on many War and post-War commissions, acting as alternate for Owen D. Young on the commission which last year produced the Young Plan. He was a Fellow of Harvard at twenty-five (youngest ever), but frequently shocked the other Fellows by his slang and profanity, the late great President Eliot once asking to have some of his remarks repeated in the English language. He married a daughter of the late Charles Francis Adams, is a member of a Boston law firm to which Archibald Graustein of International Paper & Power also belongs, is chairman of the board of the Boston and Maine Railroad. He was best man at the wedding of Nicholas Longworth and Alice Roosevelt. He is a hero-worshiper with Owen D. Young as chief hero.

Jeremiah Smith Jr. is one of the few Democrats from New Hampshire and doubtless the only Telephone director who could not by any stretch of the imagination be considered a man of means. He was little heard of until, in 1924, the League of Nations having loaned (via the House of Morgan) $50,000,000 to bankrupt Hungary, put into his hands the administration of this money and made him complete dictator of Hungarian finances. In a two-year period Mr. Smith straightened out the terribly inflated financial structure of a poverty-stricken people, refused to accept a $100,000 salary to which he was entitled, told grateful Hungarians that "If you give me a decoration I will never forgive you," declined proffered degrees from Harvard and from Yale, and left Hungary with nearly half of the $50,-000,000 still unspent. The $100,000 which he refused to accept is now being used as a scholarship fund to send picked Hungarians to American colleges.

From the Telephone standpoint Director Daniel Willard, great railroader, is considered primarily a great public servant. He was associated with Mr. Gifford on the Council of National Defense, and his telephone directorate is the only board position he holds apart from his railroad and banking activities. And Mr. Gifford, in turn, is associated with Mr. Willard as trustee of Johns Hopkins University. Other Telephone public servants are John W. Davis, onetime (1918–21) Ambassador to the Court of St. James's, and David Franklin Houston, Secretary first of Agriculture, then of the Treasury, in Mr. Wilson's cabinets. At the close of the Wilson administrations, Mr. Houston joined the Telephone company, heading the then (1921) newly formed securities company which has so successfully devoted itself to the wide distribution of Telephone stock. No longer a Telephone director, but certainly a public servant, is Owen J. Roberts, prosecutor of petroleum connivers, who resigned his Telephone position to join the U. S. Supreme Court. Added to the board in 1930 were Winthrop W. Aldrich, generally conceded as representing the Rockefeller and Chase National Bank interests and Hale Holden, chairman of the executive committee of the Southern Pacific Company; and in 1931, Samuel A. Weldon, vice-president and cashier of the First National Bank, was elected to succeed the late George F. Baker.

Of the dominantly financial membership of the A. T. & T. board, the late George Fisher Baker was of course most representative. Many years ago, on Jekyl Island, Mr. Baker used to gather around him a little group of men who symbolized all that was most powerful in American finance. That group (of which Mr. Baker was the last survivor) included J. Pierpont Morgan, James Stillman, and James J. Hill. It also included Theodore N. Vail, the man who took the Telephone company when it was little more than a promise and only left it when it was a little less than a monopoly. To his last day the Telephone company and the U. S. Steel Corporation remained the companies in which Mr. Baker took his most active interest. Since 1924 Mr. George F. Baker Jr. sat on the Telephone board. James Strange Alexander, retired chairman of the board of the Guaranty Trust; Edward Eugene Loomis, of the Lehigh Railroad, Mr. Baker's most intimate friend; and Myron Charles Taylor, of U. S. Steel, are other great names which are great Telephone names as well.

Lone operating executives on the Telephone board are Vice President Charles Proctor Cooper and President Walter Sherman Gifford. Mr. Cooper, who rose from the New York Telephone Co. ranks to the presidency of the Ohio Bell Telephone Co., is chiefly an alternate for Mr. Gifford, representing the management in his superior's absence. The Telephone company has 9 vice presidents against 19 directors, but purposely restricts its management directorate so as not to confuse the Board's position as an advisory council with that of a super-executive committee.

As for Mr. Gifford, it is difficult to consider him as a director without considering him as the president, yet any adequate consideration of this latter function should demand a separate and more extended treatment. Even if he were not a director *ex officio*, he exhibits the usual qualifications, for he was born in Salem, he graduated from Harvard (along with Clarence Dillon), and during the War ably supervised the handling of many millions of dollars in the purchase of government supplies. Familiar enough is the story of how, after his graduation (1905), he asked both General Electric of Schenectady and Western Electric of Chicago for jobs, put the General Electric letter in the Western Electric envelope, and vice versa, but got the Western Electric job anyhow and began his career at $10 a week. It was only twenty years later that he was Telephone president, at a salary reputed then to be $200,000 a year. Other men, however, have risen as rapidly as Mr. Gifford and from beginnings at least as humble. The most significant contribution that Mr. Gifford has made, not only to the Telephone company but to contemporary economic thought, has been his statement concerning the profit policy of his company. This country is crowded with corporation presidents whose corporations are making a great deal of money. Even the $200,000,000 a year which Mr. Gifford's company makes can be partially explained on the theory that under our present system some company is bound to make $200,000,000 just as some company is bound to build a skyscraper with 100 stories. What is unusual, obviously, is the corporation sufficiently self-conscious and social-conscious to believe that the position of corporations as purely acquisitive mechanisms will probably become more and more questioned. In saying, at Dallas, that the Telephone company would return excess profits to the users of its service, Mr. Gifford raised a far-reaching and fundamental issue. Whether one considers that the operations of the Telephone company are a settlement of that issue is at present beside the point. For even the statement of the proposition is new and is significant. From a superficial standpoint, Mr. Gifford is perhaps most remarkable as head of our first $5,000,000,000 company. From a more basic standpoint, he is perhaps most remarkable as the man who made the Dallas speech.

BUTCHER FOR
TWENTY MILLIONS

*The Packer Does More for Less Money
Than Any Other Industrialist. Herein
His Business is Described With Special
Reference to Pigs and to Swift & Co.,
Which has Entered the Billion-dollar
Class*

SWIFT AND COMPANY

SWIFT & COMPANY, butcher for 20,000,000 persons, buys no raw materials. Its cattle, its sheep and its hogs are finished products. Year after year it spends some $500,-000,000 for these beautifully assembled mechanisms and proceeds at once to disassemble them. By countless individual acts of destruction, Swift & Company paradoxically increases the value of products which are the result of countless individual acts of creation.

Unlike automobiles and watches, these mechanisms are easier to put together than they are to take apart. Certain kindly laws of nature aid the farmer. The hog, for example, will grow at the rate of about one pound each day and the farmer may confidently expect that his product will be more valuable tomorrow than it is today. Swift & Company deals with natural laws less kindly, if not actually hostile. Fresh meat in uncontrolled temperatures will spoil at a rate much faster than a pound a day. These two chemical manifestations, one of life and one of death, govern most of the economics of the livestock and packing business. As it is harder to deal with deterioration than it is with growth, the packer's problem is the greater.

In meeting it, the packer has created one of the largest industries in America. Standing astride the Mississippi, he reaches with his right hand into the great agricultural states, producing two-thirds of all U. S. livestock, and with his left hand hurls $3,000,000,000 worth of steaks and chops and hams toward the huge population centers of the East. The motorcar maker at Detroit puts no greater value into the automobiles he sends spinning across the earth. Nor does the movie producer at Hollywood. If the figure is too large to be grasped bring it down to terms of the individual. To each man, woman and child in the United States, some packer distributes each year 151 lbs. of meat and lard.

Chicago is the industry's center; the stockyards are its major clearing house. Into the yards, in 1929, poured a living stream of 15,000,000 animals. The stream at Omaha was half as long; at Kansas City somewhat less than half. At about 70 markets, the total reached the enormous figure of 91,862,000—a hog, a steer or a sheep for every adult inhabitant of the U. S. and several other countries.

In such tremendous mass is the packer's salvation. Swift & Company makes a profit of $\frac{1}{4}$ cent a pound on the meat and by-products it buys from the farmer and sells to the public. But it sells 5,500,000,000 such pounds, and in 1930 netted nearly $12,500,000. Compared with its something over $900,000,000 gross sales, the profit was ridiculously small, less than $1\frac{1}{2}$ per cent. In 1929, it pushed its total volume over the $1,000,000,000 mark, joining an extremely select list of gigantic U. S. corporations. Swift, like Armour & Company (which does about the same business), and the smaller Wilson & Company and Cudahy Packing Company, must have enormous volume to exist. Together, these four packers dress more than 40 per cent of the country's federally inspected meat; yet their combined net profit in 1930 was less than the profit of Ford, du Pont, U. S. Steel or General Motors. This is not a mysterious problem; it is clearly understood and bitterly fought by every intelligent packer. With livestock buyers for 1,200 packing plants competing in the U. S. markets, price levels are kept as high as demand allows. And on the other hand, these packers are buying against a consumer's market of two, three or even six months hence. A quarter-cent bargain in November may become a two-cent loss by March.

Each packer fights low returns with various weapons. Swift has built up a huge business (more than 114 plants) in dairy produce, eggs and poultry. It is one of the largest distributors of butter in the U. S. These not-entirely-meat-packing activities, together with commercial fertilizers, bring in about $250,000,000 each year, or about one-quarter of the business.

A vast organization keeps this industry in motion. More than 55,000 men and women work for Swift: about one-sixth of them in the pivotal, all-important Chicago Packingtown and stockyards; a fifth in its 450 branch distributing houses spread across the U. S.; a third in its 41 smaller packing plants; the remainder in its $50,000,000 export trade, its 6,000 refrigerator cars operating over more than 600 car routes and its other activities. After volume, motion is the prime necessity of the packing business. To Swift's plants come each year more than 17,000,000 animals. Their killing is the starting gun in a race against time, against the uncertainty of markets and the certainty of eventual deterioration. Waste of time is as great a sin in Swift's Book of Commandments as waste of material. Against both, it wages intricate and interesting war.

Roughly measured, the period of usefulness of a hog covers about twelve months. In the first nine, beginning with the farrowing, the farmer prepares the hog for market. The end of this effort of creation is the hog's sale to the packer. In the last three months, beginning with the killing, the packer prepares the hog for the public. This period ends when the last product of the hog is in the hands of the consumer. As one may go behind the hog's birth to its biological beginnings, so one may project its economic life into a chemical future. But for the purpose of studying the hog, this crucial year allows enough scope.

Each period has its own dilemmas. Of the farmer's troubles, sickness is the most immediate, and marketing time the most baffling. So steadily does the farmer consider the price he will get for his hogs that every four years he thinks himself out of many millions of dollars. In 1922, the farmer could sell 16 bushels of corn for only $9, which was the same as the price of 100 lbs. of hog. Pondering this, he decided that in 1923 and 1924 he would not sell his corn, but would feed it to his hogs and sell the hogs. Thus by 1924, the number of hogs slaughtered (under federal inspection) had jumped from 43,000,000 to 53,000,000. The price of 100 lbs. of hog fell from $9 to a little over $8, but the 16 bushels of corn, which in 1922 were worth $9, in 1924 could be sold for nearly $16.

Again the farmer pondered. Apparently his idea had been wrong. It had become more profitable to sell corn as corn than to sell corn as hogs. Reversing his economics, he so reduced the hog supply that in 1926 the hog prices went to $12, while the value of his 16 bushels of corn dropped to $12.

Added to this large cyclical problem are the seasonal ups and downs of hog marketing, with prices rising in the off months and falling when the winter runs are heaviest. There is even a day-by-day fluctuation in the Chicago market, a fluctuation which the packers and thinking live-stock producers are working to eliminate. Normal December receipts in Chicago average between 10,000 and 60,000 hogs each day. Yet one Monday, December 15, 1924, the packers were appalled to find no less than 122,749 hogs jamming the stockyard pens. In one day the price fell $1.75. Now the farmer gets market reports four times a day by radio. Quickly figuring the comparative values of corn and hogs, he decides whether to ship at once (by train or truck) or hold for a better market. If too many become frightened on a falling market, the result precisely parallels conditions on the New York Stock Exchange in October, 1929.

Here in the hog alleys is as keen trading as may be found in the world, conducted almost without the aid of speech. There is no lack of noise. Into the pens strides Fred Young, Swift's veteran buyer who looks like John W. Davis. He pokes the hogs with his stick and says "Tsa-a." Everybody pokes hogs with sticks and says "Tsa-a, Tsa-a." The hogs grunt. Mr. Young judges. Then he comes out to where the commission firm's salesman is standing. Young looks at him, waiting for a price. The seller utters one word: "Ten." Fred Young moves rapidly on. He is not ready to pay $9.10 per cwt. for hogs weighing 180 lbs. His price, set by wise Sven Lund back in the general offices, is $8.90, based on the outlook for demand for pork and the supply of hogs.

Often Mr. Young spends much time, after the market opens, in dickering before he makes any purchases. The buyer for Miller & Hart (Berkshire brand) may pay the asked $9.10 for the load. Smaller packers and order buyers frequently set the early market. Fred Young waits, telephoning the market trend back to the wise Sven, who is in touch with all the principal markets. Many times he yields to a rising market, pays $9.10 or even $9.20, because the reverse of his judgment is often true. A nod from Young, a nod from the seller, close the deal. There are never misunderstandings. Each day the packers pay in cash; Swift's *daily* average for livestock for the year is about $1,250,000.

Thus ends the period of creation. The farmer's work is done. The hog, completely assembled, is in Packingtown.

Almost everyone has seen a farm; almost everyone feels himself reasonably familiar with it. Each year 200,000 visitors are guided through the visitors' route at Swift & Company plants; not a dozen of them leave with a thorough understanding of the Chicago stockyards and Packingtown. Conceive, if you will, a square mile (640 acres) of reclaimed swamp sliced out of the middle of a city of 3,500,000 persons. Bound it on the east and northeast by the black belt, on the north by a factory district (Wrigley's, Standard Sanitary, Starck Piano Co., Henry Bosch Co. [wall paper], Certain-Teed Products Co. [roofing], Chicago Portrait Co., etc.), on the west by the foreign sections, on the south by a modern and prosperous shopping center. Within are some 50,000 men and women, absorbed in destruction. They are of all castes, all races. Once the majority were Irish; now the Irish have gone and in their places have come Slavs and blacks. Watching them on the killing floors, in the dressing plants, one notices their splendid physiques, their clever hands. Or perhaps the knives are more impressive than the hands which guide them. Hundreds and thousands of clean, flashing knives.

The eastern third of the yards belongs to the livestock men. Here they bring or send their hogs and cattle, riding up and down the alleys on fine horses to dicker with the buyers. The fencing about the pens gives the effect, from above, of a gigantic grey checkerboard. Here and there, over the pens, long grey arms point to the west. These are viaducts for men and for animals, routes to offices and to killing houses. From time to time they tremble and roar under a drive of steers. Intensely proud of their profession are these men. They trace their Scotch or English ancestry back through generations of cattlemen. In the old English dining-room of the Saddle & Sirloin Club, they are watched by the portraits of their fathers' fathers.

Only the most important livestock men ever penetrate farther west than the end of the alleys. Beyond, and in the central third of the stockyards, are the offices of Swift, of Armour, of Morris (Armour-owned), of smaller packers, Roberts & Oake, Miller & Hart and others. Here, too, are the visitor's routes through killing houses and model kitchens, through laboratories and community markets. To the east is the odor of the barnyard; here in the Swift general office building the air is washed and no windows are open. The precaution is wise, although in this central portion there are many sweet-smelling places. The smoke-room, where row upon row of Premium hams are perfumed with the smoke of wood fires. A tiny room in the sausage plant, where spices are mixed for flavoring. The huge tanks of cottonseed oil in the refinery, rich and earthy and edible. All of them fine scents, grateful after the machine-odors of any plant.

Here, too, is the locus of the Brothers Swift. Once there were Armours and Morrises as well as Swifts, but with the sale of Morris to Armour and the reorganization of Armour, the other old packing families have almost disappeared. In the far northwest corner of the yards, almost outside the gates, the Wilsons still run the business bought in 1916. But five sons of the late Gustavus Franklin Swift are now the reigning aristocrats of Packingtown, and a sixth functions in Boston.

Rich as they have become (each could retire whenever he liked), splendid as are their homes, these Swifts are not out of place in the yards. Their tradition is no less compelling than the tradition of the cattlemen or the tradition of the clever knives. Very close are the Swifts to their business. Only one, Harold, has any major outside interest. He is president of the Board of Trustees of the University of Chicago. It was Harold who went to the Yale Law School to bring 31-year-old Dean Robert Hutchins to become Chicago U.'s prodigy president. It was of dark, grave Harold that British Sir Josiah Stamp once said: "How extraordinary! It is only in America that a butcher could become a university head." He was the only Swift to go to college. He is the only Swift bachelor.

Harold is distinguishable among the Swifts by the extent and importance of his activities outside the yards. Within the yards, G. F., named for the Founding Father of the Swifts, is equally distinguishable. Boss of the plant's operations, he is the family's most practical meatpacker, a good judge of hogs and the company's logical president.

The company is very conscious of its Swifts, counts them as potent weapons in its unending duel with Armour & Co., now bereft of Armours. That a second generation should still be in packinghouse shirtsleeves fills the company with pride; that a third generation comes on (although not in great force) makes the cup of Swift joy overflow. Young Alden, son of chairman Louis, is the third-generation representative in the yards. His departments include beef, purchasing, transportation and by-products, a large assignment, but Alden has ability. In Denver, head of the Swift plant, is L. F. Jr., the other third-generation Swift, who carries on.

The Swifts breathe washed air; surrounding them are white mahogany offices, the Swift radio station, the kitchens where each day pound cakes are baked with new, Swift-devised shortenings, the refrigerators filled with pretty, packaged chops and cuts, for all the world like a confectioner's window. This is the silk-stocking district of the yards. Even the killing floor, for all its blood and guts, has somewhat the air of being on parade.

Only a few steps westward and the parade comes to an abrupt end. Few visitors venture far into the western part of the plants; they would not be comfortable there. On one hand rise the plants of a company with a euphonious name (Darling & Company) and the malodorous business of rendering meat trimmings from butcher shops. Across the narrow alley are Swift's by-product plants. Heaped outside the bone house are the heads of cattle, in awful pile; inside are grinders which belch forth clouds of dust. The odor is not pleasant. Swift supplies the workmen here with filter masks. Some use them and some do not. It is wiser to use them.

Thus the Packingtown in which the farmer's finished product finds itself.

The major adjustment which the hog makes as it moves to the last quarter of its year is of course the change from life to death. This is the only adjustment which can conceivably be of concern to the hog, and it is a curious thing that it should be of such little concern to Swift & Company. If killing is the chief function of a butcher, then the Swifts are not butchers. Exactly 25 minutes elapse between the time the live hog reaches the killing floor and the time the dressed carcass goes to the cooler. By the left hind foot he is hoisted athwart a giant wheel, then delivered to a conveyor from which he hangs, squealing, head downward. A mammoth being with a spear-like knife makes a quick, deft thrust at the hog's throat. The adjustment is made.

Beautifully certain are the ministrations of the killing room to the rows of carcasses which were hogs. An incredibly intricate nest of blunt knives scrapes every hair from the hog's skin; nearby stand government inspectors, slicing the neck-glands, to search for tiny white spots which are tuberculosis. Off comes the head; it is put to one side. One deft ripping motion and the inside of the carcass is as clean as the outside. A twist of giant tweezers and the toenail clatters to the floor. Now the procession moves through a bath of fire to singe off the last of the hair, a bath of water to cool. The rhythmic rise and fall of a cleaver rends the backbone. On and on come the carcasses, perhaps 20,000 of them, a fat pink parade curling through blades of steel.

From the killing floor the carcass moves to the cooler for twenty-four hours, then to the floors where men and machines carve it into dollars and cents. Here is a mechanical saw which grinds through the shoulder; there is a draw knife like a curved adz which scoops out the loin. Hundreds of white-sleeved arms swing back and forth. Hundreds of funnels gulp the morsels the knives flip aside. Some gulp lean trimmings; these will make sausage. Some gulp fats; these will make lard. Down one chute go the hams, trimmed to within $\frac{1}{8}$-inch of standardization; down another pour shoulders. To the waiting refrigerator cars is rushed the fresh meat, ready to travel to a branch house in Seattle or Atlanta. But the hams and the bacon must go to the curing cellars, there to remain from 30 to 90 days—and the toenails, the hair, the fats, the lips, still have long weeks to wait before their processing is complete, before the hog has been perfectly destroyed.

In this gradual dissolution there is no accident, no happenstance. When the live 250-lb. hog begins his run across the viaduct to the killing floor, he is already divided and subdivided as exactly as a suburban real estate development. Swift knows that when the knives are through with him, there will remain:

Of fresh meat (loins, Boston butts, spare ribs) .. 37.50 lbs.
Of hams (to be cured) .... 32.50 "
Of bacon (to be cured)...................... 29.37 "
Of fat backs (salted) .... 23.75 "
Of lard...................................... 22.50 "
Of picnics (smoked shoulders)................. 12.50 "
Of clear plates .... 6.87 "
Of sausage (about $\frac{1}{50}$ part of the hog live weight
   in the form of lean trimmings)............... 5.63 "
Of jowl butts .... 5.63 "
Carried forward 176.25 lbs.

Brought forward 176.25 lbs.

Of various edible products such as feet, necks, tails
(popular with negroes), cheek and head meat,
ears, snouts (often pickled) and lips . . . .   7.50   "
Of edible by-products such as kidneys, stomach-
linings (sold to pepsin makers), gullet and giblet
meat. . . . .   5.62   "

189.37 lbs.

Shrinkage accounts for . . . .   51.25   "

240.62 lbs.

There still remain 9.38 lbs. of hog to be usefully destroyed. There are hides (to be tanned into pigskin), hair
(to upholstery), bits of skin and sinew (to glue), grease (to
lubricants), blood (to stock foods), bone (to bone-handles,
buttons, bone-dust). In the by-products houses are whirling
cylinders of blood, soon to be dried to dust. Another room
is carpeted with thousands of glittering white shin-bones,
forming fantastic geometric patterns. Once they were
changed to Mah-Jongg sets; now they become knife-
handles and buttons. In the glue house, fragments of gristle
swim about in open tanks; their liquor will be condensed,
then dried, then ground to the inevitable dust: dark brown
cones of powdered glue. Fragments of fat are rendered
for lubricants (not lard) or distilled for grease. Even the
water from the tanks is partially evaporated and its grease
skimmed off, then evaporated again to make food for
animals.

But even after these by-products have been isolated from
the 9.38 lbs. of residue, there yet remains an ultimate
remnant. From this Swift prepares, in giant cooking vats
in the animal-food house, a brew which it calls digester
tankage. Its ingredients are fragments of skulls, toes, hair,

knuckles, and the ultimate remainder of every previous process in the vast Swift plant. Once these remnants went to the fertilizer tanks; thus the brew had its christening. Now they are dried and ground. In a misty storeroom are piled 1,500 tons of this tankage, macabre mountains of meal. Its protein content is fixed by law at 60 per cent; it makes good stock food. Here is the final achievement of the Swift disassembly, the visible sign of the shopworn adage that the packers use every part of the hog but the squeal. Weirdly incongruous are the heaped-up remnants which roll up to the by-products plants in bright red wagons; when they come out, they have merged their identities in useful dust, the last product of destruction.

Swift's horror of waste has produced many curious deals in Packingtown. One of the most valuable to mankind has been the supplying of pork glands for insulin and sheep glands for adrenalin. One of the most curious is the sale each year of several pounds of gall stones, collected from the killing rooms. These are bought, for well over $100 a pound, by mysterious Orientals who do not divulge their purpose. Swift supposes, but does not know, that they are used as charms or for medicines.

·The great problem of physical waste Swift has mastered. When the Founding Father strode along that evil-smelling stream known as Bubbly Creek, he would stop at the openings of the Swift sewers. If he saw any fat coming out, he knew there was waste in the packinghouse. Back he stormed and someone smarted. No fat issues from Swift's sewers today. That leakage has been stopped.

The next problem is much harder to solve, and Swift has not yet conquered it. In the chemical laboratories, in an atmosphere of test tubes and constant-temperature-rooms lies the key to Swift's immediate manufacturing problem. Having eliminated the waste in the product itself, the remaining step fairly shrieks itself through Packingtown:

Eliminate the waste in Time.

Nine months will produce an 180-lb. hog; 25 minutes will kill it and send the carcass to the cooler; 24 hours will chill the meat; 15 minutes will see it cut into its hams, its shoulders, its bellies (bacons) and its loins.

But in the curing process, in the barrels of pickle (salt, sugar and nitrate), the hams and the bacon remain for from 30 to 90 days. And some dry (or summer) sausage must hang in the drying rooms for four months before government inspectors are satisfied that no suspicion of trichina remains. By the time these have been shipped to branch houses, distributed to dealers and sold to the consumer, the hog's year is up and the period of destruction may be said to be complete. Such enormous stocks as Swift has always in storage obviously complicate its marketing situation; the packer must buy his supply in November for a conjectural demand in March. Now the Swift laboratories experiment ceaselessly with quick cures. The preservation question they have mastered; they can cure in comparatively few hours. Not yet have they found a way to duplicate the flavor of the slow cure.

In these laboratories are many odds and ends which help paint the Swift picture. Here is a room devoted to experiments with gelatin and motion-picture films. Here is another where scientists are improving the dry rendering process. Already this process (which substitutes continuous rendering by means of steam-heated coils for rendering in steam vats, with the consequent escape of odors) has made the yards a more habitable place. Swift's scientists would do more if they could, would make the Chicago plant as sanitary as the model exhibit at Toronto. But the buildings are old and there is the ever-present problem of Swift's neighbors. Swift might clean house, but would the small packers to the west? The issue rests.

These laboratories are now the scene of experiments which may have a profound effect on Swift's future. With the tremendous effort to perfect the frozen meat process, the fundamental principles of which were established by Swift in 1903, Swift makes what is probably the last and most important effort to evolve a distributing machine equal to the "disassembly" plant at Chicago.

From a production standpoint, further Swift progress would be almost an improvement upon perfection. Yet Swift & Co. itself does not at all contemplate a process of marking time, or of being content with the $12,000,000 dividend payment it has made every year since 1918. And opportunity has been provided by the partial revocation, on January 5, 1931, of the famous Consent Decree which Swift and other large packers had accepted in 1920.

The Consent Decree was the round table settlement of a threatened government suit against Swift, Armour, Morris, Cudahy and Wilson, then and now (except that Armour has absorbed Morris) the largest units in the packing industry. Facing anti-trust proceedings, the packers agreed not to handle such so-called *unrelated* lines as the packaging of canned fruits and vegetables; agreed also not to enter the retail business. The result was to hamstring them in meeting a new competitive situation. The retailer, in the shape of the great chain store systems, went into the packing business, one chain now operating two packing plants and a large sausage factory, while the smaller packers, not parties to or bound by the Consent Decree, went into the retail business. After years of argument, a modification of the Decree was obtained, which permits the packers to manufacture, sell and deal in—at wholesale, but not at retail—the so-called *unrelated lines*. Whether this belated relief is to be of material value remains to be seen.

Meanwhile, however, nothing but an unimaginable outbreak of vegetarianism can interfere with Swift's basic structure and basic prosperity. While trade commissions may investigate, while the new and cultural Chicago may deprecate and disown the square mile of stockyards, Swift remains secure in its billion dollar business, in its income of millions piled up from profits of one quarter of a cent per pound of meat. It has 48,000 stockholders (including 25 per cent of its employees) and in 1930 it announced a four for one stock split to give more investors (and employees) an opportunity to hold its securities.

Thus Swift & Co., butcher for 20,000,000 meat-eaters. When G. F. Swift, that brusque, sardonic Yankee, first came from Cape Cod to dress meat at the source of supply, he could not have visioned so tremendous a service. Volume has made it possible, and ice, and advertising. Man no longer can hunt his quarry and bring home his kill, but he is still carnivorous. Swift & Co., with the knives to cut meat, the ice to preserve it, the cars to transport it, faces the future with small misgivings. For it is the modern minister to a timeless and primeval want.

MONOPOLY

*The Aluminum Company, a Corporation
Which Paternally Includes an Industry;
Whose Best Customers Are Also Its
Chief Competitors*

ALUMINUM COMPANY OF AMERICA

~~~

THE story of steel cannot be written in terms of the United States Steel Corporation. The story of copper contains many chapters not related by Kennecott or Anaconda. But the story of aluminum in this country is solely the story of the Aluminum Company of America. With trifling exceptions, every pound of virgin aluminum produced in the United States has been, and is being, produced by the Aluminum Company. Every use of aluminum has been pioneered and popularized by this same corporation, and in its laboratories have been developed the strong alloys, so vital to aluminum's present and future. American industry now uses aluminum to the extent of more than 350,-000,000 pounds a year. For the progress and the performance of this new metal, industry has unquestionably the Aluminum Company to thank.

Yet criticism, rather than gratitude, has been the Aluminum Company's usual lot. It is commonly regarded as a monopoly, and therefore bad; and as a Mellon monopoly, and therefore worse. Radicals, alarmists, and political opponents, scenting an obscure but invidious connection between Mr. Mellon's public position and private interests, convey the impression that the nation's minor currency may be at any moment aluminized, with Mr. Mellon's aristocratic countenance emblazoned on every nickel and dime. No sooner is aluminum mentioned than the conversation turns to monopolies in general, to the Aluminum Trust in particular, and how this ogre is taking at least the aluminum bread pans out of the people's mouths.

Like all prejudices, the prejudice against the Aluminum Company represents a fact exaggerated and a truth distorted. But it is also obvious that no such feeling can exist entirely without foundation. The Aluminum Company is admittedly the sole producer of aluminum in this country. Its position as sole producer was guaranteed, between 1888 and 1909, by a patent monopoly on the basic process of reducing aluminum from its ore. The Mellon interest dates from 1890, when the Mellon family exchanged cash for Aluminum Company stock. Andrew Mellon has no position with the company now, but R. B. Mellon (Mellon National Bank, Pittsburgh), Richard K. Mellon and David K. Bruce (Andrew Mellon's son-in-law) are directors, and the Mellon family is a large (yet a minority) holder of Aluminum Company stock. The corporation's position as a monopoly is qualified by competition with a continuous stream of imported aluminum and by the large and growing supply of aluminum recovered from aluminum scrap. Its status as a Mellon monopoly is rather more than qualified by the Mellons' interest not reaching even an operating control. Yet the Aluminum Company undeniably dominates the aluminum industry, and with its progress and profits the Mellons are unquestionably concerned.

Furthermore, the Aluminum Company directs a thoroughly integrated business. The reduction of aluminum ore constitutes only a fraction of its activities. It makes and sells in semifinished form such products as propellers, pistons, and various other machine parts. There is nothing original about a producer being also a fabricator and merchandiser. But the Aluminum Company's position as chief source of aluminum does create the rather peculiar situation in which the company's best customers are also its most active competitors.

Consider, for example, the position of the General Fireproofing Company of Youngstown, Ohio, which makes, among other products, aluminum furniture. General Fireproofing's aluminum furniture is, of course, in direct competition with the Aluminum Company's own aluminum furniture. Yet General Fireproofing makes a profitable practice of buying its aluminum from the Aluminum Company and, except for the scrap market and importations, has no other source of supply. If the Aluminum Company regarded competition as an evil to be eliminated, it might put General Fireproofing in an extremely awkward position. And it is generally true that any manufacturer of aluminum products will find himself in active competition with his major source of material. "Aha!" cry antimonopolists, "Behold an entire industry in one clutching corporate hand!"

To this integration complaint the Aluminum Company has, of course, an obvious answer. Competition, says the Aluminum Company, is something to be encouraged, to be fostered. Whenever an aluminum chair or piston or skillet, regardless of who made it, is sold, the Aluminum Company observes an increase in the market for its aluminum and another forward step in aluminum's progress. At least one Aluminum Company competitor—Bohn

Aluminum and Brass Corporation—sells nearly as much of its aluminum product (Bohnalite pistons) as the Aluminum Company sells of its corresponding product (Lynite pistons). But no matter how often Bohnalite and Lynite salesmen clash, or how often Bohnalite salesmen make the sale, the Aluminum Company plans no dark methods of putting Mr. Bohn out of business. Mr. Bohn is a good customer. Mr. Bohn helps to sell the automobile industry on the merits of aluminum. The Aluminum Company has been accused of filling orders from its subsidiaries and holding up supplies of its competitor-customers. It follows, however, precisely the opposite procedure, on the theory that the production and promotion of aluminum is its main objective, to which the sale of aluminum products is incidental. To use its position as sole producer in order to become sole manufacturer and distributor would seem to the company like biting off its face to please its nose.

Thus the aluminum controversy revolves chiefly about the Aluminum Company's power as a source from which most aluminum flows. The Aluminum Company maintains that only as sole producer could it have developed aluminum, in four decades, from a laboratory curiosity to an industrial staple. Detractors maintain that all monopolies are evil and that it is inimical to any industry to have its operations so largely overshadowed by one corporate entity. To determine something of truth's elusive position between these two extremes, it is necessary to consider aluminum's past, to go back to the day when the Aluminum Company (which was as much of a monopoly on the day of its birth as it is at present—indeed, it was more of one) was considered not at all a menace and probably a good deal of a curiosity.

For certainly in 1888 the newly formed Pittsburgh Reduction Company (the present name resulted from a reincorporation in 1907) represented an intensely speculative enterprise. From 1855 to 1888 aluminum, produced in minute quantities, had sold at an average prohibitive price of sixteen dollars a pound. Typical fabricated aluminum products were a helmet of a king of Denmark, the rattle for an infant prince of France, and the shiny cap on the Washington Monument. There was no dearth of aluminum in the earth's crust (it is fifth commonest of metals) but it clung so tenaciously to its compounds that the extraction of pure aluminum was a chemical, not an industrial, process.

In 1886, however, Charles Martin Hall had discovered a method by which aluminum could be commercially produced. A common compound of aluminum is aluminum oxide, found in a dirty yellow-brown mineral called bauxite. Mr. Hall, working in a homemade laboratory (the woodshed of his father's home at Oberlin, Ohio), separated the oxide from the bauxite, added cryolite, a fluoride of aluminum, and applied an electric current. The oxide resisted the passage of the current, turned the electrical energy into heat, and eventually broke down into its aluminum and oxygen constituents. Thus, with what must have been an extremely rudimentary electric furnace, Mr. Hall solved the problem of commercial aluminum production and laid the foundation of his later fame and fortune. Both, as might be expected, were considerable.

When, in 1887 and early 1888, Mr. Hall failed to finance his pending patents for the electrolytic production of aluminum in Lockport, New York, he was introduced, through his friend, Mr. Romaine C. Cole, to Captain Alfred E. Hunt, then identified with the steel interests of Pittsburgh, Pennsylvania, and an owner in the Pittsburgh Testing Laboratory, metallurgical testing engineers. Captain Hunt interested a few of his business associates, and a company was incorporated under the laws of Pennsylvania, with a capital of 200 shares of $100 par value, to try out these patents on a practical scale. The first meeting of the subscribers to the stock of this company was held on August 8, 1888, and the name adopted was the Pittsburgh Reduction Company. The organization meeting, held on October 1, elected officers with Captain Hunt as president; Mr. Horace W. Lash, first vice president; Mr. Robert J. Scott, second vice president; Mr. George W. Clapp (also an owner in the Pittsburgh Testing Laboratory), treasurer; and Mr. W. S. Sample, secretary. These gentlemen, with Mr. Millard Hunsiker, were the first board of directors.

It was agreed between this board and Messrs. Hall and Cole that if the patents could be successfully worked the company would increase its stock to 10,000 shares, of which 57 per cent would be given for the patents, 15 per cent to the original subscribers, and 28 per cent would be held in the treasury for plant enlargement. Mr. Cole was made the first general manager, and Mr. Hall was appointed electrician. A plant site was rented on Smallman Street, Pittsburgh, between 32nd and 33rd Streets, and equipment purchased consisting of two 60 horsepower boilers and a 125 horsepower engine, with two 25 volt 1,200 ampere generators from the (then) Westinghouse Electric Light Company. The list of the company's present plants is impressive: Badin, N. C., pig aluminum (from alumina), ingot; Buffalo, N. Y., sand castings, permanent mold castings (Lynite pistons, etc.), die castings; forgings (Lynite connecting rods, etc.); Detroit, Mich., sand castings; Garwood, N. J., die castings; Massena, N. Y., pig aluminum (from alumina), ingot, wire, cable, beams for structural use, bar, and rod; New Kensington, Pa., ingot sheet, tubing, cooking utensils (Wear-Ever), foil; bottle caps (Goldy Seals, Alco caps, R-O Seals), bronze powder (Albron), molding, Mason jar caps, special equipment (tanks, coils, etc.); Niagara Falls, N. Y., pig aluminum (from alumina), ingot, sheet, planographic plates; Alcoa, Tenn., reduction plant, rolling mills.

Owing to the illness of Mr. Cole, his position as general manager was soon abolished, and Mr. Hall was made superintendent, with Mr. Arthur V. Davis (later president and now chairman of the board), then an employee of the Pittsburgh Testing Laboratory, assistant superintendent.

The first metal was made on Thanksgiving Day, 1888, and for the rest of the year, and well into 1889, production and sales alternated in importance with a constant need for additional capital for enlargement. The taking out of foreign patents and their protection, together with domestic patent litigation, occupied the time of the executives and directors of the company to a large extent so that comprehensive financing was impossible.

On September 19, 1889, the capital stock was increased to 10,000 shares and subscriptions to 2,250 shares invited. Additional capital gradually became interested. Messrs. D. L. Gillespie, Thomas L. Shields, E. M. Ferguson, and T. Chalmers Darsie, well-known Pittsburgh business men, were elected to the board, and finally on January 28, 1891, Mr. A. W. Mellon took sufficient interest in the company to finance a mortgage on their new plant at New Kensington, Pa., and to join the board. Shortly after, Mr. R. B. Mellon became identified with the company and, after the death of Captain Hunt, was its president. The settlement of the patent litigation with the Cowles Electric Smelting and Aluminum Company by decision in favor of Hall and the starting of the first plant using water power at Niagara Falls put the company well on the way to finally successful operation.

The early prospects of the Pittsburgh Reduction Company could not be considered bright. For although these were the only men who could produce aluminum, they were also the only men who had any use for it. Solemn indeed was the moment when the partners put their first week's production (100 pounds) in the safe and wondered what to do with it. Nobody wanted aluminum. It had, to be sure, certain advantages. It was light—only one-third the weight of steel and less than one-third the weight of copper. It was noncorrosive—air and rain could not reduce it to a mass of rust. It was a good conductor of heat and a fair conductor of electricity. On the other hand, it was still extremely expensive. The first selling price was five dollars per pound for 96 per cent pure, and four dollars per pound for 88 per cent to 96 per cent pure metal. The price was rapidly reduced to fifty-five cents a pound, and at present is about twenty-five cents. A comparison between eighteen-cent copper and four-cent steel illustrated the greater first cost of any aluminum product, although of course a pound of aluminum has about three times the volume of a pound of steel. Furthermore, aluminum itself was suspect and unknown. The pure metal was soft; its early alloys experimental and uncertain. Nothing could be done with aluminum that could not be done with steel or copper or even wood. Aluminum was competing with long established materials that sold for a fraction of aluminum's price and that had a thoroughly standardized metallurgical and fabricating technique. The problem of producing aluminum was solved. The problem of selling it had only begun.

The Aluminum Company was therefore forced into the fabricating field. The manufacturers of copper cable saw no sense in buying aluminum to make aluminum cable. The manufacturers of tin pots and pans were equally reluctant to shift over to aluminum. Therefore the Aluminum Company manufactured its own cables, its own kitchen utensils, and sold them to an uninterested and incredulous world. Nor was this necessity for pioneering a necessity only in aluminum's younger days. Within recent years, for example, the Aluminum Company designed, introduced, and popularized aluminum furniture. It is fair to say that in every major use of aluminum, the Aluminum Company has been compelled to demonstrate the practical possibility of using aluminum by actually making and selling the aluminum product itself. In many of its fabricating and selling activities it has encouraged other manufacturers to follow in its footsteps. In some (such as cable) it has not. Yet its early integration was necessary to its existence, and nearly every manufacturer of aluminum products today is traveling along a pathway which the Aluminum Company first explored.

Early uses of aluminum included chiefly kitchen utensils, cables, machine parts, and novelties. These last are not now so important, but they were extremely vital in the critical early period. The novelty manufacturer, often operating on the proverbial shoestring basis, will take chances with a new material and is today nursing the young stainless steel industry through its infant stages just as he was one of the supports of aluminum's childhood. An aluminumware display of 1894 included collar buttons, looking-glass and picture frames, penholders, candlesticks, match boxes, house numbers, and spoons. Other later miscellaneous uses were aluminum fishing reels, helmet and cap badges, artificial limbs, thermometers, skate bodies, hypodermic syringe cases, phonograph recorders, dog collar trimmings, and horseshoes, while earnest but unsuccessful efforts were made to popularize aluminum musical instruments, glove fasteners, combs, hairpins, and cartridge cases. There is still a considerable aluminum novelty business—aluminum playing cards, for instance, being popular with yachtsmen and other out-of-door card-players, inasmuch as they prevent the distressing possibility of having a long, established suit blown into the bay by a passing breeze.

It was in the field of transportation that aluminum really began to take rank as a major metal. The bicycle rage of the nineties constituted aluminum's first transportation phase and is still an excellent illustration of its outstanding advantage—lightness. Even the person least conscious of physics and least concerned with the formula that energy equals mass times the square of velocity can appreciate aluminum when energy is the muscle power of the rider, mass is the weight of the rider, and velocity is the speed that the exertion of muscle power produces. When the bicycle vogue vanished, only to be succeeded by the rise of the automobile, aluminum interests decided that the millennium had arrived and prepared to enlarge factories and increase production.

Unfortunately, however, the all-aluminum automobile was an illusion. There were many aluminum bodies used in early automotive days, and there never was any question that the aluminum car was superior to the steel car in that it consumed less gasoline, wore out fewer tires, and lasted much longer. But as soon as the automobile went into mass production, as soon as it became a real factory job with price a deciding sales factor, costly aluminum yielded to less costly steel. On the Continent (where cars are taxed partly on their weight, and where the automobile owner expects to drive his car for ten or twelve years instead of knocking the gloss off and trading it in) the aluminum body is well established, but in this country it is to steel, not to aluminum, that the automobile has turned. Yet although the complete aluminum automobile proved a disappointment, aluminum did find a tremendous field in automobile parts. In pistons, for instance, both lightness and heat conductivity made aluminum an ideal metal, and the general automotive field today constitutes aluminum's largest single use.

From 1912 on, and especially during and after the War, aluminum made rapid progress, particularly through the development of high-strength alloys. Aluminum is correctly thought of as soft and easily bent, but heat-treated aluminum alloys (chiefly with copper) have a tensile strength equal to mild steel. The better airplane propellers are now made almost exclusively of aluminum alloy, although, much to the aluminum people's displeasure, even aviators themselves commonly talk of their steel "props." This confusion results partly from the fact that the Aluminum Company makes propellers in a semifinished form, then sells them to a propeller manufacturer who machines, finishes, and resells the products. Thus one Aluminum Company customer, the Standard Steel Propeller Company (since absorbed by Hamilton Aero Mfg. Co., a unit of United Aircraft & Transport Corporation), sold its aluminum-alloy propeller under the name of the Standard Steel Propeller, a title from which the Aluminum Company officials would gladly have removed the second word. Aluminum alloys are standard for dirigible frames, and one dirigible has been built with an aluminum (instead of a fabric) skin.

But although an air-minded public thinks first of aviation when (or if) it thinks of aluminum alloy, it is in the more prosaic land transportation and general industrial fields that these alloys have been most important. Indeed, a discussion of aluminum alloys brings us down to the Aluminum Company of the present, for the greatest contemporary development in aluminum is its application to structural forms. Such objects as channels, girders, I-beams, and other structural shapes have been traditionally sacred first to iron and then to steel. The perfection of heat-treated alloys gave aluminum the required properties for structural employment. It was then necessary to work out standards, specifications, and methods of shop practice for the making of structural aluminum. This tabulation of data was at length accomplished and in November, 1929, the Aluminum

Company's works at Massena, in northern New York, went into operation on the making of structural shapes.

The potentialities of structural aluminum are almost fantastic. Railroad tracks, for example, will not stand much heavier loads than they now carry; at least partly aluminized must be the bigger and better trains of the future. Aluminum may lighten some of the load that skyscraper foundations of tomorrow will carry, although at present architectural aluminum is used chiefly in decorative spandrels, copings, and gratings. The navies of the world are extremely interested in aluminum, particularly since naval limitation agreements have put so much emphasis upon the displacement of battleships. A 10,000 ton aluminum cruiser, for instance, would be three times the size of a 10,000 ton steel cruiser. Of course, such an all-aluminum cruiser could exist only in the pages of a newspaper Sunday supplement, and equally, of course, the naval limitaters would be shocked and pained at what they would consider a tricky and unethical evasion of their limitations. Nevertheless, a specification is a specification and a pound is a pound, and certainly naval engineers are exhibiting an intense interest in the degree to which aluminum may be substituted for steel. Meanwhile, the Aluminum Company expects that in every structural field in which reduction of weight is an important factor (and it is a most important factor in every phase of transportation construction), aluminum structural forms will win a rapid acceptance and build up a gratifying tonnage.

Thus the Aluminum Company today, as in 1888, considers itself and its metal still in the beginning of their careers. Forty years is a brief time in a metal's history, especially in comparison with ancient copper and prehistoric iron. Constantly expanding, the business of the Aluminum Company is also constantly changing in character. As recently as over the three-year period from 1926 through 1928 the business of the company (aside from its sales of aluminum to other manufacturers of finished aluminum products) found its greatest tonnage in transportation, especially automotive parts; in cables, particularly high tension lines carrying up to 220,000 volts; and in household products, including washing machines and vacuum cleaners as well as cooking utensils. Other important uses were aluminum-capped and aluminum-sealed bottles (containing everything from ginger ale to whiskey); in the manufacture of shaving cream and tooth paste tubes; and powder, forming the pigment in aluminum paint, which, noncorrosive and highly reflective, is widely used for all outdoor and many indoor purposes. Aluminum paint is particularly valuable in the oil business as an aluminum-covered oil tank absorbs less of the sun's heat and prevents evaporation.

Tomorrow's development of structural shapes should result in a greatly increased use of aluminum in unit transportation, especially in motor trucks and street cars. Aluminum overhead cranes and aluminum electric hoists have recently been introduced. Aluminum furniture and architectural aluminum are just getting under way; and to the growing aviation business, aluminum is, of course, particularly vital.

During 1928 the Aluminum Company showed a net income of $19,279,465; in 1929 it passed the $24,000,000 mark, but 1930 showed a sharp drop to $10,868,000. In 1929 the domestic production of aluminum as given by the statistical abstract of the U. S. was 225,000,000 pounds, but 1930 figures were over 30 per cent lower.

In considering the earnings of the Aluminum Company, it must be remembered that the total earnings are by no means entirely based on the sale of ingot metal any more than the earnings of the United States Steel Corporation are confined to a profit on ingot steel. Like the Steel Corporation, the Aluminum Company has fabricating mills, railroads, power companies, and other investments, all essential to its aluminum business and all contributing to the earnings. In the very early days of the company the earnings were based on the marketing of ingot aluminum alone. Today its earnings on ingot aluminum are only about one third of the total.

Thus the Aluminum Company and thus aluminum. Whether the monopoly indictment will die down with the completion of Mr. Mellon's tenure of office as Secretary of the Treasury is perhaps debatable. As far as virgin metal production competition is concerned, the company has had no domestic competitors. Shortly before the War, a French company did plan a reduction plant in North Carolina, but the outbreak of the War brought an end to this competitive attempt. There is, however, a European aluminum combination of cartel, controlling a production of nearly 200,000,000 pounds a year. This cartel, however, does not seem to give Aluminum Company officials any great concern. They philosophically admit that overproduction abroad is bound to find the easiest market. A more important aluminum source of competition is the scrap market. As aluminum does not disintegrate, it retains its metal value.

Indeed, aluminum scrap at about twelve to eighteen cents a pound, depending on quality, has a higher market value than new steel, and can be remelted and reused with entirely satisfactory results. Aluminum experts maintain that if aluminum were still marketed only for its early uses, the supply of scrap would be equal to the entire demand. To be sure, the Aluminum Company has been accused of attempting to corner the scrap market. This the company denies, and points out that even if it were so shortsighted as to attempt such a corner, the effort would be as impossible as attempting to control any other broad scrap supply.

Meanwhile, it must always be remembered that aluminum is constantly in competition with other metals. Just as aluminum kitchen utensils to some extent superseded tin pans, so now the new stainless steels are competing for the utensil market, although the Aluminum Company feels that aluminum's superior heat conductivity will enable it to hold its position. The aluminum products always face the disadvantage of a higher first cost (an important factor in preventing the Aluminum Company from pricing its pig according to fancy); nor are there many applications of aluminum in which some other substance will not serve with reasonably satisfactory results.

It is perhaps this intermetallic competition which makes the Aluminum Company itself so free from any feeling that it is a monopoly, at least in the invidious sense of the word. Insofar as a corporation may be said to have a personality, the personality of the Aluminum Company is expressed largely in its paternal attitude toward aluminum. The Aluminum Company official does not necessarily sleep on an aluminum bed or sit in an aluminum chair. He does, however, look upon aluminum as a father might regard an only child, which, nursed through a trying infancy, has developed into a sound and healthy adolescence. That the Aluminum Company of America does regard aluminum with a certain prideful air is undeniable. It considers its critics as those who, having had no hand in the building of the temple, are now engaged in carping at the finished structure.

Yet it must be admitted that aluminum has made, in a forty-year period, an astounding progress. It must be also admitted that every step in that progress has been taken under the Aluminum Company's sponsorship and guidance. The Aluminum Company has undoubtedly been the laborer in the vineyard—a laborer who now feels himself well worthy of his hire.

BIGGEST DRUG CHAIN

The Building, Stone by Stone, of the Brilliantly Planned Structure of Drug, Inc. Herein is Told How a Share of Drug, Inc. Common Came to Give Its Owner Better Service Than He had Formerly Enjoyed

DRUG, INCORPORATED

❦

DRUG, INC. owns the largest chain drug store system in the world, and every one of you has at one time or another walked into one of its stores. Drug, Inc., being exclusively a holding company, does not advertise, but of the companies it holds you have heard of Life Savers, Inc., the Bayer Co. (aspirin), the Vick Chemical Co. (VapoRub), Bristol-Myers Co. (Ipana, Sal Hepatica). Of drug stores which it includes, you have heard of Rexall stores and Liggett stores, Owl stores on the Pacific Coast and Boots stores in England. You may have also noted from its 1930 report that its earnings for the year were $21,130,698, or over $6 per share, and heard that its sales are estimated at $160,000,000, a figure which is probably low.

Drug, Inc. is a money-maker now, it is far from through with its expansion program, and it is a good company to watch. It is also a good company to understand, because it straddles a number of fields at once, is as important a manufacturer as it is a retailer, as important a retailer as it is a distributor, and never confuses the three functions. Thus, when it bought the May Drug Co.'s eighteen Pittsburgh stores in December, 1928, it was following quite another tack than when it bought Life Savers, Inc. just one month later. And in the difference lies the key to the development of Drug, Inc. since it officially came into being on March 2, 1928.

A chart of the activities of Drug, Inc. would reveal the fact that from the corporate body of Drug, Inc. there extend two arms, quite properly terminating in two hands, each of which has many fingers. Now it would be straining the metaphor to say that Drug, Inc. does not let its right hand know what its left is doing, but it is true that Drug, Inc. is distinctly ambidextrous and that one hand is as important as the other. So far as the body itself is concerned, it contents itself with taking in the financial nourishment gathered by each of its busy hands, seeing to it that they gather more together than they could separately, and distributing the proceeds to the 26,000 stockholders whose corporate creature it is.

One hand is United Drug. The United Drug Co. was originally a red building in a street called Leon in Boston. Candy was made in the basement and on the top floor, and sandwiched in between the candy-making floors were three floors devoted to drugs and a few executive offices. Forty druggists, including Mr. Louis K. Liggett of Boston, each put up $4,000 to form it, and they didn't quite know what was going to happen to it or to their money. In fact, several of them could not even find Leon Street, and Mr. Liggett issued to each of them a printed direction slip saying that the best way to find the factory was to get off at Back Bay Station, walk to a corner, grab a cow by the tail, let her lead you to the city limits, and then somebody would probably show you the way. It was all very silly and gay-making, and it was in 1902 and it might never have succeeded and Mr. Liggett might never have had a yacht. But it did succeed, and it is now the 10,000 Rexall stores, the 706 Liggett stores, the 900 Boots stores, and the many factories of United Drug and its subsidiaries. And it is as shrewd a system of distributing and retailing as that of the Great Atlantic & Pacific Tea Co. The early history of the company, its modest beginning, and gradual acquisition are interesting but usual. You may take it for granted that United Drug was once a little red building and that it had a tough time at first. It is of more moment to tell you what it is than what it was.

Of more moment, that is, except for one thing. That is an idea which is past history because it occurred in 1901, but is current history because it operates today. In 1900, Mr. Liggett, not very successfully, was selling drugs and medicines in what salesmen call the Boston area. He saw about him many patent medicines, each popular in its own little district. Why not, asked Mr. Liggett, pool all these special formulas, invest in a central manufacturing business (the original building in Leon Street), and thus allow each druggist to have a wider line of popular medicines? Each druggist would be the exclusive retailer of the jointly manufactured products in his own district. Upon this idea was built United Drug, now one of the two hands of the great Drug, Inc. The little manufacturing business in Leon Street is now the large manufacturing business in Leon Street and in factories of subsidiaries from London to Valley Park, Missouri. The forty original Rexall (king of them all) agents have swollen to 10,000, managing 10,000 Rexall stores, and there has developed a branch of United Drug which was not foreseen in 1902. The Liggett chain began with the purchase of a Rexall store upon the death or retirement of the agent. Now it includes 706 stores, almost entirely in the large cities.

The relationships between these three major parts of United Drug (the factories, the Liggett chain, and the Rexall agents) are important to an understanding of Drug, Inc. and the difference between the purchase of the May stores and of Life Savers. United Drug, in 1927, made some 9,000 separate items of merchandise, many of them branded with the trade names of Rexall, Puretest, Liggett, etc. These included tooth pastes, some five different kinds of mouth wash, candy, shaving soaps and creams, aspirin, laxatives, bicarbonate of soda—all the staples of a drug store as well as bathing caps, hot water bottles, and the various paraphernalia of the new drug store era. They were available to the Liggett chain and the Rexall agents only, and they automatically provided these retailers with a line of highest quality trade-marked merchandise on which no competition could undersell because no competitor possessed them. For both the chain and agents, the exclusive agreement was ideal. As ruinous price-cutting (of which more later) became universal, the Liggett and Rexall managers could rely considerably upon their renewal trade in United Drug products at a maintained price. Some small town Rexall agents bought as much as 40 per cent of their entire merchandise requirements from United Drug; the average of both Liggett and Rexall chains itself was nearly 20 per cent. The plan was as successful when United Drug was a huge company with a $7,000,000 profit as it had been in the early Leon Street days.

And from the manufacturing end, the exclusive agreements had many merits. There were provided some 11,000 assured outlets. A relatively small sales staff (about 100) would bring selling costs down to the extremely low figure of 4.7 per cent of the sales price. There was also an advantage in being able to gauge the demand so exactly, particularly in a company where 9,000 products had to be kept in balance and evenly distributed over the year. But from one important point of view, the exclusive agreement applied a definite brake to United Drug progress. So long as the agreement remained in force, it was out of the question for United Drug to buy any major nationally branded and advertised product. It would be patently absurd to confine the marketing of Life Savers or Castoria or Cascarets to the Liggett-Rexall systems. Expansion at the manufacturing head of the system was sharply limited, if not altogether stopped, by the very plan which had built it. This was the situation in which United Drug found itself at the end of 1927.

The other hand of Drug, Inc. is Sterling Products. While United Drug was developing along its highly individual lines, another and quite dissimilar company was also making its impression on the drug trade. Sterling Products, Inc. began life in 1901, at about the time when Mr. Liggett was gathering his forty Rexall agents. The retail idea, which was so vital . to the United Drug scheme of things, was never stressed by Sterling. In 1906, it took over the first of the long list of patented products which were to come under its management. After Danderine (1906) came Cascarets (1909), California Fig Syrup (1912), and, in 1919, the famous Bayer's Aspirin. As it absorbed each new company, it threw in such management as was needed (often Sterling retains the old management practically intact) and steadily increased the company's profits. In 1925 Sterling earned $4,903,000; in

1926, this mounted to $5,406,000; and in 1927, it jumped again to $6,197,000. United Drug in the same year suffered a slight setback from the peak year 1926 and showed $6,763,000 before preferred dividends. The two companies were at that point approximately equal in earning power, although United Drug's volume was immensely greater than Sterling's.

Just who was responsible for the idea of the merger is one of the points which is lost in the general Drug, Inc. enthusiasm. It was either Mr. George M. Gales of United Drug or Mr. A. H. Diebold of Sterling or both. The two men were friends and men of imagination, and they were forever tossing up conversational balloons. This one took the air and for excellent reasons.

Each company was impressed by the economies possible through a joint purchasing program. As sixty-five cents of Liggett Co.'s dollar still goes to the supplier, it is apparent that this was no mere talking point. If United Drug and Sterling today could cut even 1 per cent from their joint bills, Drug, Inc. would have another $1,000,000 available for dividends.

This was a major and compelling factor, appealing strongly to both Mr. Gales and Mr. Diebold. On the other hand, each man, each company, had strong individual reasons for favoring the merger. The Sterling firm, for example, spent large sums of money advertising and marketing its proprietary remedies; United Drug could offer about one-sixth of all the 60,000 drug stores in the U. S. as promotional aids. It was indirect promotion, to be sure, for it was obviously impossible to bring the Sterling products into the exclusive agreement. Yet the Liggett stores and the Rexall agents could be counted upon to give them something more than an even break in display and local advertising.

On United Drug's side, the merger offered a brilliant way out of its manufacturing *impasse*. While it could not *itself* buy Bristol-Myers (Ipana, Sal Hepatica, Ingram's Shaving Cream, etc.) and enjoy a $1,600,000 profit on $6,100,000 sales (a ratio of over 25 per cent), there was no reason why the new Drug, Inc. should not reap the large manufacturing profits which were automatically denied United Drug. Provided always that the United Drug system, including the exclusive agreement, remained intact.

There was, finally, the factor of security values. Drug, Inc., the result of the merger, would be not only much larger but would present a far more complete industrial picture than either United Drug or Sterling. It seemed reasonable to suppose the public would give its stock a higher value (in relation to earnings) than it would give to either a manufacturer or to a retailer and distributor whose manufactured products had a closed market. If this happened, Drug, Inc. could obviously continue both United Drug and Sterling expansions more cheaply than either could continue separately. To each company, in short, the merger seemed to open up an attractive future.

Neither Mr. Gales nor Mr. Diebold nor anyone else in Drug, Inc. today sees any cause for regret. Some of their plans have turned out even better than they could have foreseen. After the break, for example, and through the early months of 1930, the assured Liggett-Rexall market was of the greatest value to the various Sterling companies, and such a product as Life Savers shows an actual 1930 gain. Expansion has of course been tremendous. In these three years, United Drug absorbed three chains (134 stores), and Sterling added close to a dozen brands known and sold throughout the U. S. After the merger was effected, Drug, Inc. used 156,500 shares to acquire retail businesses under United Drug management with estimated earnings of some $750,000 ($4.80 per share), and 1,189,009 shares to acquire manufacturing earnings under Sterling management of some $8,500,000 ($7.15 per share). This disparity is largely due to the fact that in taking over the Owl chain with sales of nearly $20,000,000, Drug, Inc. was buying sales volume rather than earnings, since Owl's preferred dividends were not being covered in full at the time that it was taken over.

One more notable result of the merger can be seen in the diversification of income which alone makes a share of Drug, Inc. such a radically different investment from a share of the old United Drug or of Sterling. Before the merger, a large part of United Drug's $4,500,000 net for common came from its retail business and followed the general retail rule of an extremely low ratio to sales (the A & P ratio, for example, is about 2.88 per cent on the dollar). Sterling's situation with large manufacturing companies enjoying open markets was altogether opposite. Their combination in Drug, Inc. provided a most happy diversification. Of Drug, Inc.'s estimated $175,000,000 domestic sales of the companies consolidated (1929), Sterling accounted for perhaps $45,000,000. But of Drug, Inc.'s $21,130,000 net for 1930, Sterling contributed some $15,000,000, United Drug $6,000,000 (based upon estimates of the respective companies prior to consolidation);

and Sterling management became responsible for dividends of $9,230,000 on 2,307,499 shares against United Drug's responsibility for $4,776,000 on 1,194,000 shares.

However sound the economic urges toward the United Drug-Sterling merger may have been, the project would have failed miserably if Drug, Inc. could not have summoned the man-power to effect its plans. In every argument pro or con the chains, the question of management plays a vociferous part. Therefore let us arrest the management of this world's largest drug business in the full swing of a busy morning and make each of Drug, Inc.'s major executives show us exactly what he is doing. As questions of rank are never posed in the Drug, Inc. offices (there having been no need to pose them), we may begin quite at random in the offices of Mr. George M. Gales, the unquestioned Drug, Inc. expert on retailing. On this particular morning, Mr. Gales is noting that sales of the Boots stores are up from the corresponding month of last year, and while Mr. Gales is agreeably impressed by the sheets before him, he is scarcely surprised. In fact, it is very difficult to surprise Mr. Gales, and when he is surprised there is apt to be trouble. For this spruce, cultivated, Southerner-turned-Long-Islander makes it his business to know just what profits each store should show and then makes it the store's business to show them. He has a notable record with United Drug; the job which pleased him most was going to England in 1920 and putting Boots on its feet.

Mr. A. H. Diebold and Mr. W. E. Weiss should be summoned together, although on this particular morning Mr. Diebold is in New York's Liggett Building and Mr. Weiss is at the great Sterling factory in Wheeling, West

Virginia. Messrs. Diebold and Weiss comprise the Sterling team. Out of Canton, Ohio, some twenty-five years ago, came a tall, mild man and short aggressive man. The tall, mild man had the ideas; the short, aggressive man put them into practice. They are today the dominant figures in Sterling, and their methods are the same. It was Mr. Diebold who conceived the tremendous Sterling expansion of the last three years; Mr. Weiss made it possible and profitable.

After these, we might interrupt Mr. Charles McCallum, to discover him thumbing through a sheaf of newspaper clippings. Each day, from every town where there is a Liggett store, come the advertised price-cuts of Walgreen or Katz—competitors. "Cigarettes—1.19 cents a carton" "Aspirin—79 cents per 100" "Ipana Toothpaste—31 cents." The lists are long, and the day's sheaf is high. Mr. McCallum will tell you that the independents are often worse than the chains. "You cannot sell below cost price and remain in business," he observes. "Our price policy is simple: the lowest possible price to the consumer consistent with good business." Sometimes Liggett will meet a competitor's campaign; more often, not. But prices are daily problems for other reasons. There are the Liggett stores' birthday sales, when you can get a fifteen-cent soda for a nickel. And a store in the South may be overstocked with candy as a hot spell approaches. United Drug studies the weather, as it studies the flu and other odd subjects. But in general its price policy is both stable and constant.

Even simpler is Drug, Inc.'s price program in England, where operate the Boots stores (founded by Jesse Boot, now Lord Trent. He chose his title from the river which runs past his estate). There a merchants' protective trade association, government organized and supervised, places a stamp (like the U. S. Internal Revenue sticker on packages of cigarettes) on all drug goods. The stamp proclaims a price, and all druggists are forbidden by law to undersell it.

Likewise in the Liggett Building in New York is W. C. Watt, treasurer and financial brain of Drug, Inc.—and, irrelevantly, perhaps the best golfer in the company. And, of course, there is Mr. Liggett in Boston. He is somewhat less active now than when Leon Street was young, but his command of figures and his extraordinary memory are still Drug, Inc. assets. He is a large, ruddy person, cheerful and convivial. As Republican National Committeeman of Massachusetts, he was stormy and vigorous and caused much comment among dry Republicans by a devout espousal of the anti-prohibition cause. He has a home in Newton, Massachusetts. He yachts on his *Ambler* and keeps hunters. But he likes his business and he likes his office, which is filled with photographs of friends and family and many an old copy of his firm's house magazine, *Rexall Advantages*. On the wall behind his chair hangs a painting of the original Leon Street building. On the dictaphone on his desk is a little brass pig.

His first business experience, at the age of fourteen, was selling for Wanamaker's. His first (and unsuccessful) venture into the drug business was selling a headache tablet. He has a flair for organization and is able to inspire both confidence and enthusiasm in his associates. In 1921 the stock of Drug, Inc. was badly depressed, and Mr. Liggett found himself unable to liquidate his holdings in order to meet certain obligations. Rexall agents loaned a total of $1,250,000 and enabled Mr. Liggett to get out of his difficulties. He is undoubtedly as well informed about the drug business as any man in the U. S.

STERLING PRODUCTS: CLINICAL NOTES ON SOME FAMOUS REMEDIES

In Port Chester, N. Y., are made Life Savers in a factory that you can see from the railroad tracks, and many a commuter to New York has cast an early morning eye at the three huge packs of Life Savers advertising the "Candy Mint With the Hole" on the lawn in front of the building. In Rahway, New Jersey, is the factory for Three-in-One Oil, first concocted by one J. Noah H. Slee, second husband of Margaret (birth-control) Sanger, who is his second wife. It derives its name from the fact that it is actually three oils—animal, vegetable, and mineral.

The origin of most of the Sterling medicines is pretty much the same. These medicines were made by local doctors, prescribed for their patients. They began to grow in popularity; they became known; they were purchased by Sterling Products; they became nationally known. In Glenbrook, Connecticut, where one Dr. Phillips first made it and sold it to his neighbors, is concocted the now famed Phillips Milk of Magnesia. California Syrup of Figs was first bottled by a man named Queen who lived in Reno, Nevada. There is Charles H. Fletcher's Castoria, a pleasant substitute for castor oil, marketed under the excellent but improbable slogan: "Children Cry for It." One Seraph Deal still enjoys royalties from the sale of Mum. In 1929, the company purchased the Bristol-Myers Co., manufacturers of Sal Hepatica, Ingrams' Shaving Cream, and Ipana Toothpaste. In 1930, it purchased the Vick Chemical Co. (VapoRub).

The effect of such companies as United Drug and Sterling upon patent medicines has been, according to the American Medical Association, which is always very doleful upon the subject, to "help toward making patent medicine advertising a little more decent and conservative." With some acidity, the A. M. A.'s Bureau of Investigation concludes that "most of these cooperative concerns make at least a pretense of giving some information regarding the composition of their products."

All the United Drug and Sterling labels, however, are acceptable under the restrictions of the Federal Food and Drug Act. In the history of United Drug, the A. M. A. has record of only one product which was declared misbranded. This was a Rexall headache wafer marketed around 1910 and declared harmless, although it contained acetphenetidin, a harmful drug. Acetphenetidin is one of the few drugs that the Food and Drug Act requires to be declared as to presence and quantity in patent medicines. The highly ethical and strict A. M. A. could not, of course, approve of any company which markets a patent medicine. But as far as this phase of its business is concerned, Drug, Inc. receives from the A. M. A. as much approval as it could possibly obtain.

Sterling Products, Inc. is itself successor to Sterling Remedies, started in 1887 by one H. L. Kramer of Attica, Indiana. Mr. Kramer in his day was a violent anti-nicotinist and developed a product called No-Tobac. In the spirit of the well-known Keeley cure, No-Tobac tasted so awful that you were supposed never to want to smoke again. The trouble was that No-Tobac was constipating. It rid you of a habit but, with something akin to poetic justice, it created an unpleasant condition. So Mr. Kramer ingeniously developed a laxative pill made of cascara sagrada to be taken after No-Tobac. His trade name was Cascarets. The Cascarets, not the No-Tobac, made the fortune. A moral may probably be drawn.

Most widely sold drug in the U. S. is aspirin. In Rensselaer, New York, a rather disagreeable town, is the Bayer Co., manufacturers of Bayer's Aspirin, most widely sold and advertised aspirin in the world. The Bayer Co. was originally owned by the I. G. Farbenindustrie, but was seized by the U. S. Alien Property Custodian (at that time the vigorous, brilliant Germanophobe, Mr. Francis P. Garvan) at the beginning of the War. Sterling bought the company from the government in 1919.

Not listed on the *American Druggist* chart, although they are Sterling companies, are the Winthrop Chemical Company and the Metz Laboratories. They are engaged chiefly in medicinal research and produce no patent medicines. They are the aristocrats of the group. They were omitted because the A. M. A. frowns dourly on the advertisement—direct or indirect—of ethical preparations. The two companies produce nothing which the A. M. A. does not approve though there was once a slight argument about the labeling of a certain product with a trade name.

The Metz Laboratories operate on a smaller scale as do the pharmaceutical laboratories of Squibb or Parke, Davis. They work out new formulas or improve old ones. They are proudest of their discovery of spinocain—an anæsthetic for major operations. It is put into the spinal fluid and causes temporary paralysis of the lower half of the body. It is used on patients whose hearts might not be able to stand ether, and its after effects are less annoying.

The Winthrop Chemical Company is allied with Germany's vast and important chemical company, I. G. Farbenindustrie. It manufactures I. G. pharmaceuticals under a perpetual contract to give I. G. a percentage of the profits.

Significant among I. G. products are chaulmestral, the leprosy medicine, and luminal, only known specific for epilepsy. Recently developed is an anæsthetic called avertin, rapidly growing in popularity among advanced hospitals. It enables the patient to sleep for some time before the operation and for several hours after it. Its after effects are practically negligible. Vigantol is an I. G. specific for rickets. It was developed by Dr. Windaus, winner of the 1928 Nobel prize for chemistry, who at the request of I. G. went to Norway to discover what in cod liver oil made it healthy. He studied the cod's food and found no clue, at length studied the light as it filtered through the water to the cod. He succeeded in isolating Vitamin D. And cod liver oil is properly called bottled sunshine. Vigantol, which is isolated Vitamin D, will cure any case of rickets.

In the whole history of medicine only a very few absolute specifics have been found. One is quinine for malaria; another I. G. produced and Winthrop-marketed, is the famous 606, better known as salvarsan, which makes war on the trypanosomes responsible for African sleeping sickness and annihilates syphilis germs. It was discovered by Paul Ehrlich, than whom no more picturesque figure ever appeared among research workers. He was born in 1854 in Silesia. At school in Breslau he was brilliant but intellectually unruly. Asked to write an essay on the subject, "Life is a Dream," he composed these sentences: "Life rests on normal oxidations. Dreams are an activity of the brain and activities of the brain are only oxidations."

His god was Robert Koch, and it was Ehrlich who showed Koch how to stain tissue and see the tubercle microbe. Dabbling with the germ, he caught tuberculosis and went to Egypt, returning in 1890 cured by Robert Koch.

He was constantly experimenting with dyes. One day as he watched methylene blue course through the tissues of a rabbit, he noticed that dye stained only the nerve endings. He decided to discover an aniline dye which would select a microbe for annihilation, avoiding the tissue and leaving it unimpaired. For several years he experimented with trypanosomes. Then he read of a poisonous drug called atoxyl, of which arsenic was the strategic substance, which had proved efficacious in a few cases of sleeping sickness. Ehrlich blithely said, "We will change it a little." Every scientist assured him that atoxyl could not be changed, but Ehrlich continued his work. The rest of the story is well known. After 605 failures, Ehrlich's 606th experiment produced salvarsan, which killed trypanosomes and left no trace or after effects. It was the result of twenty years of "mad unscientific work." It was the most important chemico-medical discovery of a century.

TIN CAN

Mirrored in The American Can Company's Dramatic Thirty-year Evolution is the Whole Trend of American Industry, the Strange Phenomenon Whereby Our Cities Rise Upon Foundations of Cans, the Change in Industry's Personnel from the Adventurers to the Administrators, the March of Technical Advance

AMERICAN CAN COMPANY

◦◦◦

THE American Can Company does not talk about itself. Nevertheless, there adheres to it (as to any large corporation) a cluster of fact plus a cluster of estimate, opinion, and rumor.

Some Can facts are matters of public record. Its most important published statement is its net income, which was $22,884,000 in 1930, up from $22,725,000 in 1929 and $19,863,000 in 1928. Its most recently publicized activity was its entrance into the British can-making field. In July, 1930, it organized British Can Shares, Inc., to hold shares in British Can Co., Ltd., large British can-maker. The Can Company, moving against the industrial trend, reported larger sales in 1930 than in 1929, also declared an extra dividend of $1.00 in September, 1930.

Otherwise, what is published about Can is largely routine. Its home is at 230 Park Avenue, Manhattan. It has fifty-three plants in forty-five cities, farthest flung plant, in Honolulu, making cans for Dole, Del Monte, and Libby pineapples. It is traded in on the New York, the Chicago, and the Amsterdam stock exchanges. It values "land, buildings, equipment, etc." at $136,843,848; it has total assets of $198,422,360 and a surplus of $69,739,471. Until 1929, it consistently put more money back into surplus than it paid out in common dividends, and in the past ten years it has invested over $70,000,000 of earnings in plant additions and improvements. Chairman F. S. Wheeler and President H. W. Phelps have been with the company since its organization in 1901. Its distinguished directorate includes Herbert L. Pratt of Standard of New York and E. E. Loomis of the Lehigh Valley Railroad. During the bull market of 1929 its common sold up to $184\frac{1}{2}$, and its turnover of more than five times the number of shares outstanding ranked it close up to Radio Corp. as a market favorite.

It does not publish sales or gross income figures. It issues annual statements only. It is undeniably the largest can-making concern, with Continental Can second, but how many cans it makes or what proportion of the business it does are matters of deep obscurity. Conservative estimates, however, are that American does over 30 per cent of U. S. can business (measured in dollars) and that it is at least twice as large as Continental. It was organized (in 1901) as a merger of a majority of all can-making companies, and for some years was popularly known as the Tin Can Trust. Today it is a conservative, soundly established, highly profitable corporation occupying in the making of cans somewhat the position occupied by U. S. Steel in the making of steel. Like U. S. Steel, it is not a monopoly, it will never again be a monopoly, and for the greater part of its life it has seen its percentage of the can-making business diminish. It represented the violent disturbances of an equilibrium which is still reasserting itself. But from this restoration of the normal order, no one has more profited than the Can Company. Its promoters have long since gone to a reward not associated with the securities of merged companies. Its financial policy has altered from the extremely radical to the ultra-conservative. It is deservedly popular with the canning industry, to the advancement of which it has notably contributed. In its first year, as the Tin Can Trust, it made $1,775,564. In 1930, in a fair and competitive field, it made $22,883,941. This comparison must be weighted with the realization that the can business has expanded tremendously during the past thirty years, as the harsh demands of an increasingly urban civilization have compressed nearly every perishable product into the safety of tin plate. Yet the company of today is making much more money on a much sounder basis than the trust of yesterday. It is probable that if the money spent in the illegal formation of the monopoly had been invested in a more legitimate expansion during the same period, holders of Can securities would have gained at least as much profit without undergoing nearly as many gray hairs. But the group of promoting insiders would not have added so quickly to their wealth.

And the American Can Company is a splendid example of high-pressure promotion. Its formation was very much affected by the circumstance that tin cans are not made of tin. They are made of tin plate, which is steel with a thin coating of tin. The tin plate industry is (and was) an important branch of the steel industry, and the tin can-maker is (and was) by far the greatest user of tin plate. Thus a simple and logical form of steel integration would be an association between a can-maker and a tin plate-maker, and indeed the Continental Can Company today has a tin plate subsidiary and the McKeesport Tin Plate Company has a tin can subsidiary. Remembering that the American Can Company was formed during the great steel integration period culminating with the formation of the U. S. Steel Corporation, it is not surprising to find that its organization was partly a move in the steel merger. Indeed, there is reason to believe that the Can Company was put together with the express purpose of combining with the Steel Corporation and that the failure of this combination to materialize was a disappointment to its founders and stockholders. The Can story and the Steel story run so closely parallel that it becomes very difficult to discuss the formation of Can without getting into the much more complicated and far-reaching discussion of the formation of Steel.

For the backers of American Can were also the backers of National Steel, of American Sheet Steel, of American Steel Hoop, and of American Tin Plate, all of which (as everyone knows) were organized just prior to the formation of U. S. Steel and became charter members of that great company. There were five prime Can movers. One, Edwin Norton, was a can-maker. The four others were promoters. They were William H. (Judge) Moore; J. Hobart Moore, brother of the foregoing; Daniel Gray (Czar) Reid; and William B. (Tin Plate) Leeds. Leader of the quartet was Judge Moore. Originally an Easterner (there is a Moore Chemistry Laboratory at Amherst), he went to Chicago, married well, practiced law (hence the legal title), and finally, with his brother, abandoned law for organizing. His first notable promotion was Diamond Match; to him also the National Biscuit Company owes its origin. But it was in the steel business that he made his greatest reputation and profit. By 1898 it had become evident that the steel industry was on the verge either of a great war or a great peace between Federal Steel (J. Pierpont Morgan) and

Carnegie Steel (Andrew Carnegie). Golden was the opportunity for the promoter who could combine steel units not identified either with Federal or with Carnegie. And quick was Judge Moore to seize it. With his brother and with Messrs. Reid and Leeds ("Two little boys from Indiana," as Mr. Reid used to speak of himself and friend), he organized what would today be spoken of as the Moore Interests. Consisting of the (already mentioned) National Steel, American Steel Hoop, American Sheet Steel, and American Tin Plate companies, the Moore group was the third largest steel consolidation, producing 12 per cent of ingots, 70 per cent of sheet steel, and 90 per cent of tin plate. The companies were all heavily capitalized, and the promoters' commissions amounted to more than $20,000,000 of stock. So when, in February, 1901, the U. S. Steel Corporation was organized and absorbed the Moore group, the Moores and their associates traded steel stocks for Steel stock and became notably affluent.

Looking back upon the Can organizers, especially looking back across a period of years notable for the decline of the monopoly movement and for an increase in industrial social consciousness, Mr. Moore and his friends appear rather more picturesque than profound. From a sober economic standpoint, they spent their time in perpetually painting the town red. One thinks of Dan Reid and Billie Leeds ordering $250,000 of tin plate machinery on the day following the promulgation of the McKinley Tariff, with its protective duty on tin plate, or of the same Dan and Billie startling old Andrew Carnegie by offering him $1,000,000 for a ninety-day option on his holdings in Carnegie Steel. Or of Mr. Reid's gay parties or of Judge

Moore's stable of seventy fast horses or his even more famous fur coat, which cost $19,000 and was the most expensive garment worn by any U. S. male. Or of J. Hobart Moore retiring to Glenwood Springs, Colorado, to take cave baths. "The Big Four from the Prairies," they were called, and it was said that not for years did J. Pierpont Morgan forget the price which they extracted for their contributions to the steel merger. Yet it would be a mistake to consider them merely industrial playboys. Judge Moore, for example, was a director of the First National at a time (1902) when its directorate included also James J. Hill, George F. Baker Sr., and J. Pierpont Morgan. He left an estate of $24,000,000; he left also a group of combinations (such as Diamond Match, National Biscuit, and American Can) which have remained of outstanding importance in their industries. Mr. Moore and his friends wound up companies and ran them (frequently at a hazardous velocity) like small boys playing with toy trains. But they were not really toy trains, and many of them have continued to run long after the departure of their creators.

This, briefly, was the background against which the American Can Company went through its formative period. The Can Company was put together in much the same manner that the Moores had rounded up the sheet steel companies and that Mr. Reid and Mr. Leeds had corralled the tin plate-makers. When operations began (late in 1899), there were about 175 can-making companies, none of which were national, hardly even regional, in scope or importance. One of the largest individual companies was, however, Norton Bros., and Edwin Norton, its president, was selected to look after the actual physical formation (by purchase) of the trust structure. And Mr. Norton did one of the very best jobs in monopolizing history. In from six to eight months after he had begun securing options on can properties, the American Can Company was in existence as a merger of ninety-five can-makers, and within sixty days after its organization (March, 1901), twenty-eight additional concerns had come into the fold. Excluding canners who made their own cans, the companies forming the American group produced more than 90 per cent of the entire can output, and no company of major importance remained outside the organization.

Mr. Norton must have been an excellent persuader thus to assemble nearly an entire industry in less than a year's time, but his accomplishment was perhaps more thorough than extraordinary. The period was the high noon of the monopolizing impulse; many a small independent was well satisfied to sell out to the trust former, and many another was afraid to remain out by himself. The relationship between the Tin Plate Trust and the proposed Tin Can Trust was perfectly obvious and universally realized, and the possibility that the can-maker who did not join the Can Trust would have a difficult time buying tin plate was one compelling inducement. As a matter of fact, the Can Trust did make a preferential agreement with the Tin Plate Trust, although the two companies did not work together as closely as might have been expected, since by the time American Can was actually organized, Tin Plate was a portion of the Steel Corporation, and Mr. Morgan and his associates did not approve of anything in the nature of trade discrimination. But before Tin Plate joined the Steel Corporation, the position of Tin Plate as a near-monopoly controlled by the Moore management and the prospective position of American Can as a near-monopoly controlled by the Moore management must have been extremely suggestive. Furthermore, Mr. Norton collected, in addition to can-making companies, companies that made can-making machinery and was known to be negotiating with other machine shops for either preferential or exclusive supply contracts. The independent who was not sure of being able to buy raw material on a fair basis was equally unsure concerning the chances of getting machinery in anything like an open market, and as a matter of fact the Can Company after its organization did pay one of the largest can machine makers the sum of $100,000 per annum to sell to American Can its entire output of certain can-making machinery and also to waive certain disputes concerning patents. Thus the Tin Can Trust, in addition to a dominating manufacturing position, seemed likely also to enjoy at least a marked advantage with respect both to machinery and to material.

Yet, in fairness to Mr. Norton, it should be added that the Can Company was not assembled chiefly through any coercive process. Mr. Norton's success resulted primarily from his being willing to pay can-makers from one and one-half to twenty-five times the replacement value of their plants. There was never a more generous purchaser than Mr. Norton. One can-maker got $500,000 cash for a plant in which he had originally invested $70,000. Another can-maker built a $16,000 plant, and before he had ever made a single can in it, sold out for $80,000. As one discussion of the Can-forming period puts it: "The ratio between the real value (of properties purchased) and the price named depended more upon the nerve and the impudence of the seller than upon any estimate of the property's probable worth to the new combination." According to later government estimates, Mr. Norton's shopping trips resulted in an expenditure of about $25,000,000, probably twice as much as it would have cost him to have bought land and built and equipped factories capable of producing many more cans at much less cost per can. One of the strongest evidences that Mr. Norton was not interested in expansion but in elimination was that within two years of Can's organization, it had shut down eighty-four of its 123 factories—an extreme instance of "concentration" which is difficult to explain on any basis other than the theory that dead lovers are faithful lovers. Can-joiners were also required to sign an agreement not to reënter the canning business, within 3,000 miles of Chicago, for fifteen years. One can-maker, offered $300,000 for his plant, refused so to commit himself, whereupon the purchase price was increased to $700,-000 and the reëntrance prohibition was accepted. It would therefore appear that nearly all the independents who sold out to American made themselves a most profitable bargain and emerged from it with no complaint.

But of course it was not Mr. Norton's money that was being so generously distributed, and in the long run it was not exactly Mr. Moore's either. Most of the sellers took part or all of their payment in stock of the projected company, and the spectacle of a can-maker who had not yet made any cans selling his business for stock in a company which had not yet been incorporated was an unsurprising and normal procedure in the promoting process. Some cash, however, Mr. Moore and his friends did put up, but the funds thus invested were emphatically bread upon the waters. As soon as enough options had been secured to guarantee the success of the incipient trust, the American Can Company was incorporated, March 19, 1901, under the laws of New Jersey, and proceeded to authorize itself $88,000,000 capitalization (of which $82,466,600 was issued), half in common and half in preferred. The common and the preferred each had a par of $100, but the stock was actually traded in on a basis of $100 for a share of common *plus* a share of preferred, so that the $82,466,600 issued represented a market value of $41,233,300. Of this amount, the promoters took $39,000,000, in return for which they turned over their ninety-five can companies, plus $7,000,000 in cash to supply the new company with working capital. As the ninety-five companies had cost about $23,500,000, the total promoting expense (including the $7,000,000 cash for working capital) amounted to $30,500,000, and the promoting profit to the difference between $39,000,000 and $30,500,000, or $8,500,000. By the middle of 1901, therefore, the can-making industry in the U. S. had been almost entirely transformed into the American Can Company, and Mr. Moore and his friends had been repaid for their time and interest at the rate of something better than $1,000,000 a month.

Probably their profit would eventually have been even larger had they joined American Can (like the rest of the American family) to the Steel Corporation. But the Steel company was organized about a month before Can, so that Can could not have gone in with Tin Plate and Steel Hoop and Sheet Steel. To be sure, the two companies might have merged after Can's formation, but Mr. Morgan had already paid a high price for Mr. Moore's other properties and furthermore it would have been difficult to regard the acquisition of the Can Company as purely a further step in steel integration. At any event, although the Can Company was described shortly after its formation as being "closely allied to" and to be "ultimately absorbed by" the Steel Corporation, the closeness did not continue and the absorption did not occur. Otherwise, however, the Can formation would appear to have been an unqualified success. The promoters had their profit, the company had its business, and from every outside indication American can-making and American Can seemed to have become permanently identical.

And yet the tower had hardly been erected when it began to topple. The Tin Can Trust, although powerful, was also poverty-stricken. In the first place, it was notably overcapitalized. To balance its $82,000,000 of outstanding stock, its chief tangible assets were the plants which, as we have already seen, were bought for less than $25,000,000 and had a replacement value of possibly less than $15,000,-000. In the second place, its $7,000,000 of working capital disappeared almost instantaneously. The purchase price of the absorbed companies did not include the actual inventories of these companies at the time of purchase, and for these inventories the Trust paid nearly $6,000,000. It also purchased, a few months after its formation, about $1,000,-000 of its own stock, so that between these two transactions it began operations almost literally without a dollar to its name. For year after year it paid only partial dividends on its preferred (which were 7 per cent cumulative) and paid no dividends on its common. It took sixteen years to catch up with the preferred dividends (largely because of War orders, the company finally getting even on dividends in 1917). And the first common dividend was paid in 1923, or twenty-one years after the company's formation. It is no wonder that the stock of the company was long regarded as a highly speculative investment and that its market value went so low that for some years its promoters' paper profits remained purely paper. From the Trust's initial hard times and the resultant decline in its securities has arisen the story that George F. Baker Sr. purchased large quantities of Can stock at $3.00 a share. Such stories are always impossible to substantiate, but it is true that Mr. Moore and Mr. Baker were fellow directors in First National and that the Can did slump to the $3.00 figure, at which Mr. Baker might well have accumulated it.

But a more significant result of the Trust's proud but poor situation was a compulsory advance in the price of tin cans and the resultant revival of competition. All monopolies are popularly supposed to celebrate their position as such by price-raising. The Can Company, however, did not raise can prices to collect any exorbitant profit. It was merely attempting to keep itself in business in spite of unfortunate structural deformities. But the motive did not influence the result. The higher price of cans made canmaking profitable; promptly there followed just as wild a rush to get into the can business as there had been a rush to get out of it. A small tin can business did not require very much capital, and an industry which could be bought up for $25,000,000 could be reëstablished again at the same or a smaller figure. Soon it seemed that everyone was making tin cans. The Trust bought up some of the new tin can companies and also bought up 1,000,000 or so cans, but tin can concerns continued to multiply, although some of them made very bad containers which were no help to the canning industry. Not until 1904 were prices stabilized, and by that time the damage had been done. Not all of the little can companies went out of business again after prices had been restored to normal. The canning business was itself expanding. More fruits and vegetables were being canned; more people were eating canned foods; the Trust was attempting the impossible performance of continuing to monopolize a constantly expanding industry.

And in 1904 there came additional competition in the shape of a single strong competitor. Mr. Norton left the Trust and proceeded to organize the Continental Can Company. There are, of course, many stories as to why the man who was the Trust founder (from an operating standpoint) should so soon have parted company with it. Perhaps the simplest explanation is that Mr. Norton was growing old, that he was looking forward to his retirement, and that he had a son whom he wished to set up in business. There was also a Mr. Assman, friend and associate of Mr. Norton, who was in much the same position, there being an Assman Jr. to complete the parallel. So out went Mr. Norton and Mr. Assman and many another good Trust executive, and in came Continental as new and vigorous can competition. By 1913, when the government got around to prosecuting the Trust under the Sherman Act, the 90 per cent monopoly of 1901 had dwindled to 50 per cent, and healthy and growing was can competition.

The government's suit was the final chapter in the decadence of the Trust's character as such and very nearly resulted in the dissolution of the combine. It was ruled that Can had been formed in violation of the Sherman Act, and even after its organization it had indulged in certain objectionable practices, notably the concealment of subsidiaries. Yet by 1913 the Can Company had been for some years under the control of the more constructive elements in its composition. If it had been a bad trust, it had also become a good manufacturer, and its services to the canning industry were of inestimable importance. If an industry suffers from the presence of a company that is too big, it suffers also from the absence of a company that is not big enough. Before the advent of the Can Company, the canner purchased his cans from month to month, and the price of cans, low in the winter, increased through the spring and summer and reached its apex during the harvest season, in which the canner needed large and immediate deliveries at no matter what cost. The American Company offered the canner a seasonal contract, at a fixed price and with a guarantee of prompt and ample deliveries. Furthermore, the American Company, early in its career, went very thoroughly into the research problem of scientific canning and has been the foremost supporter of the National Canners' Association since the formation of that canning research organization. During the suit against the Can Company, a great many canners were asked whether they thought the Trust should be dissolved. None spoke in favor of dissolution; many spoke emphatically against it. And the trial judge himself, in the course of rendering his opinion, said: "I am frankly reluctant to destroy so fine an adjusted industrial machine as the defendant has shown itself to be." Even competitors of the Can Company said that they had no objection to the manner in which it carried on its business and that they felt no undue pressure from its power and scope. Thus by the time that the Can chickens came home to roost, they were not to be birds of such a very wicked feather. It is true that if the Can Trust (like the Oil Trust or the Tobacco Trust) had been organized by the juncture of large units which could have conveniently been separated, such separation might have been ordained. But no court could restore the 175 can-making companies as they existed in 1901, and any attempt at reestablishing the *status quo* would not only have been obviously unsuccessful but would have plunged the entire canning industry into a chaotic demoralization. Thus the court refused the government's petition for dissolution, and it does not appear likely that the American Company will ever come into court again on Sherman Act charges. For the leopard not only changed its spots, but found itself much better off without them.

After its escape from governmental dissolution, the American Company entered upon its modern period—a period begun by War-time prosperity, a period which has continued through a conservative management, a sound financial structure, a steady increase in revenue and in earnings. As its early history stands out against a background of stocks and promoters and manipulation, so its recent and present history stands out against a background of Iowa corn and Maryland tomatoes and Wisconsin peas and Hawaiian pineapples and California peaches. It should be remembered that the American Company is a can-maker, not a canner, and has no commercial interest in the packing of foods. But its business is of course directly dependent upon the canning business, which has increased probably far beyond even the vivid imaginations of the Can organizers. In 1905, about 41,000,000 cases of foods were packed in the U. S. In twenty-five years the pack had increased to 200,000,000 cases. As there are on an average twenty-four cans to the case, the packers are using 4,800,000,000 cans, and though all can companies appear extraordinarily sensitive as to the number of cans they manufacture or the proportion of the total represented by their production, an estimate of 45 per cent for American would appear reasonably correct. The cans themselves (those that are food containers) cost a little less than two and one-half cents apiece, the business representing therefore the infinite multiplication of infinitesimal profit. Like all industries that have to do with agriculture, the can-making business is somewhat affected by crop fluctuations, but the possibility of all crops going off the same year is sufficiently remote. Furthermore, the can-makers are rapidly developing what is known as the *general line* of business. A general line can (as distinct from a packer's can) is a can not containing fruit and vegetable products. Paint cans and oil cans, for instance, are conspicuous examples, and today nearly half the business of American and about 30 per cent of Continental is in the general line field. A somewhat startling example of the general line can has been furnished by Canadian distillers who have been putting up their whiskey in highly lithographed cans, the theory being that the bootlegger who so readily imitates labels on bottles cannot duplicate the expensive and complicated process of multicolor lithographing on tin.

And the American Company serves a business which is

still expanding. The canner has been one of the notable gainers by the shift in population from farm to city. In 1900, only 40 per cent of the U. S. population lived in cities. In 1930, the urban dwellers were nearly 60 per cent of the whole. And during this thirty-year period there has also been a constant increase in the number of apartments as compared to the number of homes. There is a strong kinship between the kitchenette and the can. There is an equally obvious relationship between the large city—particularly the large eastern city, far removed from farm lands and their harvest—and the consumption of canned rather than fresh fruits and vegetables.

Trite is the quotation concerning our having been given memories in order that we might have roses in December. Applicable is the adaptation that we have been given canneries in order that we might have peas and tomatoes and fruits in the barren months of winter. Many a modern city meal not only begins with canned soup and ends with canned pears and peaches, but may well include canned asparagus and corn and perhaps even present, as the *pièce de résistance*, some such canned specialty as beef *à la mode*. Vegetables such as artichokes, hominy, and pumpkin; fruits such as grapes, strawberries, and grapefruit; fish such as anchovies, shad, and clams; specialties such as Boston brown bread, fig pudding, and Irish stew—these and many other tinned products have unquestionably given the American diet a marked variety, have also saved many hours otherwise spent in the cooking of fresh products. As for the ancient prejudice against canned foods, that feeling dwindled along with the feeling against bakers' bread, and certainly the home canner is no menace to the canner of commercial nature. Just as the Campbell Soup people have long pointed out, the housewife today can buy a virtually ready-to-serve product for less than its raw materials would cost her.

To the prosperity of the canner, the can-maker has constantly contributed. He has developed the open-top (solderless at top and bottom) can to replace the old container in which there was the possibility of solder particles appearing in the contents. Through his own laboratories and through his contributions to canners' research, he has supported the experimental work in many new methods and processes. American has recently developed the vacuum process, through which it hopes to make the canned foodstuff virtually identical with the fresh. Among other large American customers are Del Monte, Beechnut Coffee, Lipton Coffee, Hormel, Van Camp Packing, and Patton Paint companies. Large customers of Continental are Campbell's Soup, Standard Oil of New Jersey, and William Underwood companies. Other can-makers are likely to specialize in general line cans. Thus the Metal Package Co., third largest can-maker, makes containers for the following non-foodstuff companies: Standard Oil of New York, Colgate-Palmolive-Peet, United Drug, Gulf Refining, and McKesson and Robbins companies. With the exception of the milk canner, few large canners manufacture their own cans.

Largest U. S. companies have also expanded into Great Britain. In July 1930, American formed British Can Shares, Inc., through which it acquired a large interest in British Can Co., Ltd., which manufactures about 25 per cent of the metal containers made in the British Isles. Continental Can has also entered the British field through the purchase of something less than 20 per cent interest in Metal Box & Printing Industries, Ltd., which does more than 50 per cent of British canning. The British have developed the lithographed can to a point beyond the best practice in this country, but their ordinary packers' tin cans are not so satisfactory, and the British canner is as likely as not to make his own cans. Thus American and Continental expect to learn valuable lithographing lessons, expect also to demonstrate in Great Britain their ability to turn out the standardized container in great quantities, at low costs.

Out of the wreckage of the old Trust, therefore, the Can Company has retained the leading position in an industry that has been consistently prosperous for many years and that looks confidently forward to an even more prosperous future. Back in 1908 its common could have been purchased at $8.00 a share; in 1926 its high was $130\frac{1}{2}$, at which point the $100 par was reduced to $25 and the stock split six for one (a 50 per cent stock dividend). The new stock was one of the speculative favorites of the 1929 market, reaching a high of $184\frac{1}{2}$, though breaking to 86 in the crash. During 1929, 13,463,200 shares changed hands, or more than five times the total outstanding, a rate of turnover about twice that of U. S. Steel and not greatly exceeded by Radio Corp., whose six to one ratio of sales to shares outstanding was probably the highest of any major company.

There is perhaps no moral to be drawn from the Can story. The fact that its success came after it had ceased to be a monopoly is of course no monopolistic argument, since much of that success came from consolidating the position which it derived from its original character. Its present management—Chairman Frederick S. Wheeler and

President H. W. Phelps—have been with the company since its organization, and the company is today markedly reticent concerning both the story of its past and the gross business of its present. On the other hand, it has been and remains of tremendous service to the canning industry. Its original promoters may appear to have been governed more by the acquisitive instinct than by social or economic considerations. Yet out of their extensive but terribly ramshackle structure has grown the sound and substantial corporation of today. From an industrial standpoint, it would appear that the good men do lives sometimes after them and that it is the evil which is interred with their bones.

DANGER IN MILWAUKEE

In the Great Milwaukee Plants of the A. O. Smith Corporation, Where Automobile Frames are Made Without Robots and Sold Without Salesmen, is the Supreme Example of the Automatic Function—and a Threat to the Old Industrial Regime

A. O. SMITH CORPORATION

By Stuart Chase

JEREMIAHS of monumental profundity wring their hands and tear their beards lamenting the conversion of men into robots in the age of the machine. They adduce no figures, but the impression given is a wholesale operation, affecting nearly all of us. Elsewhere I have sought to verify, quantitively, the strength of this indictment. With the Census of Occupations as a base, I found that of 42,000,000 Americans gainfully employed, not more than 10,000,000 spent their working hours in close contact with machinery. Further analysis discloses that only about 5,000,000 can properly be called robots at all in that they surrender their personalities to the machine.

The other 5,000,000 either are handicraft men and other helpers about factories who have little to do with machinery, or—and this is important—they themselves *dominate* the mechanism, and thus let some of its energy into their own veins. Air pilots are not robots by any stretch of the imagination, and neither are operators of motor cars, locomotive engineers, or structural steel workers. Lastly, of those who might be termed robots—some 12 per cent of the gainfully employed—the number is actually declining, and for two reasons. Due to technical improvements in output per man, factory employees are growing fewer.

Second, the automatic function in industry is steadily gaining ground, displacing machine-feeders and nut-screwers by skilled designers, inspectors, dial-watchers. A large number of so-called robots give way to a small number of workers with reasonably intelligent and independent jobs.

In order that the Jeremiahs may see exactly what I mean, I take pleasure in presenting in some detail the most advanced single exhibit of the automatic function in the world. The honor belongs beyond peradventure to the mill which makes automobile frames practically by itself on the premises of the A. O. Smith Corporation in the city of Milwaukee. And I take pleasure in presenting one or two additional aspects of this extraordinary company which ought to give the machine age philosophers, both gloomy and cheerio, enough to reflect on for quite a while to come. This plant not only threatens to end the scourge of the robot; it threatens to end industry itself—in the form that we have hitherto known it. There is a mixture brewing here which, if it explodes, will make Milwaukee more famous than ever did its beer.

The company was founded over half a century ago with the commendable purpose of fabricating baby carriages. In due time, babies were abandoned for bicycle riders. About 1900, Mr. A. O. Smith, the son of the founder, gave the first recorded example of that policy to which the company now dedicates itself. He had been following the early flounderings of the automobile. Bankers and other sensible folk knew it for what it was—a crazy, impracticable contraption. Not so Mr. Smith. He was convinced that the motor car had a future. Some day it would be made in large quantities. It would need a frame on which its engine would rest. That frame might be made of wood, iron, or pressed steel. He pondered over these three alternatives as the one-lungers gurgled, backfired, and frightened live stock out of its wits. He concluded his ruminations in favor of pressed steel. With a group of men from the bicycle shop, he proceeded to design and erect special machinery for making steel frames, *a full year before there was any call for them, or indeed any evidence that America would take to making automobiles in a determined way at all!* He had thought out his problem, designed and set up his equipment in advance of the world's recognition that there was a problem. This is the sort of thinking which is coming out of Milwaukee today.

In 1902, the orders—more or less on schedule—began to arrive, the machines were put at productive labor, and the first frames shipped out. They came from the shop at the rate of ten per day, and Mr. Smith offered a house and lot to the foreman who could get out twelve. (Now they are coming at 10,000 a day.) It was hand and machine work, much of it robot work, if you please. The business prospered. The grandson of the founder, Mr. L. R. Smith, took the helm his father laid down. He looked at the rows of men handling heavy steel side bars, performing a single operation. "It's stupid," he thought, "and wasteful. It costs too much; it's bad for the men. Men have too much innate ability to be condemned to such work as this." He turned to his engineers, a growing corps and one upon which he came more and more to depend. (He is himself an engineer.) "Could we design a machine to do this whole job automatically, a machine as big as a factory, to pick up the raw steel and throw these things out at four or five thousand a day? I know it is a crazy idea, but can we do it?" His engineers had learned to expect anything from this man. The T squares spanked and the drawing boards groaned. Ten times the plant was built on paper, and the cost of the crazy idea had mounted to $1,500,000.

Finally, after incredible labor and some of the boldest mechanical thinking ever done on this planet, a plan was evolved which looked as though, by the grace of God, it might work. Bankers were called in and their advice asked. The rosy-gilled fraternity was petrified, and advised, whatever it was, not to do it. They were thanked politely, and the metamorphosis of paper into concrete and steel was promptly begun. Fortunately, money in the home stocking was still available.

Beyond the technical incredibility of the project was the whole question of the potential market. Suppose the plant could be built, who was to buy frames in lots of 7,000 each and every day; 2,000,000 frames a year? Competitors were in the field, and in 1916 only 1,500,000 motor cars were manufactured the country over. The blueprints called for more frames than there were engines to mount on them. But even as his father had sensed the beginning of an industry in 1900, the son sensed the post-War automotive boom. "We were aiming at million-lot machinery, million-lot production, and million-lot costs, and lo! the market came to meet this million-lot expectancy. The plant was built in 1920. Soon afterward the roaring twenties, building 3,000,000, 4,000,000, 5,000,000 motor cars a year, were in full swing and demanding Smith frames.

"By the time the mill was built, $6,000,000 had been sunk in it, including the drawing paper. Would the damn thing work? The blueprints were optimistic, but how about

Madam Nature? Here were 552 separate operations to be performed on every frame. If any one of them went wrong, the whole gigantic mechanism might jam.

"I will never forget that moment when it became necessary for me or an associate to throw on the power. Both of us were stalling, one waiting for the other. Neither can remember clearly which one threw the switch. But for an hour and fifty-seven minutes, the unit functioned without a hitch. Then it shut down for want of raw material!"

The damn thing would work. It has been working ever since. And, of course, for all the palpitations when the first switch was thrown, Mr. Smith and his engineers *knew* it would work. Too much sound research had already gone in to permit of failure. It was no miracle nor are the subsequent achievements miracles, spectacular as they appear. It is the sort of thing to be expected when engineering takes the place of rule of thumb, and its possibilities developed *to the limit*. In due time production was stepped up from 7,000 frames a day to 10,000—and the end is not yet.

One goes through a guarded gate into the great enclosure upon which the company's property stands: a company which sells $60,000,000 of tonnage products a year, moving out on 30,000 freight cars. The buildings are not huge but squat and grim, full of noise and full of power. There is an air of spaciousness and cleanliness, but no hint of lawns, flowers, and the tra-la-la-la school of mill design. Clean, muscled, and stripped to the waist is the dominant note. But stop a moment. What is this partly finished building of peculiar steel construction with black granite base and fluted aluminum creeping up over the stanchions? It is the new Research Building, equipped to house 1,000 engineers. It could have been built for $400,000 but is costing $1,500,000.

And why, pray, the extra $1,000,000? It is expended to make as just and lovely a temple to the god of science as devoted hands have reared to other gods in other ages. Engineering research is the chief business of this company. Frames for motor cars, pipes for oil fields, pressure vessels —these are by-products.

We enter a door in one of the squat mills and are suddenly drowned in sound. We are in a room perhaps 300 feet long and 200 wide, with walls of glass. Its floor is one solid mass of glittering steel, a thousand shapes which rush and stop, rise and fall, advance and retreat, dancing to some gigantic rhythm, yet to a counterpoint which sets up no vibration. One quadrille offsets the other, leaving the building without a tremor. The multiplicity of moving shapes confuses us, but as we mount a platform, a sense of discipline, of patterned harmony, becomes apparent. Wide, clean aisles separate the moving groups. There are no towering mechanisms, no belts; the whole upper part of the building is clear. The largest single shape is near the door by which we entered. It is also the noisiest. With drum-shattering gasps it is solemnly picking up pieces of steel, fitting them to a pattern, dropping the unit down for some attention (the seat of the noise apparently), raising it up, placing it on a little carriage of delicate steel rods . . . carriage after carriage, which rush and stop, rush and stop, rush and stop, in our direction.

Comprehension dawns. Upon each carriage is obviously a motor car frame; the hissing mechanism has assembled the various side bars and cross bars which compose it, and the dropping motion—our guide assists us here—is the automatic insertion of 100 rivets into their waiting holes. The assembled frame moves towards us for the job of heading the rivets and so locking the parts finally together.

As the frames advance and stop, two batteries of steel dragons, with jaws like those of stone Aztec serpents, move forward upon them, one from either side. Their round metal eyes glitter, their jaws are distended to cavernous proportions, they nuzzle into their victim's vitals, select each a sought-for rivet, then slowly, relentlessly, even softly, the great jaws close. The final crunch of 40,000 pounds upon the rivet head is effortless. Gently the jaw opens; gently and solemnly both batteries retreat. The frame moves on to another group of monsters, where the process is repeated with a second set of rivets. One hundred rivets require about 100 dragons, and only about six can operate comfortably at one "station."

Sometimes, if you please, the beast opens its mouth to bite, thinks better of it, retires, rears up into a more ferocious position, and then comes dreadfully down. It is reported that Mr. Otto Kahn could not be budged from his entranced survey of this deliberate animal. "I have seen many ingenious machines," he said, "but this is the first that ever I saw which started to do a job, stopped, spit on its hands, hitched up its overalls, and then went to work!" This is a good story—but dragons, my dear Mr. Kahn, really, dragons do not spit on their hands.

There are nine units in the total process. In each unit are a number of stations—connoting a single operation. What I have described is but the operation of several stations on unit No. 6, the general assembly line. As we walk along our platform which runs the length of the building, each unit is identified between its dividing aisles, and its general function, if not its bewildering detail, made plain. A little table tells the story:

UNIT　　　　　　FUNCTION

No. 1.—Picks up the raw steel strips, examines them, throws out those which do not meet the required standards of length, breadth, and thickness.

No. 2.—Douses the admitted strips into baths of pickle for cleaning.

No. 3.—Fabricates the longer strips into right and left side bars—bending them, turning up their edges, punching holes for future rivets.

No. 4.—Fabricates the shorter strips into cross bars.

No. 5.—Assembles the various parts of the side bars.

No. 6.—Assembles the whole frame, inserts and drives home the rivets—by virtue of monsters altogether fabulous, as we have seen.

No. 7.—General inspection of the assembled frame, a partly human job.

No. 8.—Automatic washing, painting, and drying.

No. 9.—The snatching of the painted, dried, completed frame by the left hind leg, as it were, and bearing it, like a hog in a packing house, to a vast overhead storage space. There it hangs, in carload lots, until a man in a little underslung crane, which crawls like a busy beetle among these towering heights, drops it, kerplunk, into a waiting freight car.

One hour and a half from raw steel to suspension by the hind leg, and a minute or two more to freight car if there is any rush. Every eight seconds a completed frame goes swinging into storage, 420 an hour, 10,000 a day. Frames for Pontiac, Chrysler, Chevrolet, Buick. For each type of frame, the great dance stops for a few hours. Skilled mechanics swarm out from the tool shop at the end of the building and reset the dragons' jaws and the other mechanisms to take care of the new size. Given an overall length and width, any variety—past, present, or future—of frame can be made. About thirty different styles are now fabricated, but the total variety is virtually limitless. The goal of standardization with *flexibility* has been won. In nine years of operation no automobile maker has ever had to shut down his assembly line for lack of frames, this in spite of eleventh-hour increases in orders on the part of customers.

Are the Jeremiahs answered? Academically no. Practically yes, if this sort of thing is to expand. Mr. Smith admits his mill to be an engineering failure though a huge commercial success. He set out to build a machine that would make frames without men. He did not quite succeed. At one or two stations, men touch the frame with their hands, thus breaking 100 per cent performance, though this is still the goal. The Jeremiahs, I among them, find other objections in the thought of ex-robots walking the streets. As technological unemployment advances, a technological solution must be found. I was glad to hear Mr. Smith say that shorter hours offered one remedy from the long swing point of view.

But consider the tangible achievement. Not a stone's throw away is the old "hand" mill. I went through it, and the contrast was staggering. Here are 2,000 men in long assembly lines, drilling holes, driving bolts, twisting shapes, conveying the growing frame by hand from process to process. Yet work as they may, they can make no more frames a day than can the automatic mill with a scant 200 men, not more than fifty of whom actually touch the product. Two thousand dreary jobs against 200 amusing ones, for an identical output! Ponder this well, ye Jeremiahs. The cost of the automatic frame to the hand frames is as two to three (and rather less in total than a good pair of shoes), with a very large absorption of development overhead. Some day when this overhead cost is all absorbed, the automatic cost will fall into the subcellar . . .

Few men ever voluntarily leave the automatic mill. There is a long waiting list. They appreciate it as "something different"; they appreciate the boldness of the boss in designing it, and their jobs are certainly far more independent and interesting than those in the hand mill. One man sits in a little tower, the control switches of a whole unit under his hand; another resets the gape of the dragons' jaws; another adjusts the "nailing machine," the automatic riveter which shoots by compressed air a hundred tiny bars of steel at once. (To skilled technicians this is the supreme mechanical achievement of the mill and the engine of which Mr. Smith is himself the proudest.) Skill varies; some jobs can be taught in a few days, others require months and months of intensive training, while in design, erection, and repair we have as skilled a group of crafts as this, or any other age, has ever glimpsed. The whole building is one vast integrated machine. Another major job remains, however, before the Jeremiahs are completely routed. There is, I believe, too much noise in that place for human ears to stand indefinitely without injury.

I asked Mr. Smith if the process were applicable to other industries. "Yes," he said, "almost everywhere when the demand is great enough to warrant 'million-lots.' Even automobiles could be assembled automatically if we were sure of their general style long enough to spend the time and money."

All the eggs of the A. O. Smith Corporation are not in one basket. Far from it. If frame-making be depressed, there is still the pipe business. Nor is the demand for pressure vessels likely to fall in the doldrums, due to its close association with the developing chemical industry.

This leads us back to the War. The company was conscripted to make aërial bombs. It devoted all its time to the art—dust even gathered on the frame mill blueprints in 1918. It made a lot of bombs, but far more important, it worked out an electric arc-welding process with which to seal up the bombs. This was later applied to couplings for joints in oil well pipe. The art of drilling was distinctly improved. Why not make bigger and thicker couplings, still by the welding process, put heads on them, and use them for stills in which to crack gasoline? Why not make all sorts of vessels capable of withstanding great pressures and high temperatures? The lowly casing coupling began to swell into the most fantastic shapes. One walks through the pressure vessel building as through some Mesozoic zoo. It is a custom department; each Megatherium is built to order. Here they are in all stages of construction: a round bellied monster sixty feet long, eight feet high, with a hide four inches thick; a vertical specimen twenty feet high, with a bloated stomach and amazing protuberances at cock-eyed angles; another with the tapering head of an anteater—except that it is thirty feet in circumference. About these monsters play skilled men in goggles and gloves, roweling their vitals with blinding flares. The fumes are borne away in boa-constrictor conductors which writhe about every job, and the air is clear. The steel bubbles, fluid as water when the arc comes down, and when it cools, the healed breach is as strong as any part of the vessel.

Perhaps you do not believe the latter statement. Indeed the local engineers were not absolutely sure of the strength of the early vessels themselves. There was nothing to do but to put them under pressure until they cracked, and find out where they cracked, and why. Great vessel after vessel was taken out in an open field and pumped full of water until—at 20,000 pounds or more to the square inch—it exploded, with instruments to measure and assess the yielding point.

This was unheard of. The Smith engineers not only found that when their welded vessels exploded the break was never at the point of welding, but they found out so many new things about "factors of safety" hitherto assumed by other vessel builders that they were forced to change the term to "factors of ignorance." They found that the behavior of steel at high temperatures under a long continued stress is far weaker than its behavior in a short test. They found out how openings and ends affected the strength of vessels. They made exhaustive studies of fatigue in steel. They made their pressure vessels impregnable (no one has ever failed) and at the same time added certain new and highly important laws to general science.

As a result of this research, the company is building the largest high pressure vessels ever known—one of them seventy feet long. Observe, too, that this process is yoked firmly to the almost unlimited future of the dawning chemical industry—ready to fabricate its stills, towers, digesters, and autoclaves, strengthened for unprecedented temperatures and pressures.

We go back to aërial bombs for the last major commercial product of the company. Lying in the Florida sun, a few winters ago, Mr. Smith had a pipe dream. Why not fold up long sheets of steel and arc-weld them where the edges joined? Why not give the pipe industry, which had scarcely moved for thirty years, a jolt? Within four months of his return, a new mill had been designed and built, and the pipe was coming through. Soon it was emerging to the tune of eight miles a day. Now it emerges at the rate of thirty-two miles a day. Presently . . .

It is a process noisy but simple to follow. Here come the big sheets of raw steel, sliding along on rollers. Three great bending machines force them into circles. The open seam is then welded by men in what look like gas masks, plying their flares high up in the middle of the shop—a Dantesque row of figures—while the pipe slowly moves beneath them. Each section is then subjected to terrific pressure to test its strength, with milky water to show possible pin hole leaks. The show then turns completely automatic and the thirty-foot pieces are washed, painted, dried, and rolled up a causeway into a storage bin even more fabulous than that designed for frames. It is a steel skeleton, 100 feet high, packed solidly with packages of pipe, one package to a carload. The cars roll under the great crane, and a package, specially designed to meet the shocks of traveling, drops neatly in.

The American oil industry—and its bankers—were

shown how they could, with this particular kind of pipe, build transcontinental lines for gas and gasoline at a cost lower than had ever been thought possible. Sceptics were turned into believers when they saw this pipe standing up under the hands of great torturing machines which tested its strength by crushing, twisting, and accordion-pleating; when they saw it required 134 less joints to the mile than the old twenty-foot pipe required; when they saw gangs of specially trained Smith Corporation men sinking it into the ground at unbelievably low costs per mile. In brief, the engineers demonstrated to the oil men how to make money in their own business, and the great pipe line boom was on. Gas is coming to Chicago from Texas, 950 miles away; gasoline is pumped over an 800-mile line.

What particularly pleases Mr. Smith and as a fanatic on economic waste particularly pleases me is that by virtue of these pipe lines, gas hitherto blown off into the atmosphere is to be collected and salvaged. It is more valuable than any manufactured gas known. Yet one well in California blew off enough gas, day after day, to meet the daily requirements of the entire city of San Francisco!

This is not the end of the story, only the beginning. Other pipe builders have been aroused from a generation of lethargy to develop competing processes. In small-diameter pipe, competition has long been hot and heavy between the several large producers. Now the electrically welded pipe monopoly of A. O. Smith (for a time, they were largest American steel users) has been challenged by Steel's subsidiary, National Tube, which has fought hard and fairly successfully to improve the old seamless pipe to meet A. O. Smith pioneering and which has begun to produce electrically welded tube. Youngstown Sheet & Tube has installed equipment for a process of its own; Republic has completed a $10,000,000 plant to make electrically welded tube in sizes from eight to sixteen inches. Not yet, however, has any steel company actually broken A. O. Smith's hold on the big (sixteen to twenty-four inch) electrically welded pipe market. And in 1928 Mr. Smith turned his laboratory hounds loose to develop a way of making pipe which would antiquate his competitors' ways before they got fairly started. Behind one high wall in the plant I was not permitted to go. Have the hounds run down the quarry? I do not know. But nobody in the organization seemed particularly worried.

One last field observation before we move to general principles. In a rambling wing I found the very efficient safety department and the department of preventive medicine equipped for as complete a physical examination as the best hospital can give. This is said to be the most thorough-going medical study of *normal* persons ever conducted. As the records grow and the years go by, it will be profoundly helpful in telling the well person what he must do to keep well . . . There are scientists of steel in this company and scientists of flesh and blood.

The Smith dynasty has a guiding star. It employs seven salesmen—I counted them—and not far from 600 engineers. Presently the new research building will house 1,000 engineers in quarters equipped with facilities beyond their wildest dreams. Their work is not primarily to keep the present output increasingly efficient, but to develop new varieties of output, and totally new processes for fabricating them. A program of industrial depth bombs, but geared to three basic principles:

I.—The product must lie in the field of mass production, with an established market, or one which the economic research staff knows can be established.

II.—A product to be made so much better and cheaper than anything else in the field that it will sell itself on its engineering merits alone, with no outlays for high pressure salesmanship or advertising.

III.—A product profitable enough to liquidate its fixed investment in not longer than a year or two. (The success of this principle hitherto is reflected in the company's luxuriant profit and loss accounts. I speak as a sometime C.P.A.).

The product having been determined according to these principles, it is put through three stages, or stations as Mr. Smith calls them. First comes the "pencil sketch" station. It may die there. But if the figures look sound, it goes to the "test tube" station, of laboratory analysis. If it survives this manhandling, it goes to the "pilot plant" station—a miniature factory where it is actually produced under normal operating conditions, and its performance, and particularly its costs per unit, accurately determined. The pilot plant answers the question: can it be made in the expected quantities at the calculated costs and how big must the real operating plant be? This delimits the design of the proposed plant and makes its construction practically automatic, with everything accounted for in advance. If the answer is in the negative, whatever the time and money spent upon the idea, it goes down the trap door. "I can get out of a business faster than anyone in the country," says Mr. Smith—an art which few executives have learned.

Lloyd Raymond Smith comes honestly by his face, his trade, and his name. Steelmen were his father and his father's brothers, and these were in turn the sons of a steelman. Not far from the A. O. Smith plant is another monument built by this family—the Geo. H. Smith Steel Casting Co. Altogether the Smiths have played a large part in Milwaukee's life. Lloyd Raymond Smith has always lived there in a big, comfortable house at 410 Terrace Avenue, has raised six children there, and has added to the city's wealth a fortune whose size can be measured only by the value of the business he directs and largely owns. So swift has been the company's recent rise (net income, year ended July 31 1928—$2,830,000; 1930—$5,500,000) that its value almost defies calculation. He has never dissipated the great force of his concentration upon this enterprise by accepting scattered directorships.

Certain by-products of profound industrial significance arise from this program. The production of a given article under these principles of engineering research, automatic fabrication, low costs, tends to insure high quality. If the mill is not to jam, every incoming piece of raw material— as we saw in the frame plant—must pass rigid tests of inspection. The delicate controls demand an absolutely uniform product, without flaw or break. Engineering and its handmaiden, mathematics, are sciences to which the word "elegance" has been frequently applied. In full control of the job, other things being equal, the output will share that perfection and that elegance. Mr. Lewis Mumford, the distinguished architectural critic, has been hinting at this for a long time. I am glad to supply him with concrete evidence of the soundness of his stand.

A second philosophical by-product—and not so exclusively philosophical either—is the factor of obsolescence. The Smith policy is ruthlessly to scrap anything which is not a jump or two ahead of the rest of the world; to scrap indeed when it *is* ahead, if the research staff has developed a better process. Certain great corporations buy up, or develop, improvements and file them in their safes. Mr. Smith puts them to work instanter; ground for the new plant is broken before the signature of the patent office is dry. "I grant it is wasteful, I grant the overhead cost is enormous, but it is far more wasteful to burn up men and materials in the old way when a better way has been found."

It all boils down, of course, to the margin of economy in the new way. If the margin is demonstrably greater than the cost of installing the method, it is cheaper to the company and to society to scrap the old; aye, to throw uncounted millions of investment on the dump heap. The only trouble is in locating the marginal point. Aging boards of corporate directors have some difficulty in the premises, but to a stripped, flexible organization with every executive ready to go through hell and out again with Mr. Smith, and 1,000 engineers supplying the facts, the point is easier to determine. Nine times out of ten an organization like this will succeed, where the ordinary manufacturer, regarding engineers as so many expensive plumbers, will fail if he attempts to flirt with the ballistics of obsolescence. "How can you afford to spend so much for engineers?" these gentlemen ask our hero. "I can't afford not to," says a lean, brown man in the upper forties, with a face like a Yankee skipper's.

I regard Milwaukee as the most dangerous area in the

U. S. It promises, in the persons of the Smith dynasty, to deal American industry a wallop beside which the stock market crash was a chuck under the chin. Any determined adoption of its principles will turn the economic structure upside down and inside out, scrap billions of dollars of investment, shatter the nerves of untold bankers, and set the exalted profession of high-pressure salesmanship in a roadside ditch.

But when the hurricane is over, we may find a world where poverty has disappeared, where robots are unheard of, where working hours have been cut in two, where waste is at a minimum, and where the era of the salesman has given way to the era of the engineer.

MR. GRIFFIN AND MR. PECK

Their Friends and Competitors; Their Busy, Profitable Day; Their Place in a Community of 17,000 Jenningses, Palmers, Burrs, and Nemeczkys. A & P's 15,700 Stores, Its Three Brobdingnagian Subsidiaries; Its Dedicated Cows; and Its Rich, Modest Hartfords

THE GREAT ATLANTIC &
PACIFIC TEA COMPANY
OF AMERICA

⟨ ∾∾ ⟩

THROUGH Fairfield, Connecticut, runs the Boston Post Road. Near Fairfield's economic center, just beyond the railroad tracks as you motor toward Bridgeport and the Yale Bowl, Mrs. Frank Saum, widow of Fairfield's late favorite barber, owns a property. As a woman of sound judgment she has leased part of her frontage to the world's largest grocer, who pays her some $250 a month for the use of a double-fronted red-brick store mortared blue. The two fronts have been merged into the Great Atlantic and Pacific Tea Company "combination" Store No. 820 under the management of one Thomas F. Griffin (groceries) and A. B. Peck (meats).

Mr. Griffin and Mr. Peck are popular. Nearly one-twentieth of Fairfield's 17,000 population—the exact average is 802—drop in to see them every day. Every day these visitors carry away with them packages to the value of $641.66 or eighty cents per customer; and on these sales Mrs. Saum's tenant makes an average net profit of nearly two cents per customer, or a daily total, after all charges, of $15.97. Since the store is open six days a week, the two managers "send out of town" profits of $95.82 during that period; about $400 during a month; something like $5,000 a year.

From the right-hand screen door of Store No. 820 there emerges every five minutes or so a tall figure in starched white jacket and apron, a shining pink face, a head nearly bald, an earnest, dignified demeanor: Thomas F. Griffin, grocer par excellence. Imperturbably courteous, somewhat lacking in sense of humor, Mr. Griffin carries before him a box stuffed with packages of every shape and size, often very heavy. Beside him walks the lady who has just made the purchase, glancing up and down the street a little more nervously than the manager as they cross through the traffic. Whether the customer's income is $2,000 or $30,000 (for Store No. 820 has both), Mr. Griffin deposits the package in her car, bows with dignity, and returns. Approaching his own windows his severe blue eyes note the displays that he arranged early that morning: a large pile of dark green Del Monte cans priced to meet the Grand Union cut five doors below; a case of Cliquot Club dry ginger ale—a fancy item; a coffee sale—Bokar for twenty-nine cents; a butter sale—twenty-five cents a pound; Long Island ducks (Mr. Peck's department) for twenty-three cents a pound— a knock-out. The three windows, with chickens in the small center one, are about equally divided between A & P products and other products, except in the matter of coffees and teas. For many months, the tea and coffee displays have been exclusively A & P. Mr. Griffin vanishes.

Behind his counter he knows all his usual customers by name, but converses with reserve. Not only does he look like a grocer in an advertisement, but his quiet ability has been recognized by A & P, who have made his store a training school for other managers. For this reason, and because his is a combination store, instead of receiving the average $50, Mr. Griffin's salary is probably considerably more. The responsibility is an honor to Mr. Griffin. It is also a chore, since the Fairfield staff must always include a transient clerk who will move along to some store in the country as soon as he is trained. There are six other clerks in the Fairfield store, none of them much above twenty. Each takes care of some hundred customers a day (about ten an hour); but to this figure allowance must be made for time out at meals and for the rush hours when the store is crammed. Mr. Griffin is sincerely proud of his store, but his A & P activities are not confined to its threshold. Not long ago, with charcoaled face, Mr. Griffin was interlocutor in a minstrel show given by the A & P Managers' Benefit Association at Bridgeport, where Mr. Griffin has his residence. Now, more than five years in the employ of the company, he is eligible to buy A & P common nonvoting stock, when and if more is issued, and his family is protected under the A & P life insurance system.

It is a matter of some concern to the more community-conscious citizens of Fairfield that both Mr. Griffin and Mr. Peck live in Bridgeport. Not only, they say, is the A & P profit taken out of town, but its two largest salaries are spent in the metropolis six miles to the east. Mr. Griffin and Mr. Peck are trained to take this hurdle also. The former arrives in Fairfield about half-past seven in the morning, unlocks the store, supervises the uncrating of newly arrived vegetables (which come from New Haven). He leaves the store about six o'clock at night, nine o'clock on Saturdays. Twice a week he stays late to fill out a vast sheet called a goods order blank. The sheet is so composed that the order may be filled at the A & P warehouse with the greatest efficiency. It is placed on a warehouse hand-truck labeled "820," and this moves past goods which are stacked in the same order as that in which the items are listed on the sheet. When the truck reaches the end of the order, it is at the end of the warehouse departments. The load of groceries is then transferred to a motor truck for delivery to Fairfield on Tuesdays and Fridays, arriving about eleven o'clock in the morning. The Atlantic Commission Company truck stops every day.

The life of Mr. Griffin is a series of visits by superintendents and assistant superintendents of this and that. The inspections are so frequent that they hold no terror; there is no last minute primping because the boss is coming. Every day an assistant superintendent, with a dozen stores to inspect, drops in; his immediate superior, the superintendent, visits Mr. Griffin about once a week. A sales manager and an advertising manager introduce new products, engineer spectacular sales, arrange for space in the Bridgeport newspapers, widely read in Fairfield. This Bridgeport advertising does well enough since the prices announced are identical everywhere in the 315 stores served by the New Haven warehouse. Opened in 1914, Store No. 820 has never advertised in the weekly Fairfield *News*, another hurdle which Mr. Griffin and Mr. Peck are trained to leap. Every month Mr. Griffin makes an inventory of stock on hand and tallies this against receipts. The daily receipts are deposited in the Fairfield Trust Company, withdrawn at regular intervals, cleared in New Haven, whence they are checked to Boston, central office of the New England division.

Within the screen door it is cool and the air smells of produce. Just beyond the entrance a square wooden pillar painted green is surrounded by three pyramidal shelves displaying the day's perishables. The shelves are divided into compartments about a foot and a half long, and on the bottom shelf oranges occupy six compartments—the largest display. Likewise on the bottom shelf are onions in three compartments, apples in two, potatoes in two, cabbage and lettuce in two, nuts in one. On the second shelf, smaller in circumference, are grapefruit, cantaloupes, bananas, an old battered cash register, vegetables. The top shelf is very small. On it are cucumbers, a couple of small pineapples (the main demand for pineapples is in cans), more grapefruit and cantaloupes. On the floor beside the post are two green wire baskets filled with lemons; three or four empty spinach baskets, one half-empty; a basket of green peppers, full; a basket of peanuts, full, and another half-full of apples. All this was deposited when morning was yet gray by a big red Atlantic Commission Company truck that glided in from the warehouse at New Haven and piled crates on the sidewalk. Much of the produce is bought from local farms. In the vicinity of his green pillar Mr. Griffin sells $400 a week; $66.66 a day, in vegetables and fruit.

Business is larger along the right-hand side of the store, where five wide shelves are stacked with cans, packages, bottles, and jars. Near the front window pickle and relish bottles gleam. The leader in this section is catsup, whose various brands, including tomato-cocktail, fill six feet of shelf. Halfway down the store are stacked teas. Beyond the cash register are a couple of yards of canned milk—White House (canned by A & P), Magnolia, Borden's, Van

Camp's. Canned milk is to the shelves along the wall what oranges are to the shelves around the green pillar. The topmost shelf, seven or eight feet high, carries a complete line of cereals. This unit of the store, including all canned goods and packages, together with the National Biscuit Company display near the front door, turns over $970 a week; $161 a day.

Set into the back wall of the store a large refrigerator contains butter, fresh milk, cheese, yeast. In front of the refrigerator is a second counter stacked with eggs, in boxes and loose. Near-by is a rack of brooms, a rack of garden seeds— both racks made somewhat inaccessible, on busy mornings, by the large piles of cardboard bakery boxes containing Grandmother's Bread, the empty boxes pushed aside in all directions. This is the "sales" corner, and on busy Saturdays it is not easy to follow the movements of Bokar cans, unpacked as sold, A & P Bartlett pears, or Del Monte peaches.

Detached features of the store are tobacco, located near the front, with a total weekly sale of $100, nearly 3 per cent of the business; a glass case built out from the main counter containing pastries; candy beside the cigarettes.

The following are Mr. Griffin's total sales (approximately):

	Weekly
Jars, packages, cans	$970
Produce, fruit, vegetables	400
Butter	265
Sugar	170
Coffee	130
Eggs	125
Bread	120
	Carried forward $2,180

Weekly

Brought forward $2,180

Tobacco	100
Soap	85
Milk (canned)	75
Flour	50
Tea	40
Total	$2,530

The turnover of Mr. Griffin's end of the business is about $2,530 a week; along the left-hand wall Mr. Peck brings this total up to some $3,850 a week by doing a $1,320 butcher business. Mr. Peck is a kindly man with wrinkled face and spectacles. Since he is a trained butcher, his salary is likewise probably well over $50 a week, and he has two clerks, William Banyas and George Cole. Mr. Peck's emporium was formerly a butcher shop owned by Johnny McGarry. McGarry moved up the street to his present white-tiled store; his shop was annexed to the A & P, its walls torn down. That was in 1927. Mr. Peck's counter is of glass for the display of cuts, with those Long Island ducks a feature. Shelves on the wall toward the rear are stacked with canned fish, especially A & P salmon. Though high in rank, Mr. Peck is not officially the manager of the store. Responsibility for locking up, cleaning, and accounting falls upon the adequate shoulders of Mr. Griffin. Besides doing a major part of the business, Mr. Griffin's "sales" are larger and more complicated than Mr. Peck's. The sales and advertising managers at New Haven are constantly adjusting the price of his rice or arranging to turn over a larger amount of butter when butter is cheap. They must keep in touch with the prices of his competitors— Grand Union, First National (formerly Davey Brothers), and Logan Brothers—on canned asparagus, tomatoes. Consequently the store's windows are more important to him than to Mr. Peck, and not content with the window on the grocery side of the store, he overflows into Mr. Peck's window quite at random. Mr. Peck is left with a little window between the two doors, where chickens are hung and bright cards daily announce the prices of the meats.

The gross business of Store No. 820 is $1,500 more in summer than in winter. This is not only because of the tourists and picnickers, but because its largest customers are persons who winter in New York City and do not appear at their estates in the vicinity of Fairfield until spring.

This is an old town, settled in 1639 amid the burning of witches. The British burned it in 1779. Fairfield citizens are proud of their history to the point of shifting the Post Road away from their old church and village green in order that the clattering main street might not disturb their dreams about their ancestors. Nevertheless, with the help of the factories and the city of Bridgeport, to which Fairfield is practically a suburb, the dreams have been disturbed. The chains are capitalizing, not only from the extremely rich and the extremely poor, but from middle incomes of $5,000 or so, whose earners commute from Fairfield's suburban homes to Bridgeport or even New York. The town's growth has been from agriculture through industry to real estate. Development of suburban real estate, now the Fairfield phase, has added 6,000 to the population in ten years.

However, between the housewife and her grocer there is a subtle link—the husband. He will comment on the food; he will pay the bills. Between the housewife and Mr. Griffin of Store No. 820 this link is missing; she carries money in her purse that is apparently her own, while Mr. Griffin is unable to offer her anything of especial tastiness, chosen with pride by himself. It is by the preservation of this link that the two big independent stores in Fairfield thrive: Mercurio's, the luscious Italian grocery; McGarry's, the old traditional meat market. In a sense neither of these stores is competing with Store No. 820, because their stock is of a deliberately superior kind. While A & P is displaying canned peaches Mercurio's devotes a whole window to nonalcoholic vermouths. Mercurio's asparagus is dear, but it is green almost to the very end. At McGarry's you will find the finest, most expensive cuts of meat. Epicures are inclined to go to the chains for their staples and to run up prodigious bills for luxuries at these more fashionable independents. Besides the epicures and the careless rich, the independents do well with the conscience trade. Every man engaged in a business that touches the town retailers must trade with the independent merchant. Edward Brennan, publisher of the Fairfield *News*, and Howard Comstock, its editor, not only trade with the independents, but also put in a good editorial word for the policy of buying from the locally owned stores. This paper waged an antichain "trade with your own taxpayer" campaign a few years ago.

Johnny McGarry has a good trade. As Postmaster William Gould says, he could carry on very well with the accounts of Walter B. Lashar (American Chain Co.) and the Jennings families alone. There are fewer Jenningses in Fairfield than Cheneys in South Manchester, but their paternalism is the same in quality, and they are rich. O. G. Jennings, who was born in Fairfield, made his money in Standard Oil. He has been a McGarry customer ever since he married. Likewise his son Lawrence, whose wife is the daughter of Witherbee Black (Black, Starr & Frost-Gorham). Besides these big accounts, McGarry has Mrs. Charles Le B. Homer (sister-in-law of Owen J. Roberts); Robert H. Leach, general manager of Handy & Harmon.

Mercurio's grocery is first class, with a great display of fat fruit and vegetables in front of it, and many chauffeurs crossing in and out. It opened some thirty years ago, with the family living above and the innumerable children spilling over into the shop. A few years back the business was formally turned over to four children—Dominic, Frank, Sally, Jimmy—whose average age is less than thirty years. Sally is the boss, Dominic is the president and drives one of the five trucks. He continues to drive because he is known to housewives in that capacity. Mercurio faces are entirely irresistible. They have for customers, among others, Mrs. George Waldo, wife of the editor of the Bridgeport *Post and Telegram;* all the Sturges families—Henry S., Frederick, Clarence B. (and his smart Tide Mill Tavern, which is a plum to any tradesman); the Jenningses; Mr. Jennings' sister, Mrs. Hugh D. Auchincloss; the Warners (corset manufacturer at Bridgeport); the country clubs; the Standard Oil and Corn Products Bedfords; Horace B. Merwin, Bridgeport banker and president of the Fairfield Trust Company.

It would be convenient to be able to divide the buying public of Fairfield into two groups: this distinguished, die-hard society which clings to its extravagant independents, and the penny-wise middle and lower classes patronizing Messrs. Griffin and Peck. Convenient, but untrue. For A & P straddles Fairfield as indiscriminately as the postman. Among Mr. Griffin's customers, for example, are:

Mrs. Carleton H. Palmer, former president of the National Junior League, wife of Squibb-President Palmer, active citizen of Fairfield, interested in the cultural life of the town. Store No. 820 offers everything she needs at prices within her budget. Her only complaint against the A & P is that it does not buy its vegetables from Fairfield truck gardeners whenever possible (in season). Vegetables for Store No. 820 come from truck gardens near the New Haven warehouse; but in general Mrs. Palmer roots for A & P and does all her shopping there. At the first of every week she deposits a budgeted sum of money with Mr. Griffin, and her chauffeur collects her daily orders. Mrs. Palmer does not believe in charging things. She thinks Macy's is the most marvelous store in the United States.

Mrs. Donald Perkins, whose husband is a special representative for *Standard Statistics*, says that she must shop where she can get most for her money. That is, she finds, at Store No. 820.

Selectman Frederick A. Burr, who, like Napoleon, is first selectman with two other selectmen under him, rules Fairfield with the unofficial title of "mayor." He shops all about town, affably including both chain and independent, and is inclined to prefer Logan Brothers and First National to A & P, because the two former derive from Bridgeport. Nevertheless, he drops in on Mr. Griffin now and then. His only comment on the competition between chains and independents is directed against Mercurio's, because it keeps open all Sunday. " 'Tisn't decent."

Charles S. Munson, vice president of the Air Reduction Company.

Arthur R. Womrath, of the circulating libraries, who sends his chauffeur.

Emery Nemeczky, who burns Fairfield's garbage behind his own little farmhouse for $100 a month. Emery is a gargantua who arises at 4:30 in the spring, plows gardens until dusk, when his horse is exhausted. He weighs 290 pounds, and as he plows his hand merely rests on the handle. He moves with a jovian majesty. He accumulates money, holds mortgages, and will trade with no one but the chains. He gets wistful about wealth. "Even if I plow the whole world, I never be *really* rich."

Postmaster Gould best expresses Fairfield's attitude toward chains. He withdrew without bitterness from the grocery business in 1915, foreseeing that chains were inevitable, economically sound, that the A & P was only the beginning of the invasion of non-civic stores. He points out that in the 1880's Fairfield was initiated to the Smith chain, called the Village Stores and started near Bridgeport by George Gilman for his adopted son, G. W. Smith. It is a fact to remark that this same George Gilman was co-founder of A & P with old George Hartford on Vesey Street. Whether the Smith-Gilman combination was imitating Hartford, or whether Hartford was imitating Smith in establishing grocery chains, history does not relate. Fairfield buys nevertheless and is still talking about millionaire George Gilman, his fabulous house, his legended women, his tallyho.

The Great Atlantic and Pacific Tea Company, like Ford, General Motors, U. S. Steel, and Swift, had in 1929 gross sales of more than $1,000,000,000. Of these five, A & P was the only one to sustain the billion dollar mark in 1930. The Great Atlantic and Pacific Tea Company, largest chain organization in the world, has 15,700 stores which dispense about one-fifteenth of the food sold by retail stores in the United States. Its little red shops whose black signboards always bear the gilt lettering

THE GREAT **ATLANTIC AND PACIFIC** TEA COMPANY

reported a net profit last year of \$30,742,775, and here again we merely record that this is some $4\frac{1}{2}$ million dollars in excess of 1929. Its volume of business is ten times that of Liggett and $11\frac{1}{2}$ times that of United Cigar. Add Sears, Roebuck to Montgomery Ward and then include J. C. Penney—the total of business will be \$100,000,000 less than the Great Atlantic and Pacific Tea Company total.

But the truest token of gianthood has not yet been revealed. It is this—the Great Atlantic and Pacific Tea Company makes just 2.88 cents on each dollar of sales. No other contestant, pigmy or elephantine, in the retail field can make so few cents and still call its business profitable. Swift makes only 1.39 cents on the dollar, but Swift is principally a wholesaler. Ford, popularly supposed to have the nethermost profit rate, makes $5\frac{1}{2}$ per cent on sales to dealers; General Motors makes 15 per cent.

When throughout the United States the Chain Store issue is perennially and violently discussed, it is natural the A & P, by all odds the biggest chain, should be the most savagely attacked. Popular small-town outcry defines the issue as Chain Store vs. Independent. And on this line Mr. Henderson of Shreveport, Louisiana, erected his Ku-Klux-Klan-like antichain organization. But this is *not* the way that Big Business defines the issue. For Big Business the issue has an entirely different definition. For Big Business, the issue is Chain Store vs. Manufacturer or Chain Store vs. Wholesaler. Specifically it becomes A & P vs. General Foods, or A & P vs. California Packing Corp., or A & P vs. Any Number of Others or our Hugest Corporations which deal in commodities or branded articles. Big Business may well define the issue so. For A & P has been a fierce economic opponent. Whenever it could not buy from other huge corporations the things it wanted at the price it considered fair, A & P has gone out and produced or assembled these things itself. Hence, quite as exciting as its 15,700 stores are its innumerable fisheries, canneries, bakeries, or the innumerable cows and hens whose lives are completely dedicated to A & P.

Thus it is that an understanding of this giant company must begin with its three great subsidiaries. Each a giant in itself, they are:

The American Coffee Corp.
The Atlantic Commission Co.
The Quaker Maid Co.

The American Coffee Corp. is the largest coffee concern in the world, the only one controlling coffee from Brazilian tree to U. S. housewife, and it accounts for nearly 60 of the 1,000 million dollars which A & P takes in every year.

The Atlantic Commission Co., world's largest buyer of fruits and vegetables, makes A & P the supreme Master of the American Map. Of this, more later.

It is perhaps through the eyes of Quaker Maid that we can best visualize the magnitude of the Brobdingnagian picnic which A & P is daily preparing for this nation (A & P feeds, of course, the equivalent of many complete nations). Quaker Maid has, for example, salmon. That is, they are hers when her own fishermen catch them on Alaskan mornings and her machinery squeezes them into cans on Alaskan afternoons. One plant cans 70,000 fish a day. A & P sells 26,000,000 cans a year, half of them supplied by A & P's own Quaker Maid.

A scattered herd of 75,000 cows in Wisconsin, carefully chosen but not owned by Quaker Maid Co., supplies two huge canning factories where over 130,000,000 cans of evaporated milk are packed each year. In 1921, before A & P had begun to can milk, a customer in an A & P store could buy eight cans of evaporated milk for a dollar. Of this, twenty-seven cents represented raw milk; and the farmer's profit, manufacture, distribution costs, and profits took up the seventy-three cents. Now, if the consumer asks for White House milk he gets fifteen cans for a dollar— fifty-two cents' worth of milk plus farmer's profit, and forty-eight cents for distribution and manufacturing costs and A & P's 2.88 cents profit.

In Brooklyn a vast Quaker Maid factory packs a vast assortment of foods: 72,000 pounds of jams and preserves ooze into jars every day; 70,000 pounds of cereals; and hundreds of thousands of pounds of baking powder, rice, lentils, and split peas are put into dated paper packages every day. Veritable conduits of mayonnaise, vats of olive oil, cauldrons of pickles and cauliflower (for relish) are jarred. The Brobdingnagian picnic preparations also include hundreds of pounds of noodles, miles of spaghetti, hundreds of pounds of mustard, peanut butter, maple syrup, extracts, cocoa, candy, spices, and ammonia. In Terre Haute, Indiana, a similar factory pours out a similar assortment of foods and adds to it a daily production of 10,000 cans of baked beans.

Yet Quaker Maid's deluge of food, amounting to some $25,000,000 a year, accounts for only a small per cent of A & P's total. At least two-thirds of the shelf space in an A & P store is dedicated to nationally advertised, better known brands like Del Monte canned foods and Blue Ribbon mayonnaise. Quaker Maid products act as a reserve to the national market.

Besides what it gets from its three great subsidiaries and besides what it buys from other manufacturers, A & P has other making and assembling activities of its own. For example: butter, eggs, bread.

A & P owns no dairy, but selects its Wisconsin sources of butter, supervises and inspects them regularly. Largest butter dealer in the world, A & P sells over 177,000,000 pounds annually. It is excessively vain of this product, for it pays one-half cent more than necessary to assure itself of good quality. Every grocer knows that his reputation depends chiefly on the quality of his butter, eggs, and coffee.

If every person in New York City were a hen and laying regularly, there would not be enough eggs to fill the A & P demand. The 7,500,000 hens supplying A & P are not owned by A & P. Buying is done directly from carefully selected farmers who sell their whole output to A & P.

Every hour of every working day some 153,717 loaves of Grandmother's Bread are sold across A & P counters. This amounts to more than 500,000,000 a year, baked in thirty-five widely distributed A & P bakeries, after the direct purchase from the mills of 5,000,000 barrels of flour. A Federal Trade Commission study tends to show that A & P (and other chains who do their own baking) sells bread to the public for less than the average baker can sell it to the retailer.

Butter, eggs, bread, salmon, jam, pickles, rice, oil, noodles, mustard: surely there is some place where the wearied mind may come to rest and find coherence. There is. There is a man named John Hartford. He is the son and heir of the Founder. He is the only man who has complete authority over the incredible, inconceivable, unimaginable activities of the A & P which seem, to the unthinking customer, so simple, so commonplace. He has a brother named George, less active than he. He lives in a vast, wooded estate at Valhalla, New York. And that is all that is known about him, except that he is pleasant to talk to. And except that he must be one of the really richest men in the United States. For last year (as similarly in other years) there must have gone to his credit a great part of A & P's $30,000,000 net profit. For if it did not go to him, then to whom did it go? The A & P company has a little over 2,000,000 common shares outstanding. Of these only 120,000 have seeped out to the public (via the Curb), and some 240,000 have gone to employees, leaving more than 1,500,000 shares or three-quarters of the company in the hands of—whom? Presumably the Hartford family. Even if this family owned only a third of their company, it would be necessary to talk of Rockfellers, Fords, Mellons, before you could be sure you had named richer men.

The immensity of A & P finds center and unity with John Hartford. But quite as extraordinary as that one of the greatest enterprises in history should be controlled by an Unknown is the fact that the origin of this enterprise lay in a product of secondary importance. The late John Hartford's father began with tea.

In 1859, in the days of John Brown of body fame, tea was selling for $2.00 and $3.00 a pound. This outrageous price induced George Gilman, a leather merchant located in the Swamp of New York City, to buy a cargo. He hired a store at busy 31 Vesey Street, stocked it with the tea, and added some coffee and spices. The humble façade he painted red. His partner was a young chap named George Huntington Hartford. This man Hartford saw farther than Gilman; he soon bought out Gilman's interest, popularized the store by the use of premiums—gaudy china, glassware, crockery. Then he induced ladies to form clubs and pool their premium coupons.

Clubs sprouted as far away as New Jersey, and this led Hartford to open a new store for the convenience of outlying club members. He found he could operate two stores as easily as one. It became apparent that if he had more outlets, he could sell wholesale tea in five-pound packages; by 1867 he had conceded to selling one-pound packages, always at wholesale prices. This was undercutting other retailers about $1.00 a pound. Hartford already had the idea. In *Harper's Weekly* for May 11, 1867, he advertised in dreadful hodgepodge type: "The proprietors of the Great American Tea Company became fully convinced, several years ago, that the consumers of tea and coffee were paying too many and too large profits . . . and therefore organized the Great American Tea Company to do away, as far as possible, with these enormous drains upon the consumers." He then proceeded to list eight profits between China and the American consumer and claimed to eliminate them.

From this beginning the chain store principle developed very rapidly. By 1876 there were sixty-seven so-called "branch retail houses . . ." Eighteen of these were in New York City, four in Philadelphia, three in Chicago. Stores farther away were those at Rochester, St. Paul, St. Louis, Indianapolis, Louisville, and Baltimore. But it took many years for Hartford to get rid of the tea merchant idea. Other items were added cautiously, and the company's growth was retarded by an elaborate delivery system. Still, the "economy" policy of making little percentages on a swift turnover (A & P net working capital of $102,600,000 turned over more than ten times last year for a gross business of $1,065,800,000) was deeply appreciated in the boisterous days of Fisk, Gould, and "the public be damned." Mr. Hartford continued to expand, continued to add staples, and by 1910 owned 372 stores. In 1912, when he had 447 stores, he instituted the cash-and-carry system and began to grow in very earnest. When the War broke he was in the thousands; when the Armistice was signed A & P owned 4,000. But old Mr. Hartford died in 1917 without reaching the Pacific Coast.

He had founded, as above noted, the greatest coffee concern in the world. But he had not made the United States drink tea. The Great Atlantic & Pacific Tea Co. is proud of its tea business. From the auctions at Ceylon it buys huge quantities. But, unlike Sir Thomas Lipton, it does not own its own tea gardens. And whereas the Britisher drinks nine and one-half pounds of tea per capita, the Australian eight and one-fourth, the Irish seven and one-half, the Canadian five, the U. S. citizen still drinks only seven-eighths of a pound per capita.

In fact, if you split up into rough divisions the billion dollars' worth of food which A & P sells yearly, tea comes at the bottom of the list. Here is the breakdown, roughly estimated:

Jars, packages, cans, misc.	$320,000,000
Fruits and vegetables (fresh)	150,000,000
Meats (in about 4,000 of the 15,700 stores)	100,000,000
Butter	75,000,000
Sugar	60,000,000
Coffee	60,000,000
Eggs	50,000,000
Bread	45,000,000
Tobacco	40,000,000
Soap	40,000,000
Milk	25,000,000
Flour	25,000,000
Tea	10,000,000
	$1,000,000,000

To get all this food and drink to the right place at the right time so that each of the 5,000,000 families will daily make its sixty-five-cent purchase, is, needless to say, a triumph of organization, for which, in a war, all the orders of all the crowned heads would be pinned on somebody's breast. Among the phases of this organizing triumph, great is the synchronization of coffee. But greatest of all, perhaps, is the triumph of the aforementioned subsidiary: Atlantic Commission Company.

It is first of all a buyer, choosing fresh vegetables from truck gardens all over the country. It often becomes a packer and shipper; but where growers' coöperatives exist, as in the case of oranges (Sunkist in California; Sealdsweet, Blue Goose, Indian River in Florida), the company buys goods already packed. It then becomes both consignor and consignee, shipping carload lots to its various warehouses, specially equipped with refrigerating and heating devices, and corresponding geographically to fifty-two A & P warehouses. The two sets of warehouses are seldom under the same roof, but almost always in the same cities. The vegetables are transferred from the freight siding to the commission company's warehouse, where the chameleon-phœnix is broker, commission merchant, jobber, wholesaler. The food is sorted, the orders of individual stores are filled, charged, consigned, loaded on trucks which deposit them at the A & P stores in the morning before the manager's alarm clock has stopped ringing.

In its intense desire to eliminate unnecessary profits on goods between the field and the shelf, the Atlantic Commission Company has mastered the great American garden. Unless the difference in season requires it, potatoes from the Kaw Valley of Kansas are not shipped to Grand Rapids where potatoes grow; nor are onions from near Grand Rapids shipped to Dallas, where onions are plentiful. By shifting vegetables around, a continuous supply of them is obtained throughout the winter, but theoretically Dallas onions supply the southern division only. Each A & P division of the American garden is self-supporting to an amazing degree, in its season. But items like the sleek green watermelons of Georgia and Florida, the great shaggy potatoes of Idaho, the lazy tomatoes of western Tennessee and Arkansas, the Oregon broccoli, the princely Oregon apples, the sturdy New England apples about which Robert Frost rimed, and the bitter cranberries of the Massachusetts cape are examined, purchased, and shunted around the country in an economic strategy of which Nature never dreamed.

The Atlantic Commission Company may perform miracles of distribution; the American Coffee Corp. may be wonderful in scope and scale; the Quaker Maid Co. may perform incredible conjuring with bottles and tin cans. But these cannot detract from the awesome achievements of the parent company. Its various feats demand various tributes, but in the staggering international task of assembling and consigning all its imports and domestic staples it has earned another title—Master of the American Map. In the final estimate, and no matter how sensitive one's ears may be to hyperbole, the name of the Great Atlantic and Pacific Tea Co. can by no means seem too grandiose.

Mainly it has become what it is simply by growing— one little store after another. But there was one year, 1925, when the giant took special cognizance of its size and shaped itself into its present form. In that year was formed the great produce subsidiary which we have described. And about that time, the management of the stores was divided into geographical divisions. These autonomous divisions, subject only to the Hartford rule, have headquarters at Boston, New York, Pittsburgh, Detroit, Chicago, and Philadelphia (for all the South), and Los Angeles. There is still a huge geographical gap: the Great Basin (from Kansas to California) is peopled with many another chain, but not A & P. At the head of each division and of various central activities, there are, of course, a great number of skilled merchants and organizers. It is notable that nearly all have risen from the ranks. Of the six divisional presidents, four started in white aprons, one as an errand boy without even an apron.

Also, from about 1925 may be dated another change. Beginning then, stores were remodeled, enlarged, moved to more economical locations and, above all, adjusted to their communities. Thus, in Ardmore, Pennsylvania, "richest township in the United States," an A & P *de luxe* store has been developed with fluffy pastry, caviar, crabs, wicker furniture. Except for its red façade, the Ardmore store bears little resemblance to the A & P at Second Avenue and Twenty-second Street, New York, or even to that at Fairfield, Connecticut. So, to its basic principles of price reduction by rapid turnover and the elimination of middle profits, A & P has added another: adjustment to the public taste. It would not be surprising if the skillful execution of this policy became the source of its greatest strength. Not only in its competition with the Independent. But the manufacturer may discover that if A & P becomes Master of the American Taste as well as of the American Map, then A & P's terms become, practically, Economic Law. And, doing unto others as it would be done by, A & P may graciously permit the manufacturer to make 2.88 cents on the dollar, even as A & P.

The A & P is the greatest coffee merchant in the world. And to be the greatest coffee merchant in the world is to stand at the center of the food industry. Any grocer will tell you that the three basic commodities in his store are eggs, butter, and coffee. If the eggs are good and the butter is good and, above all, if the coffee is good, the customers will return for more. And they will take the canned soup and the noodles with them.

The winter of 1929 A & P customers began buying coffee in quantities theretofore unknown in the trade. They bought 1,000,000 pounds a week more than they had been buying—an increase of 30 per cent in the sales of the company. They bought not only *Eight O'Clock* (A & P's lowest priced) and *Red Circle*, but *Bokar*, the pride of the roasting plants. And they kept on buying.

The reason was not that A & P's coffee-tasters had developed more subtle palates and a more delectable brand. But simply that the price of A & P's coffees had fallen because the A & P promptly gave the public benefit of the falling market prices. And the reason for that was Brazil.

Back of this spectacular price cut was the threatened tragedy of an entire people, and its purpose was not to absorb the coffee trade (though A & P has no reluctance to an increase in its own sales) but to sell more coffee. It was, and it still may be, the conviction of Mr. Berent Friele, president of the American Coffee Corp., subsidiary of A & P, that the consumption of coffee in America could be increased, that lower prices would increase it, and that greater exports at lower prices would take the strain off the warehouse girders and the bank statements of São Paulo.

What had happened in Brazil had been happening for a long time—since 1888 to be exact. No one knows when coffee came to South America. Legend in Brazil has fixed upon the year 1727. It was in that century that the shrub, which first came to human notice through its power of intoxicating sheep, was transported from Batavia to Amsterdam and to the Jardin des Plantes in Paris. It came to the new world by way of Martinique and French Guiana. And it quickly established itself in the state of São Paulo in Brazil. In 1888, with the abolition of slavery in that nation and the importation of cheap labor from Italy, trouble began. There were shortly 40,000 plantations, crops increased, prices declined. By 1925, overproduction had reached such a point that the São Paulo Coffee Institute was created to store coffee in the interior at the planters' risk and lend money to the planters on the security of warehouse holdings. But though the market steadied for a time, the carry-over in São Paulo after the 1927–28 crop was 11,672,000 bags (half the world consumption for a year); and the 1929–30 crop added a carry-over as of July 1, 1930 of 18,000,000 bags. Which meant that the planters could not be paid for the 1929 crop for almost two years and that $315,000,000 worth (at the then price) of coffee was tied up with loans on much of it at 9 per cent.

Consequently it was not altogether wonderful that the São Paulo coffee market collapsed after the stock market break in New York. The Secretary of Finance of São Paulo and head of the Coffee Institute resigned, rumors were circulated in New York to the effect that the banks in São Paulo had refused further loans, and the renewal of a large English loan to the State was in doubt. At this juncture Speyer & Co. of New York and J. Henry Schroder, Baring Brothers, and Rothschild, of London agreed to underwrite a $97,330,000 bond issue secured by 16,500,000 bags of coffee in Brazilian warehouses valued at the time at $198,000,000. The state agreed to undertake no more such schemes. Thus the price of coffee was to seek its natural level, excess production to find its own market, and the world encouraged to drink more coffee.

This loan has not solved Brazil's coffee problem. The crops continue large, and although huge piles of coffee are actually burnt in Brazil, the visible supply has continued to mount. Consequently, coffee over the A & P counters stays cheap.

The American Coffee Corporation is the only coffee dealer which purchases its own coffee in South America, imports it, roasts it, and sells it itself. It has twenty-seven offices in Colombia in direct contact with planters and in a position to supervise crops; in Brazil, it has buying offices at Rio de Janeiro and Santos and attempts through them a certain direct contact with the planters. A & P purchases directly in the belief that it can thus secure personal supervision of grades and the maximum of economy. General Foods (Maxwell House), Chase & Sanborn, etc., purchase through local brokers who are constantly in the market, in the belief they can buy at least as inexpensively in that way. The difference is one of business judgment and practice.

A & P at once began to buy cheaper coffees and ship them to New York, Boston, and New Orleans, from which points the green coffee is carried directly to its eight roasting plants. To avoid two separate transportation charges (dock to plants and plants to storehouses), A & P has induced the railroads to publish regulations by which a through rate for coffee applies from port to warehouse with a stop-over privilege for roasting in transit.

And the cheaper coffees were put on sale at prices below

those charged by competing brands of comparable quality. And A & P coffee sales have soared.

The reason for the difference in price is not far to seek. A & P are retailers of coffee as well as roasters of coffee. Maxwell House and the rest are roasters only and retail, *inter alia*, through the A & P. In accordance with the time-honored custom of grocers by which coffee is the bait for other sales, A & P are willing to forego their roaster's profit, take their retailer's profit alone, and dazzle the world with cheap coffee.

Whether A & P will be able to continue to lead all its competitors in volume of sales depends ultimately on the answer to the question whether coffee consumption has reached saturation point. If it has and if production is not materially reduced in Brazil (and it is easier to suggest the burning of trees than to decide whose trees are to be burned), then cheap coffee may be here to stay.

The real difficulty of comparing A & P and, say, Maxwell House is that as a coffee manufacturer, A & P is and always will be a grocer. And to the grocer coffee isn't coffee. It is the gate to soup.

BEHN
BROTHERS. . . .

. . . *was, First, the Scribbled Daydream of a Ten-year-old Boy, Now is the Energizing Force of One of the World's Largest Corporations. I. T. & T.'s First Decade; Its Growth; Its Projections in Asia; Its Skirmishes in South America. The Behn Plan and the Cabinet of the Brothers Behn*

INTERNATIONAL TELEPHONE
AND TELEGRAPH CORPORATION

A TEN-YEAR-OLD boy sat at a table scribbling. Some one strolled over and glanced at the paper. He read: "Behn Brothers—Sosthenes and Hernand Behn." The boy looked up. "Hernand and I are going into business," he said.

The new century was in its swaddling clothes when Sosthenes Behn grew his beard. It was a protection rather than a gesture; his entire career seemed momentarily to hang upon it. For Sosthenes was a New York banker, the acting head, in fact, of a foreign exchange department. And he didn't look like a New York banker. Thus the beard grew, a mark of dignity and maturity. It accomplished its purpose, and its possessor was both amused and proud. The year was 1901, and Sosthenes Behn was not yet quite twenty.

Infinitely complex forces had been at work upon the boy. There was, first of all, the matter of his blood. His curious name derived from the Greek and meant "life strength"; he was born on the little West Indian island of St. Thomas; but the principal strains which coursed within him were French and Danish. Together with Hernand, he had gone to Europe to be schooled—first to Corsica and later to

Paris. By birth and training, these Behns were cosmopolites. They were adepts in nearly every tongue spoken by civilized man. And deeper than their multi-linguism lay the rich mixture of their inheritance. Upon this they could draw at will, and upon it they have drawn freely throughout their lives. Than Sosthenes Behn is no Frenchman more French, no Englishman more British, no Spaniard more Spanish, and through it all, no American more American. Today, when the International Telephone & Telegraph Corporation negotiates in the world's capitals from Bucharest to Nanking, this world-sympathy and world-understanding are of incalculable value. The Behns travel incessantly. But they are never foreigners.

Sosthenes rather fancied the beard, and he kept it a long time. Through a trip to Mexico for a group of New York bankers, through the beginnings of his career in Porto Rico. Here, in 1906, the brothers realized their ambition. They took over their stepfather's sugar business, incorporated themselves as Behn Bros., Inc., and became successful sugar factors. As such they were favorably, but not conspicuously, known in New York. Their entrance into the communications business, which came about when the Porto Rican Telephone Company fell into their hands through a friend who had taken it in payment of a bad debt, caused no international stir. Presently, when Cuba invited them, they had two telephone systems instead of one. But when the War came, they were still bankers. Sosthenes was thirty-two, and Hernand was thirty-four. The brothers were verging on middle-age and their records, while respectable and successful enough, were not really as glittering as one might have forecast on that day in 1901.

They had double claims to American citizenship. They had sought and obtained citizenship in their own right, and the U. S. purchase of St. Thomas from Denmark automatically enfranchised them. Sosthenes did distinguished work for the Signal Corps in France, was the chief of staff for General Russell, the A. E. F.'s chief signal officer, and just before the Armistice moved to the First Army. Later, in Paris, he sat with three other colonels (including Colonel A. H. Griswold, later to become one of the Behn lieutenants in I. T. & T.) upon the adjustment board which liquidated the Signal Corps' European property. Both France and the U. S. decorated him.

It was in 1920 that the brothers began to move in a large way. In that year, they made their deal with A. T. & T. to lay a cable from Cuba to the mainland, connecting the growing island system with the telephones of the mainland. It had been projected before the War, and preliminary work on the mainland end had been started. But not until 1920 were the negotiations closed. This deal, which was small enough in comparison with the brothers' later operations, at the time was of the most tremendous significance. It gave them confidence. It crystallized their plans into the immediate organization of the International Telephone & Telegraph Corporation. Sosthenes and Hernand were encouraged to come to New York to look for support. The whole vast plan was set in motion.

It was to tap a deep wellspring of initiative. In Madrid, in 1924, Sosthenes battled for the Spanish concession. The Dictator and his advisers insisted that the company which reconstructed Spain's telephones should use Spanish equipment, made in Spain. Sosthenes was no manufacturer. The telephone plant in Cuba and Porto Rico had come from the large companies in the U. S. But Sosthenes signed the contract nonetheless. He went to his good friend A. T. & T.: "Will your foreign manufacturing subsidiary, International Western Electric, put up a plant in Spain and make the equipment for us?" It would not. He turned to his great competitors in Europe: "Will you make equipment for us?" They would not.

The entire Spanish deal seemed on the verge of collapse. Sosthenes pondered, had a thought, rejected it as wild, found no other alternative, formed his resolution. Again he went to his good friend A. T. & T.: "Very well, you will *sell* us International Western Electric?" Yes, they would. How much? Thirty millions. It was a staggering price for the young company, but Sosthenes paid it. In bonds which A. T. & T. turned over to J. P. Morgan & Co. Thus at one vigorous stroke, the Behns had become large manufacturers and had attached to themselves the most powerful banking support in America. And not at all by design, but because the terms of the Dictator's concession had to be met. And because of the Behn resourcefulness and the Behn daring.

Sosthenes is a tall, military figure of a man. The luxuriant beard has given way to a grayish mustache which one does not notice much. In his magnificent French oak office in the tower at Broad and Beaver Streets, he is very much the American industrialist. Of tremendous energy, he also energizes others. The most noticeable quality of the I. T. & T. building is its vigor. Here are the many executives whom the Behns have gradually drawn to them. Almost without exception, their offices reflect the nervous electric energy of Sosthenes's office. The man has infused himself everywhere, whether because one likes him or because one is dominated by him. His concentration upon his work is phenomenal; he is without competing interests. And one may make an appointment to see him as easily at seven in the evening as at ten in the morning. He is sure to be still at his desk.

Yet no one was ever more charming or more suave than Sosthenes Behn. From day to day and from year to year, he is unchanged. However volatile the Latin blood within him, the face he presents to the world is always composed, pleasant, confident. He has few enemies; he himself will not admit that he dislikes a half-dozen people.

Sosthenes is an arresting figure, a great industrial adventurer whose light is too strong to be hidden under even the bushels of his own modesty. But he is only half of Behn Brothers. He is, to be sure, the more exciting half, the more glamorous half, but still only half. For across from his office in the high tower is the office of Hernand, and Behn Brothers is today as real in spirit as it was when the ten-year-old boy scribbled it on paper, as real in fact as when the two proudly set up business in Porto Rico. The brothers are in perfect balance. If Sosthenes has more daring, Hernand has more intuitive caution. If Sosthenes has boldly seized each successive opportunity, gathering property after property into the huge I. T. & T. system, Hernand has quietly taken into his care the real first-born and has made the Cuban Telephone Company the most successful telephone unit of them all. Hernand is no industrial Don

Quixote. He is cerebral, even reluctant. But his loyalty to his brother amounts to a passion. And his functions as half of Behn Brothers are not to be underestimated.

Behn Brothers have built one of the world's most spectacular enterprises. In the process they have become both famous and rich. Their offices are perched on that conventional pinnacle of wealth and success, the skyline of Manhattan. But Sosthenes and Hernand Behn have not lost their inheritance. Their faces turn often to the east and to the south. To the warm islands which nurtured them. To St.-Jean-de-Luz, where their villas are bright under Latin suns. To Paris, where their houses stand beside the houses of other Parisians. They are still world dwellers, and other strains than the Anglo-Saxon still disturb their blood.

They are, withal, Americans. The enterprise made possible by their partnership, however closely attuned to the spirit of a score of nations, is yet an American enterprise, and they themselves do not confuse their internationalism with the essentially American framework upon which it now hangs. This framework is something far more substantial than their accustomed New York life, more significant than their American wives or their children. In May, 1921, when he stood at the threshold of his career, Sosthenes married blonde, lovely Margaret Dunlap of Philadelphia. They have two sons, Edward and William. This family provides Sosthenes's one major interest outside the company. But even more American than this normal life is the driving plan which embraces the Behns' every project. As they are the dominant personalities of I. T. & T., so is this plan the vast system's dominant theory. It can be described briefly as an American communications system. What this means and how it is being realized are told in the following pages.

In 1921, the Brothers Behn came to New York to launch the International Telephone & Telegraph Corporation. The Cuban and Porto Rican telephone companies had made steady advances through the War and post-War years, adding telephones at the rate of 4,000 a year and bringing net income from under $400,000 in 1915 to over $1,000,000 in 1920. But this was of interest chiefly to the Cubans (and Spaniards) who shared ownership with the Behns. Impressive as was the company's name, substantial as was its income, it operated in a territory where depression was almost a general rule, and it was enriching no one who could open up the vast credit reserves of Wall Street. The Behns wanted New York support for an American stock issue. They had an exceedingly hard time getting it. The National City had brought out the Cuban bond issue of 1921 and was their friend, but did no business in stocks; the Colonel's own Guaranty was going through a hard year; Morgan was not in the picture at all. While the Behns had an assured position in New York, sponsors for an issue of the new company's common stock were not easily found. It was not until the brothers met an able young man by the name of Cutler, just back from the War and with big ideas, that they began to see light. Cutler was then a most aggressive factor in the house of E. B. Smith & Co. He was profoundly impressed by the Behn personality and the Behn plans, and he devoted the best part of 1922 to the effort to give them a footing in the Street. At length, he convinced his partners that the project offered their house a big chance, he persuaded Dominick & Dominick to go along with him, and in April, 1923, these two houses brought out an issue of 50,000 shares of I. T. & T. common at $68.50 a share ($3,425,000). This was the real beginning of the years of expansion. The Behns never ceased to be grateful, and Mr. Cutler did his house the best single turn it ever enjoyed.

With the surface record of I. T. & T. progress in the next eight years, American investors have become gradually familiar. The record has been dazzling. Between 1924 and 1931, plant and property account went from $26,650,-000 to $342,300,000 and total assets from $38,300,000 to $604,400,000. Gross earnings were $5,850,000 in 1924, and $104,470,000 in 1930. Net income followed with a jump from $1,930,000 to $13,750,000. And these figures, staggering as they were, represented a program of acquisition which could only be described as sensational.Its chronology appears elsewhere in this article. In general, it transformed the International Telephone & Telegraph Corporation from a telephone operator in two semitropical islands to the largest telephone operator outside the U. S., the second largest telegraph operator in North America, a cable company with one arm vigorously competing across the Atlantic, one arm across the Pacific, and a third stretching to South America, an active participant in the radio scramble, and a manufacturer doing a business of some $80,000,000 a year.

That such spectacular growth should have excited the investor in the boom years is not at all surprising. When, on September 3, 1929, the common sold for $149.25 a share, it was being valued at forty-eight times earnings. On the same day, A. T. &. T. sold at twenty-three times earnings, Western Union at sixteen times, and Radio at sixty-four times. A. T. & T. was and is, of course, the world's premier common stock, Radio has enjoyed (or suffered) constant bull manipulation, and Western Union is as much a colorless stock as it has been a colorless company. I. T. & T.'s tremendous market prestige was due neither to the public's suspicion of concealed earnings nor, in its early stages, to such organized popularity as Mike Meehan can give a stock. It was due almost entirely to the repetition, month after month, of stories of I. T. & T. mergers, purchases, concessions. In 1930, the New York *Times* carried more than fifty stories about the company, a notable publicity record for any organization.

As public confidence in expanding companies continued to mount in 1929 and lifted the stock to what now seems unjustifiable levels, so later public pessimism knocked the stock to levels astonishingly low, an amazing reversal of general opinion not entirely explicable by such discouraging factors as the Spanish and Latin-American revolutions or the fall in the peseta. Rather, it was the realization, in some quarters fostered, that I. T. & T. had had to pay full prices for its properties, that interest and dividend requirements on the expanded capitalization had increased even faster than the earnings, and that nowhere in the statement of the company could there be found figures to show increased profit on each dollar invested. The world-wide depression had, in fact, overtaken the company and thrown its earnings per share of stock to a level lower than in any year since the company was founded.

While these doubts were not unnatural, they were founded upon an incomplete understanding of the I. T. &

T. record and the I. T. & T. plans. The record of the Behns in Cuba had much to do with the enthusiasm of the early sponsors of the company. The Cuban record was even then a ten-year record; other records must also be ten years old before the picture will form completely. Next oldest and most typical of I. T. &. T. developments is the Spanish concession. Some idea of progress may therefore come from its study.

When Miguel Primo de Rivera y Orbaneja announced himself "at the Royal Feet of Your Majesty" and besought Alfonso's signature to a decree authorizing the closing of I. T. & T.'s contract, he bore witness to a number of highly important things. First of all, he paid tribute to the extraordinary talents of Sosthenes Behn. Although Colonel Behn had hastened to Spain after the first, ground-breaking stock issue in 1923, he found both the Ericsson Company (Sweden) and Siemens & Halske (Germany) bidding for the Spanish telephone system. He immediately took a hotel suite, sent for a corps of engineers, accountants, and even typists, and proceeded to turn himself into a combination of a social Spaniard and an industrial American. Negotiations were long and tortuous; over a period of nearly a year, the terms of the proposed concession were continually being modified. One of the principal reasons for I. T. & T.'s ultimate success lay in the fact that after each modification, Colonel Behn and his staff would sit up all night and have a new contract ready for the government's consideration on the morrow. It was the first application of direct method as Colonel Behn understands it, and it was justified on August 26, 1924, when the contract was signed.

Another fact to which the Dictator testified in his petition to the King was the breakdown in governmental telephone operation in Europe. He spoke of "the heterogeneous character of the system . . . antiquated legislation . . . mosaic of administrative contracts . . ." but he did not do justice to the situation. At Vitoria, a city of some 36,000 inhabitants, the switchboard dated back to a time just fourteen years after Alexander Graham Bell invented the telephone. While some of the 90,000 scattered telephones were operated by private companies, the government controlled the Madrid and Barcelona long-distance systems, producing the most impossible confusion. Subscribers could make calls within the city from their own houses, but if they wished to call another city, they had to go downtown and wait their turn at the long-distance station.

They might wait an hour and they might wait half the day. When at length their calls were put through, they were often cut off with a few seconds' conversation, clearing the circuit for a newspaper or a bank which had leased the wire for fixed periods daily. Even worse than the service was the plant itself. Iron and copper wires paralleled each other in the same circuit. Repeaters, to strengthen weak currents, were unknown. Underground cables did not exist. Wires were strung along housetops and terminated in huge open-work baskets.

It was altogether hopeless, as the Dictator realized, and it was worse than most of the European systems. Hence Spain became the first nation to turn over its entire area to private operation. Italy followed, dividing its territory among four companies (of which Ericsson, later to become an I. T. & T. ally, was one). Rumania was 1930's I. T. & T.

convert. Others will make the change when national politics permit.

So far as Spain itself is concerned, the experiment must be considered an unqualified success. Instead of the contract's stipulated "average delay of not more than thirty minutes" in inter-station conversation, the new service was quite as rapid as any in the world. The contract called for completion of the system within five years, and while the last provision was not met until one week before August 26, 1929, I. T. & T. had in fact bettered its promises by some 30 per cent of plant. Further, this plant has a good claim to be called the world's best. It is of course idle to compare a 215,000-phone system with the 15,700,000 phones of A. T. & T., but in point of mechanical perfection the Spanish unit surpasses any similar unit now in existence. Telephone service in New York City, for example, is today only about half automatic; Spain is now about 75 per cent automatic. Everything is brand-new and of the most advanced type. On the personnel side, the Dictator was naturally anxious that the company should be directed and staffed by Spaniards. While in the peak years 1926 and 1927, Colonel Behn sent into Spain a flying squadron of about 260 Americans and other non-Spaniards—his own engineers, engineers borrowed from A. T. & T., accountants, skilled workmen of all sorts—he also succeeded so well in training the old Spanish employees that there are today only four Americans among the 10,800 on the pay roll of the Compañía Telefónica Nacional de España. One is executive vice-president, another is chief engineer, a third is comptroller. In spite of its relationship to New York, the Spanish company is an essentially Spanish institution, financed in large part by Spanish investors, operated by Spaniards, and making a substantial contribution to the well-being of the Spanish state.

Thus the physical and personal achievement in Spain. It remains to be demonstrated that this rationalization of a country's communications is accompanied by a corresponding increase in traffic. The number of telephones in service has more than doubled, from under 100,000 in 1924 to about 215,000 at the end of 1930. This is an important check on the total I. T. & T. increase from 156,000 to around 700,000. In 1925, Spaniards poured the equivalent of nickels and dimes to the extent of 275 pesetas into each telephone. The flood of coins has since mounted to 415 pesetas, and total revenues have jumped from 29,000,000 pesetas in 1925 to 79,295,000 in 1930. A large part (24,500,-000 pesetas) of this gain, of course, can be found in the revenues from the toll service. Most visible, perhaps, of the signs of this tide is the traffic over the Madrid-Barcelona circuits. Before I. T. & T.'s entrance into Spain, four iron wire circuits connected these busiest cities. I. T. & T., with some misgivings but with an eye to 1935, put in ten circuits, over which service was instantaneous. Three years later, it had to install twelve more. The toll call, as a practical proposition in Spain, was invented by I. T. & T.

This has obviously cost money, and the total investment in Spanish telephones (apart from the Spanish factories) grew from 140,000,000 pesetas in 1926 to 740,000,000 at the end of 1930. This tremendous pace was dictated by the terms of the concession, and it would not be extraordinary if the investment had grown faster than revenues or profits. Under the terms of the concession I. T. & T. *may* earn 8 per cent (plus 2 per cent for a general reserve) and may adjust the rate structure to bring such a yield. The revamping of the rate structure has proved to be a long and delicate job; it has been complicated by the instability of the peseta and, of course, by the revolution; it is not yet complete. But there is every reason to suppose that it will eventually be accomplished.

The figures reveal at once the great size of such an undertaking and the eagerness of the Spanish response to it. Spain is still in the kindergarten grades so far as telephone *use* is concerned. Its 8 phones per 1,000 population compare with Cuba's 21, England's 41, Germany's 50, Canada's 142, and 164 in the U. S. And Madrid's 43 phones match 81 in Havana, 119 in Berlin, 300 in Chicago, 408 in San Francisco—highest ratio of all cities.

When local money markets and earnings of the national companies become sufficiently stable, I. T. & T. takes into partnership the people of the countries in which it operates. The Cuban company has $6,071,000 preferred outstanding, for the most part in Cuban hands, and its funded debt of $7,430,400 is held both in the U. S. and in Cuba. Spanish investors took up a 300,000,000 peseta issue of preferred stock and about 20 per cent of the common stock in the national company organized to operate the nation's telephones. And the Spanish company has outstanding a funded debt of 100,000,000 pesetas, floated to pay back the I. T. & T. loans.

Thus I. T. & T.'s financial policy in foreign countries begins to take outline. First comes a drive to create earnings, no expense being spared to build for future national development. Then comes local refinancing of a part of

I. T. & T.'s investment. But I. T. & T. keeps its equity in the business. The effect of this policy can be seen from a comparison of I. T. & T.'s commitment in the various systems. In Cuba, the I. T. & T. controls a system of 75,000 phones with an equity holding of $14,000,000. There are more than 200,000 telephones under I. T. & T. control in both Spain and in the Argentine. Yet I. T. & T.'s investment in Spain is some $47,000,000 against an estimated $88,000,000 in the Argentine. Presumably I. T. & T. intends to finance further Spanish growth locally and to finance a portion of the Argentine growth in the Argentine investment market as soon as possible.

Through the media of Cuba and Spain, we see stretched out the main lines of I. T. & T. policy and the high spots of I. T. & T. experiences in world-wide telephone operation. Since Cuba, Spain is the first job which has had time to show results. In South America, where it now operates over 50 per cent of all telephones, I. T. & T.'s most important South American company (the River Plate Company in the Argentine) was acquired only in 1929, after four years of negotiation. The Spanish performance is the I. T. & T. model, as to contract, nationalization, equipment, etc.

For all the activity of I. T. & T.'s competitors—the Siemens & Halske group, Theodore Gary's General Telephone and Electric Corp. with its ally, Transamerica Corp., (Ivar Kreuger's Telefonaktiebolaget L. M. Ericsson, formerly a great potential rival, is now an I. T. & T. ally)—the most urgent competitive problem of I. T. & T. is neither in the business of telephone operation nor in the business of making telephone equipment. When, in 1928, the Behns bought the telegraph and cable companies headed by Clarence Hungerford Mackay, they stepped into an exceedingly puzzling situation. Postal Telegraph was then doing only about 17 per cent of the domestic telegraph business, conceding the rest to Western Union without much murmur. After the War, in fact, Postal's principal function was to act as a feeding and distributing agent for Commercial Cables, and while its business increased with the normal trade increase, Western Union was taking the lion's share of each year's new business. The Behns, buying Postal as a necessary step in their world plan (of which more later), were determined to make the company a real power. Mr. Mackay, whose capacity for awakening and holding personal loyalties is exceeded by no American business man, naturally remained as chief, but about him I. T. & T. put four aggressive young men with A. T. & T. training. Most notable of the four is Colonel A. H. Griswold, a direct-action man who ran the telephone and telegraph systems of the A. E. F. and in that fierce school learned the value of record communications (telegram, cable) as against the telephone.

This new management has created a new company. Postal is now making a determined effort to merchandise itself. It is establishing schools for its messenger boys, it has taken advertising schedules in the country's chief newspapers, and it is attacking, one by one, the industries which carry large telegraph files. A typical effort has been directed at the florists' delivery-by-telegram business. First comes a kind of rabbit-out-of-hat performance. At the speakers' table, during a florists' banquet, sit (preferably lovely) operators, each in front of a typing telegraph device known as a printer. Messages go out to florists all over the world;

a Postal official explains what is happening, continues to speak until the answers come in. A tremendous hit was registered at the convention of the Florists' Telegraph Delivery Association when a Buenos Aires confrere telegraphed his regret that the florists could not see his exhibition of an obscure azalea. The most spectacular of all the shows, of course, was that evening in June, 1930, in San Francisco, when I. T. & T. sent a message around the world in five minutes, thirty seconds, beating the record by some two and one-half minutes. The show (for the N. E. L. A. convention) followed Owen D. Young's great speech on surpluses and in spite of the handicap was a howling success.

On the heels of the show, Postal advertised in the trade papers and stirred its agents to special efforts. The florists responded with about $100,000 additional business in 1930, turning a 70–30 advantage for Western Union into a 60–40 lead for Postal. This is smart merchandising, and it is being carried into the most unexpected corners of industry. Postal is trying to convince companies with large sales forces to have their men in the field report each night by telegram. National advertising by telegram is another Postal goal. A move which Western Union *had* to copy was the Postal hook-up with the Standard Oil group, establishing 4,460 telegraph offices in as many gas service stations scattered through the marketing territories of the S. O. companies (New Jersey, Ohio, Kansas, California, Indiana, etc.), which can be expanded to cover the total 70,000 stations of these companies. This was no sudden, happy inspiration; it proceeded directly from the chief thesis behind all recent Postal activity, i.e., that the telegraph should be made available to the public, as available and as familiar as the telephone. Postal's move in changing its New York offices into Theatre Ticket agencies, had its difficulties, but certainly increased Postal traffic.

Hurdles in the path of this scheme are many. One is the psychological barrier erected by the ten-word limit. The Chicago executive who thinks nothing of lifting his telephone speaker and calling San Francisco yet tries to keep his telegrams within the fateful ten words. Rate schedules are now being very carefully studied, and the ten-word taboo may disappear as completely as Spain's thirty-minute limit.

But the most serious hurdle and the problem which is at the heart of the domestic telegraph situation is the competition between Postal and Western Union. It is permissible to debate the merits of the competitive *development* of the telegraph as against the monopolistic development of the telephones, but the inefficiency of that competition today is obvious to everyone—even to the principal cause of its continued existence, Mr. Newcomb Carlton.

Duplication between the two systems already costs millions and in prospect costs tens of millions. Example of current waste: a duplicate rent bill of $1,000,000 a year in New York City alone. Example of prospective waste: the $70,000,000 printer exchange. Every telegraph man agrees that there should be and will be a printer exchange. It will mean that these long-distance typewriters, which now connect your Cleveland (or Boston) office with your Detroit (or New Orleans) office and also link your office with the company's telegraph and cable dispatching offices, will be interconnected with each other all across the country and, eventually, through Europe and South America as well.

Thus the exchange will plug you in to your advertising agency, to your bank and your lawyer and your customers and the sources of your raw materials and your friends in Europe and coffee headquarters in Santos. A typist will pound out your orders, your directions, your questions, and the record will be both in your files and in the files of the office at the other end of the wire. As will be the records of that office's acknowledgments and answers.

Such an installation will cost somewhere around $70,-000,000, which is a sizable investment. Neither Postal nor Western Union is willing to make it. For when one starts, the other must follow or go out of business, and the absurdity of having *two* printer exchanges could be matched only by the absurdity of having *two* U. S. mail systems, one of which included Minneapolis and Camden, the other St. Paul and Philadelphia. So, faced with the dilemma, the companies make plans on paper and content themselves by feverishly installing free printers to connect with their own offices. Thus an enterprising New York office could to-day get itself six printers, from Western Union, Postal, R. C. A., and A. T. & T. Costs of installation to the four companies would total $3,000, but for only one (the A. T. & T. intra-office printer) need the customer pay a cent.

Emphasis is here laid upon the telegraph rather than the cable systems, for the underwater competitive situation is complicated by the real threat of Britain's Cable & Wireless combination. In the telegraph field, competition has become ruinously expensive and a real barrier to progress. Mr. Carlton, whose feeling toward Western Union is distinctly patriarchal in character, has greeted all talk of consolidation with bluff, abrupt opposition. This, and not the restraining White Act, is the real reason why a single U. S. telegraph and cable system is not nearer realization today. "Not," observes Mr. Carlton, "till I die."

Mr. Carlton is still in his early sixties, and a very hearty gentleman indeed. In the meantime, the new and aggressive Postal is cutting into his business and his prestige. With the return of normal activity, Postal should begin to make money again and pull a vigorous oar for the I. T. & T. boat.

Looking at Spain and observing the success of that large telephonic enterprise, noting the rejuvenation of Postal, it is apparent that the glitter of I. T. & T.'s record is by no means all on the surface. The Behns have not only eaten largely and very rapidly; they are also digesting their food. Clear evidence of digestion is to be found in Spain, in Postal, and in the factories of International Standard Electric. I. T. & T., which became a manufacturer almost by accident, now owes the bulk of its revenues to this aspect of its world plan. Sales of $32,500,000 in 1925, when the Behns bought International Western (later Standard) Electric, in 1930 climbed to about $61,000,000. And nearly half this increase has come from internal development, not from the mere purchase of going businesses.

Now this is not to say that I. T. & T.'s rate of growth has been ideal. Manifestly 1930 would have been an easier year if expansion could have been financed out of earnings. But the hammer-like strokes with which the Behns made the decade ring were not the results of either intoxication or whim. When a San Franciscan sets out to buy a country place, he may pick Burlingame, and then if he can't make a good deal in Burlingame, he may wander on to Menlo

Park. But telephone systems are not often on the market, and if the Behns hadn't bought the United River Plate Company in 1928 they might never have had it. And they needed it. Not for their 1930 income account, to be sure, but to fill in the outline of their broad plans.

For the Behns have just started. They have a vision of world communications which many decades can scarcely realize. It may be outlined:

First of all, a unified modern South American telephone system. At the end of 1928, when the River Plate Company was bought, telephone development south of the U. S. border roughly paralleled U. S. conditions in 1895. There was less than one telephone for each 100 inhabitants, against the present U. S. quota of 16.4. Only a few months earlier, I. T. & T. had strung its highest-in-the-world telephone wires across the Andes to introduce Chile to the Argentine. Never before 1928, had one South American capital spoken with another. The influence which modern telephone communication could have on internal trade is obvious and tremendous. Equally tremendous the I. T. & T. opportunity. Hence the Behn entrance into the A. B. C. countries; hence also their entrance into Peru and Uruguay. One large network, serving Rio and São Paolo, is linked with the local traction company, is owned by Canadians, and is not likely to join the I. T. & T. group. But some 55 per cent of South American telephones have already been brought into the system, and I. T. & T. is working at top speed to make this polyglot collection as efficient a communication unit as the new, compact network in Spain never deviating from the principle of nationalization, first formulated in Spain. Although U. S. capital and U. S. enterprise actually build the continental system, yet each company retains its nationality.

South America to be linked, via All America Cables, with the U. S. And through the U. S., with Europe. Here is a problem, and here is where Cables & Wireless, Ltd. rears its head. For this young British merger, freed from the lazy, smothering paternalism of the old British post office régime, has very vigorous ideas about control of world communications and about trade following cable and radio routes. In the great British drive for South American trade supremacy, a drive which enlisted the able d'Abernon commission in 1929 and which later called upon the super-salesman Prince of Wales, Cables & Wireless, Ltd. plays a prominent part. Cable rates are vital factors in the placing of South American business, and a rate difference of one cent a word or a time difference of two seconds a message carries more weight than one might suspect. The time problem, I. T. & T. (through its All America-Commercial hook-up) is more than able to meet. Although a message from Rio to London via I. T. & T. companies covers 11,000 miles, All America Cables will give the Rio business man minute service. Cables & Wireless, with a 6,000 mile direct line between the same two cities, cannot better the guarantee. But the rate war is very much a problem. I. T. & T. had no choice but to follow Cables & Wireless rate cuts. The eventual British goal, which is fortunately unattainable, is to make the South American-London service actually cheaper than the South American-New York service, and thus move not only cable files but trade itself from American to British markets.

Here, however, one begins to see the Behn plan in its

full proportions. The South American telephones; the cable links with the U. S., Europe, and Asia; the radio telephone; the European factories and telephone systems; radio across the Pacific to Asia, where the Shanghai telephone company also provides an outlet for the Chinese manufacturing unit, China Electric, and where I. T. & T. is in a position to build a South China system should that ever be possible and desirable; and, finally, the nerve-center of this living, vibrating organism in the U. S. This to be a unified telegraph service, if and when the government and the Western Union agree; until then, a constantly improving Postal company. This was to be also a unified Radio service, if the government permitted R. C. A. to accept 1,200,000 shares of I. T. & T. stock in return for its communications systems. But for two years this 1929 plan awaited government approval, then, opposition still persisting, the plan was dropped and the companies planned instead further competition with each other. Whatever the issue of the merger efforts, the final result cannot be in doubt. An American communication system is certainly in the making, and, just as certainly, the Brothers Behn are making it.

I. T. & T.'S DIRECTORS

Reaching out through the air and under the waters, the Behns did not, of course, find only wires or cables or factories. They also found the men who strung the wires and laid the cables and built the factories. And the chief of them, the Behns, sat down at a long deal table in front of a pattern of $20 goldpieces. Already at the table were gathered another group—the men who had been prophetic enough to guess that bread cast upon the waters in 1921 (or 1916 or 1923) would return in bountiful measure before they were too old to enjoy it, and, indeed, before the decade was out. Year by year, others came to join the group (1929 was the first year to see no new face at the table); a few dropped out. By 1931, there were twenty-one such men in the cabinet of the Brothers Behn. The chronology of their arrival at the May meetings at the directors' table reflects very accurately the progress of I. T. & T.'s fortunes:

1923.—Hernand Behn, Sosthenes Behn, George H. Gardiner, Henry B. Orde

1924.—F. Wilder Bellamy, Edward J. Berwind, John W. Cutler, Allen G. Hoyt, John L. Merrill, Charles E. Mitchell, Walter E. Ogilvie, Bradley W. Palmer

1925.—Marqués de Urquijo

1926.—Arthur M. Anderson, Conde de Güell, Russell C. Leffingwell, George E. Pingree, Wolcott H. Pitkin

1927.—R. Fulton Cutting, Lansing P. Reed

1928.—Clarence H. Mackay

In May, 1923, when I. T. & T. published its second report (for 1922), its directorate included only two men, besides the Behns themselves, who are now to be found at the long table. Mr. Orde and Mr. Gardiner were destined to become the leaders of the two groups—the management group and the advisory group—which are to be found in most directorates. Henry B. Orde was a stocky, thick-haired, Canada-trained banker when he first entered the American Colonial Bank in Porto Rico. He met the Behns, liked them, became one of the first converts to their telephone plans, and in 1916 found himself director and treasurer of Behn Bros., Inc. In 1920, Behn Bros., Inc.'s function was complete and when I. T. & T. was born, Mr. Orde assisted at the delivery. Today, he ranks next to the Behns in I. T. & T. management, is a close-mouthed, open-faced, vigorous man, completely absorbed in the company's affairs. George H. Gardiner, by way of contrast, is absorbed in many another enterprise, being the fourth man in the law firm headed by John W. Davis, and a great comfort to that firm's most profitable client, the House of Morgan. Nonetheless, Mr. Gardiner drew the original papers of incorporation for the brothers and mailed them to the Secretary of State of Maryland, and his name has always been printed twice among the directors, once in its proper alphabetical position, and once at the end of the list, as "General Counsel." The title is more general than specific. I. T. & T. has many legal advisers and a law department of the first rank. But while Mr. Gardiner would not now draw up articles of incorporation, he remains the company's guide, philosopher, and friend, and despite the glittering figures which later took their seats at the table, perhaps the most indispensable I. T. & T. director today.

When Mr. Orde and Mr. Gardiner came to the meeting of May, 1924, they found eight new faces at the table. The year 1923 had, in fact, marked the most significant step yet undertaken by the Behns—the entrance into the New York credit market. To the board, then, there came Charles E. Mitchell and Allen Grey Hoyt of the National City. The Mitchell history is well-known. Hoyt's career had closely paralleled that of Frank A. Vanderlip—each was born in Aurora, Illinois; each began his work in Washington; they came to the City within a few months of each other, and they worked together to develop the bank's young bond department. It was Hoyt who convinced Mitchell that in spite of a disturbed market, the City should finance the Behn's projects in Cuba and Porto Rico.

Together with the City's representatives there appeared, of course, the comparative youngsters who had ventured to underwrite the issue of I. T. & T. common in April, 1923. John W. Cutler and F. Wilder Bellamy left Harvard and Yale in 1909, two tall, slim, polite, and eager young men. Cutler had been a famous Harvard athlete, stroke of the crew in his first year, and in his fourth, All-American quarterback under Percy Haughton. Afterwards he became a Boston (Lee, Higginson) banker, a distinguished ordnance officer in France, and a talented amateur artist. Not until the War ended did he join E. B. Smith & Co., where he opened a successful career with the I. T. & T. deal. He is president of the Hangar Club, an ultra-smart, ultra-rich group of aviators and friends of aviators, including Colonel Behn, H. P. Davison, Marshall Field, W. A. Harriman, Gordon S. Rentschler, and others. Bellamy was first a lawyer (O'Brien, Boardman, Parker & Fox), then a banker. He was the Dominick & Dominick partner assigned to I. T. & T.'s affairs. Like Cutler, he has kept his slimness, his distinction, and his love of sport.

Also in this crucial year, to the board table came that grand old man, Edward Julius Berwind, whose chairmanship of the Berwind-White Coal Mining Co. heads an almost endless list of distinctions, who adores the husband of his niece, Mrs. Sosthenes Behn, and who, past eighty, is the best-loved of all who sit, noon after noon, at the cheerful tables of the Recess Club. And in this year, Bradley

Webster Palmer, Harvard '88, fisherman, bachelor, chairman of United Fruit's executive committee. And Walter Ellsworth Ogilvie, a potent railroader in Cuba, yachtsman in America and England, Republican and Baptist. And John L. Merrill, who began his career as a $5.00-a-week errand boy in the two-room office of that daring enterprise which had drawn 5,000 miles of cable from Texas to Peru; who finds himself, in 1931, president of All-America Cables with 30,000 miles of underwater cable and handling 5,250 messages a day; whose record of service now covers half a century.

The year 1924 saw the signing of the Spanish contract; when May, 1925, arrived, a great grandee had joined the group about the Behns. Don Estanislao de Urquijo y Ussia, Marqués de Urquijo, is perhaps the richest man in Spain, is certainly that nation's foremost banker and financier. Interminable are his names, his orders, and his children. The proudest and most embarrassing moment of his life (and in the life of his lovely Donna Maria) arrived when his heir turned out to be twins. But in time, the meticulous Marqués was satisfied that Don Juan had preceded Don Luis by some moments, and in the due course of events, Don Juan came to America to prepare himself for his great financial responsibilities. The Marqués, who bears the title of president of the Compañía Telefónica Nacional de España, is of course not the operating chief. His Banco Urquijo, however, led the list of Madrid underwriters of the company's preferred stock.

With the Marqués de Urquijo had been elected the Marqués de Comillac. This almost equally rich and illustrious grandee died, however, within a few months of his election and was succeeded, at the 1926 meeting, by his nephew, the Conde de Güell. The Conde was an intimate friend of Primo de Rivera, whose cordial support was at that time of the greatest assistance to the Behns. He had also followed his uncle as president of the Compañía Transatlántica, operating as many as twenty liners and freighters between Spain and the Americas.

Conde de Güell belongs to the 1925 (Spanish) vintage. But 1926 did mark the appearance of a new and important group at the I. T. & T. table. This included Mr. George E. ("Ping") Pingree, who had been the boss of International Western Electric under A. T. & T. management, and was to remain its boss under the new name of International Standard Electric and the new management of the Behns. And as the purchase of this huge manufacturing enterprise had brought J. P. Morgan & Co. into the I. T. & T. picture, it surprised no one, in 1926, to find two Morgan partners on the board. One of these, of course, was Russell C. Leffingwell, the expert on international finance who had come to Morgan three years earlier, the other was Arthur Anderson. These Morgan men represented the first new financial interest since the arrival of Cutler and Bellamy. The relations of the various banking houses had been thoroughly worked out, however, and neither E. B. Smith & Co. nor Dominick & Dominick lost the position they had so shrewdly won. In this year, there came to the board a new face to many, but an old friend of the Behns—Mr. Wolcott H. Pitkin, one-time Attorney General of Porto Rico and a most able lawyer. A quiet, deliberate man, close adviser to the Behns, Mr. Pitkin's prestige in the company has steadily grown.

The next group to find seats at the table came directly from All America Cables, which had been added to the I. T. & T. system in 1926. W. Emlen Roosevelt headed this group, and with him was that persistent social crusader, Mr. R. Fulton Cutting. In 1929, when Mr. Roosevelt died, Mr. Cutting became chairman of All America. From behind his great beard have come, upon occasion, rather startling remarks. One such was pronouncement, as president of the trustees of Cooper Union, in favor of "some sort of unemployment dole." In this year, together with Messrs. Roosevelt and Cutting, the board table received Mr. Logan N. Rock, now one of I. T. & T.'s vice presidents, but no longer on the board; and one of the most active of Wall Street's corporation lawyers, Mr. Lansing P. Reed, who follows Mr. Gardiner in rank at Davis, Polk, Wardwell, Gardiner & Reed.

Last of all to the I. T. & T. table there advanced, in the sprightliest possible manner, a trim, dapper gentleman who is the most puzzling phenomenon in Wall Street. It is perfectly easy to say that Mr. Clarence Hungerford Mackay is a charming, accomplished dilettante. Stemming from that rough and lucky miner, old John W. Mackay, and the proud woman who was his wife, Clarence Mackay was far from rough and had no need to be ambitious. He was and is one of the best squash-tennis players in the world. His peerless collection of medieval armor (which requires the constant services of one man plus silver polish) is internationally admired and envied. He is the godfather of the Philharmonic-Orchestra in New York. Yet Mr. Mackay is deeply attached to that country from which he sprang— the graceless, dirt-rich hills of Nevada. That state will never again enjoy such a benefactor as Mr. Mackay. He supports its university; in 1930, he opened its school of mines. Debonair as he is, his dilettantism surprisingly extends to those homely roots which are not usually remembered on Long Island.

In the offices of the Postal Telegraph Co., Mr. Mackay is at once the armor-collector and something altogether different. He is casual, unpredictable, often inconsequential. But there is not a man in I. T. & T.'s great building at Broad and Beaver Streets who does not like him, listen to him, and become increasingly loyal to him. And there is scarcely a door in downtown New York through which he cannot walk, unannounced and welcome. He built the Postal into a great company. Others are the executive chiefs today, but Mr. Mackay is very much there, very much needed, very much loved.

CAMELS OF
WINSTON~SALEM

Which "are not Disconcerted by the Advance of Any Competitor"; Which Have Poured $175,000,000 Cash into the Pockets of Stockholders; Which in Seventeen Years of Happy Fertility Have Never Once Failed to Multiply

R. J. REYNOLDS TOBACCO COMPANY

In Patrick County, Virginia, just above the North Carolina line, a sizable hill goes by the name of No Business Mountain. Beneath it there was once a tobacco plantation and factory owned by H. W. Reynolds, whose son Richard left the shadow of No Business Mountain as soon as possible, wandered southward, and set up a business for himself in Winston-Salem, North Carolina. That was in 1875. Thirty-eight years later, in 1913, we find this man, just released from the American tobacco trust which James B. Duke created, revolutionizing the tobacco industry with a cigarette whose name he chose (1) because he liked animal names; (2) because this one connoted the Orient; (3) because, of several thousand suggestions, Camel was easiest to pronounce.

Yet he did not merely create the world's greatest cigarette. Second only to James B. Duke, he is the father of the modern $1,000,000,000 tobacco industry, out of which have sprung such fortunes as those of Anthony Brady, Ryan, Widener, Whitney, Payne, and Duke. With one stroke he started a cigarette landslide, which has not yet stopped sliding. A bit of fine paper imported from France, wrapped tightly around a new combination of tobaccos, and sold under a somewhat unlikely trade-mark, created a revolution in the tobacco industry that shifted the emphasis from Virginia and Kentucky to North Carolina, from pipes and plugs to cigarettes, and from men toward women. Before Camels were invented, America was producing about 10,-000,000,000 cigarettes a year, a large proportion of them Turkish. Leading domestic brands, such as Piedmont and Sweet Caporal, were made of unblended Carolina leaf. The higher-priced Fatimas alone were pointed toward the future with a blend of some 60 per cent domestic leaf and 40 per cent Turkish. Let us not be ingenuous enough to propose the famed Camel blend as sole and sufficient cause for the Reynolds revolution; for the success of Camel is based quite as much on great merchandizing, efficient machinery, and foresight as it is on tobacco; and Camel participated, besides, in the amazing luck that fell upon the tobacco industry during and after the late War. Yet the fact remains that the year the Camel blend appeared, cigarette consumption leaped to 15,500,000,000. Today, with three other major brands having adopted the fundamental Camel idea, it is 120,000,000,000.

And again, as a result of that blend and merchandizing, the R. J. Reynolds Tobacco Co. has been America's most profitable tobacco concern, doing a business unofficially estimated at $300,000,000 a year, frequently paying enough daily federal taxes to build Winston-Salem's spanking new post-office in the morning, and another one just like it in the afternoon. Its manufacturing is 100 per cent concentrated in this quaint, provincial, tobacco-scented town, where many houses are of old Moravian brick laid up in irregular bond. From the narrow, hilly streets, from the crooked roofs (under one of which the ubiquitous father of his country spent the night), there rises the spruce spire of the R. J. Reynolds Tobacco Co. building, Carolina's proudest skyscraper, with automatic elevators and twenty-three floors (the thirteenth, eliminated). And gathered in a crescent around it, within a three-minute walk, are block upon block of Reynolds factories, the older ones with old-fashioned sash windows, and connected by flying passages upon which are painted the flaring announcements that CAMELS LEAD THE WORLD.

There are other industries in Winston-Salem, notably Chatham Manufacturing Co., famed for its blankets, and P. H. Hanes Knitting Co., famed for its cotton underwear, but were they all but Reynolds removed, Winston-Salem would still be an important spot on the map of the U. S. This second-largest city in North Carolina, with a population of 80,000, is known as Camel City; its bus line is Camel City Coach Co., and there is a Camel City Cleaners, and a dozen such. More than half the resident families are directly connected with the Reynolds Co., and it is a rare family of consequence that is not interested in Reynolds stock. The activity of the 12,000 Reynolds employees is quite prodigious. The Reynolds buildings are heavy with machines from which jet forth all day long hundreds of white cigarette streams, each at the rate of 800 smokes a minute, totaling some 38,000,000,000 a year; and besides this there are compounded and cut millions of tins of Prince Albert, the nation's most popular pipe tobacco, and millions of pounds of Apple, Brown's Mule, and Day's Work chewing tobaccos. The Winston-Salem Southbound Railway, Norfolk & Western, and Southern Railway carry away an average of seventy-five carloads of Reynolds products a day, in trains named *Camel Special, Prince Albert Special, George Washington Special, Torch Light,* and *Brown's Mule:* such that the railroad revenue derived from this area, due to the high class of freight handled, rivals that of busy Birmingham or metropolitan New Orleans.

It is a tobacco town, first and last. There is tobacco in the air and tobacco in the minds of most of the citizens. So characteristic is the smell that the true Winston-Salem citizen is restless and ill at ease when away from it, sniffs the air with pleasure upon his return. And it is probably impossible to indicate, in any mere outline of its premier corporation, the spell that this weed has cast upon the people who grow, sell, handle, and manufacture it. The Indians worshiped tobacco as sacred; the southern planter or tobacconist does no less. Toward any leaf presented to him for inspection he is critical at first, but if it meets with his approval he loves it in a fatherly, knowing way. He feels it with his fingers, smells it with his nose, measures it with his eye. He loves its texture, its shape, its odor, its taste. He loves and he knows.

Now if the Camel cigarette is based on any one thing more than another, it is upon this knowledge and this love. For R. J. Reynolds grew right out of the tobacco fields; his younger brother, W. N., who is now chairman of the board, did no less; and not a single executive has been with the company for less than a dozen years. There are no outsiders in Reynolds, nor can its remarkable career be credited to any single man. It is a directors' company, and—what is even more remarkable—every one of the directors is at the head of a department in the company's immediate employ. A description of the leadership would be a description of these twelve men, headed by Chairman W. N. Reynolds and President Bowman Gray,* it is true, but exhibiting a remarkable genius for the distribution and coöperation of power. Chairman Reynolds himself is the tobacco buyer-in-chief, and he is known throughout the length and breadth of the Carolinas and Kentucky as the most expert leaf man who appears on the auction floors.

For this sacred inspiring weed is never sold. It is auctioned. It is brought into town every fall by the farmers and piled in neat geometrical designs in the wide flat baskets that the auction companies provide. On each appointed day farmers, buyers, and auctioneer assemble—the latter one of the most picturesque figures in American industry. Hat on the back of his head, hands in his hip pockets, his body swaying, he sings and croons down the long aisles of tobacco baskets. The buyers follow him, bidding, sometimes by signs, sometimes aloud. The action is extremely fast, extremely accurate, but from one end of the warehouse to the other the trailing uninitiate will not understand a word of that perpetual, urging song as it rises and falls.

Onto these busy floors at the height of the buying season steps six-foot Mr. W. N. Reynolds, just as he did before his company revolutionized the tobacco industry. W. N. Reynolds knows tobacco leaf, and he knows the supply and demand on any tobacco market. He has under him keen buyers in Kentucky, Tennessee, Virginia, Georgia, the Carolinas, and these are officially headed by T. H. Kirk,

---

* Since this analysis was written, Mr. Gray has become Chairman of the Board and Mr. Reynolds has taken the chair of the finance committee. Able, energetic Samuel Clay Williams, formerly vice president and general council, has been elected president.

vice president and director of the business. As a result of this buying shrewdness, the Reynolds inventories present an interesting study. Since tobacco must be kept for two years to mellow and sweat, inventories in the tobacco industry are somewhat staggering. In the case of American Tobacco Co. and Liggett & Myers, they have shown a tendency to increase in direct proportion to the increase in sales. But this is not the case with Reynolds, except over a very long stretch of time. Reynolds is an opportunist, buys heavily in years when the desired leaf is plentiful, buys scantily when it is scarce. A profound knowledge of leaf and markets may thus effect a saving of millions. In 1927, for example, Reynolds's inventory was $108,000,000 —highest for all time. That was a year of Reynolds leaf. Since then inventory has declined to $90,000,000, while those of the two great rivals have steadily climbed to more than $100,000,000.

There exists in America no more competitive industry than this one of buying, manufacturing, and selling tobacco. The competition was a deliberate creation of the mind of James B. Duke, who built up the tobacco trust and, by order of the federal court, unbuilt it again. His achievement is unique in the annals of American industry, and in the study of any major tobacco company except Reynolds would have to be investigated in some detail. The tobacco trust owned a majority of Reynolds stock, but the Reynolds company was never absorbed, is still the same corporate entity that it was before the trust was formed. All that Reynolds inherits from the trust is competition so fierce that even the simplest figures of manufacture and sales are withheld. The whole tobacco business is in that primitive industrial state in which the publication of production figures is thought to be harmful, and consequently the embattled terrain of cigarette manufacture is riddled with speculation, guess, and unjust conclusion. No one really knows how many Camels, Luckies, or Chesterfields are produced every year. The figures used in this discussion are frankly mere estimates, drawn from the most reliable sources, yet without any official character. If one had the patience to add together all the estimates, a figure considerably in excess of the total national production would be reached.

Because of this situation, the Reynolds inventories have been studied with some care. It is accepted in the tobacco world that Camel buys only the highest grades of leaf; how then, some may ask, unless Camel production is falling off, did the inventory fall some $17,000,000 in two years? The Camel answer to this question is simple, catholic, and unanswerable: Camel production did not fall off. Indeed, it seems unquestionable that in the first seventeen years of its existence Camel has never failed to gain—a somewhat unique fact in industry. One is forced to conclude that here at Winston-Salem stands a very substantial monument to the coöperation of talent and knowledge. If Reynolds figures were made public, the last tobacco season would probably be found to be typical. It is the habit of most large companies to stand off from the market a little, when the crops first come in, but in August, 1930, when the tobacco crop ripened in Georgia, the Camel buyers decided to buy. Since then, 1930 turned out to be more expensive for late purchasers, and while Vice President Kirk's requirements of these tobaccos in October were 80 per cent filled at low early-season prices, other companies were scrambling for good leaf on the auction floors of the Carolinas.

As has been stated, the blend which Reynolds buys with such astuteness was revolutionary to the tobacco business when it first appeared and has had much to do with the fantastic growth in popularity of the cigarette. It is based upon bright tobacco, which now grows in North and South Carolina, Georgia, and Florida. The properties of this leaf were first discovered in 1852 (another tobacco revolution) when Eli and Elisha Slade, on a farm near Durham, North Carolina, heated some of their crop over hot flues. The tobacco emerged from the curing process a wonderful, clear, rich gold; it was sweet to smoke, and most miraculous of all, no other tobacco in the world would so react to the alchemy of the flues. This leaf became famed, not only for its color, but for its mildness; was already the basis of Bull Durham, Duke's Mixture, Piedmont, Sweet Caporal, and many another brand when R. J. Reynolds based his new blend upon it. He then added rich brown Burley from Kentucky—a step which was perhaps as radical to the cigarette business as any other—and enough Turkish to constitute less than 25 per cent of his cigarette. The whole mixture Reynolds sprayed and dipped in certain flavors, than which nothing is more secret except the Camel blend itself. Less than a dozen men in the world, perhaps no more than half a dozen, know the complete Camel formula. A knowledge of it would mean an absolutely expert knowledge of tobacco, for into it go from twenty to twenty-five distinct types of leaf, each type having three or four subdivisions—up to 100 different tobacco classifications.

Tobacco, like wine, has its special crops, special flavors, and aromas, but the American people are not educated to tobacco as the French are to wine. Consequently even the finest blend in the world could never become the pacemaker without merchandizing and advertising, and in order to understand what Camels did in this regard, it is necessary to remember what James B. Duke had done.

Mr. Duke started life on his father's tobacco farm near Durham, with pardonable envy in his eye for the flourishing business of one John Ruffin Green, whose trade-mark was Bull Durham. Spurred on by a desire to overtake Bull Durham, he developed his father's W. Duke Sons & Co. at an alarming pace; finally moved his headquarters to New York, where he waged a buccaneering, price-cutting war, and advertised on a scale that the nation had never seen and has never yet surpassed. In one year his advertising bill was exactly double his net income, and just before his competitors crumbled he was spending 20 per cent of gross on advertising. Thus was planted into the tobacco business the advertising tradition, whose most active exponent today is George Washington Hill with his Lucky Strike. Thus also—and this is the important point with regard to Camels—there was planted the tradition of premiums, coupons, and pictures of baseball players for which little boys nagged their fathers. As the American tobacco trust absorbed more and more competitors, this advertising abated somewhat. But in 1911 when the courts dissolved the trust, the costly premium mania was born anew.

It was at this point that R. J. Reynolds conceived the idea, unheard-of and unique, of marketing a cigarette without premiums or even so much as a picture of a Pensacola

Rifleman. Tobacco value was to be the slogan; the Camels smoker was to be given his money's worth in tobacco, not in pictures for his little boy. The American public saw the point. Even to this day the Camel package carries the announcement: "Don't look for premiums or coupons, as the cost of the tobacco blended in Camel cigarettes prohibits the use of them." By 1917, four years after this idea was launched, Camel was the largest selling cigarette in the country, doing about 40 per cent of the nation's cigarette business.

But the Camel merchandizing idea was triangular—the novel policy of issuing no premiums was only one apex of it. The selection of a single brand upon which to expend all advertising strength and selling ingenuity was an innovation almost as radical, and was the first step in the concentration of the modern cigarette industry into three or four leading brands. The gap between any one of the "big three" —Camels, Luckies, and Chesterfields—and their less emphasized brethren, such as Lord Salisbury, Piedmont, Tarryton, or even Fatima, runs into the thirty billions. And this second angle of Reynolds merchandizing leads directly into the third, namely, an absolutely national distribution. Before the appearance of Camels, the leading cigarette manufacturers sought such distribution by the marketing of a large number of brands, each emphasized in and favored by particular territories. R. J. Reynolds was the first merchant to attempt the popularizing of one brand in all districts of the country, and succeeded so far that to this day Camel is known for its thorough distribution in rural districts and in A & P stores. Other manufacturers have imitated Reynolds in this regard, the most recent aspirant being P. Lorillard with Old Gold. It is certain that some of the recent gains by Lucky Strike have been accomplished at the expense of American Tobacco Co.'s smaller brands which are being replaced in odd sections of the country by George Washington Hill's star performer.

The advantage of concentrating all efforts on one brand is that every new customer for the brand is a new customer for the company. When one company manufactures a number of brands, this is not the case; and such a manufacturer is further handicapped by the fact that the discontinuance of any brand is a total waste of all the advertising and sales efforts expended upon it. Reynolds daringly pushed Camels out in front and announced that everything the company knew about tobacco would be devoted to that brand. As a result, when the World War came, Reynolds was established in the minds of smokers. While all manufacturers in whatever lines object to the statement that the War benefited them, nevertheless, it becomes more and more apparent that many an American industry grew up to long trousers through the War. The tobacco companies grew from sizable younglings to giants.

What is the connection between war and tobacco the psychologists may know: we do not. But it is certain that during and after every war the consumption of tobacco leaps ahead. The cigarette itself, which Russians and Turks had smoked for generations, came to Western civilization from the Crimean War. During the Civil War Sherman's troops looted the tobacco factory of John Ruffin Green in Durham, temporarily ruining a lively war-time business. But in a few months, after peace was declared, the looters and their friends began writing back to Durham for more smokes. The factory was enlarged, and not so much at the expense of other manufacturers as by an actual increase in the taste for tobacco. Durham took its place on the industrial map, Bull Durham on the nation's billboards. Thereafter North Carolina's federal taxes began to climb, until now she pays more than any state except titanic New York; and in cigarette taxes pays vastly more than all other states combined.

Every cigarette manufacturer benefited by the tobacco taste which the late War created, but Camels benefited outstandingly because they were doing 40 per cent of the cigarette business. Government contracts to supply smokes to the soldiers were allotted to various companies in proportion to current sales; hence, willynilly, many a soldier smoked Camels. While cigarette consumption more than doubled from 25,000,000,000 in 1916 to 53,000,000,000 in 1919, the Camel ratio to the total remained constant; and as a result Camels emerged from the War producing more than 20,000,000,000 a year—nearly as many as all manufacturers had in 1916.

Camels have since continued to boom—the old 1919 levels have fallen away into the limbo of childhood; and Reynolds stock has made many a millionaire, such that, before the crash in November, 1929, there were half a hundred of them in Winston-Salem. A purchaser of Reynolds stock in 1913, when the Camel was first brought out, would have paid $270 a share. Had he taken up the 1918 rights at $100, each original share would now have become 100 shares worth some $5,150 and he would have received dividends totaling nearly $2,000. Since 1917, nearly $175,-000,000 has been declared in cash dividends on the two common stocks. The company has no bonds, and retired its preferred stock in 1926. With substantial reserves built up from past earnings available for expansion, and with the inherent stability of the business, Reynolds has in late years greatly liberalized its dividend policy. Of $125,700,000 earned from 1927–1930 inclusive, $107,500,000 has been paid in dividends, or about 85 per cent. This is a slightly larger slice of the earnings than expanding American Tobacco Co. has been able to spare and considerably larger than conservative Liggett & Myers can afford.

The asset value of this fabulous earner is certainly enormous, but has little to do with the printed balance sheet. Most of it is intangible. The depreciated value of the plant and real estate is given as but $17,000,000—a figure very slightly in excess of one year's advertising bill, but the brand value of Camel is one of the most valuable properties in American industry. It is lumped into goodwill and written down for $1.00, but some idea of its worth can be obtained by considering that millions of smokers cannot tell one blend from another and rely chiefly on the impressions of the eye for the formation of smoking habits; and by considering, also, how difficult it is to persuade a smoker to change from one brand to another. For purposes of equalization of profits-taxes the U. S. Government estimated the value of Reynolds's trade-marks at $100,000,000. Such is certainly an under-estimate.

And this glittering domain was mostly created by a wad of weed rolled into a little piece of tissue paper—an article that stands out in American industry as one of the simplest, the cheapest, the most preposterously taxed. Cigarettes of the Camel type are quoted at $6.40 a thousand, which, with discounts of ten and two, yield $5.65 per thousand to the manufacturer. On this, the federal tax is no less than $3.00 per thousand, which is to say that the balance left for tobacco, paper, manufacturing, packaging, distribution, advertising, and profit equals about $2.65 per thousand— about one-quarter of a cent per cigarette, or just about five cents per package of twenty. The actual cost of manufacturing one Camel is as secret an item as the Camel blend or the Camel production, but it is obviously the merest fraction of a cent. The cost of Camel advertising is somewhere between three and five one-hundredths of a cent per cigarette. Were it not for the extraordinary tax, cigarettes could retail at eight cents a package and produce even larger profits than are now being made.

Ownership of Reynolds is divided into $10,000,000 of Class A common stock, which carries the vote, and $90,-000,000 of B, which does not. The latter is Winston-Salem's most popular stock, the former is Reynolds's most cherished child. At the dissolution of the tobacco trust, every trust stockholder received his share of the control of Reynolds that the trust had owned; consequently the stock was widely distributed. But the Reynolds company pays large bonuses to its employees, and for purposes of unity and concentration, the size of each bonus is proportionate to the amount of A stock that the employee owns. Employees of whatever rank are encouraged to buy A, and the result has been to place such a premium upon the voting stock that few outsiders find it profitable to hold. Little by little it has drifted back into the organization; outside the company walls it has been largely replaced by the equally profitable B, with the result that while the vote is concentrated in Winston-Salem, a great proportion of the Camel dividends are sent out of town every quarter, and notably to New York.

The grand old merchant and tobacconist, R. J. Reynolds, died in 1919, leaving one of the largest estates in the South to his widow, his two sons, Richard and Smith, and his two daughters. The children's portion of the estate is handled by the Safe Deposit & Trust Co. of Baltimore. Neither Richard nor Smith Reynolds has entered the Reynolds business, and both of them are considered somewhat unruly by the conservative citizens of Winston-Salem.

But if the younger Reynolds generation finds other occupations besides tobacco, not so their uncle, W. N. Reynolds, whose leading passion is for this pungent, somewhat temperamental leaf. He can "read tobacco," which is the farmer's way of expressing a knowledge of texture, shape, weight, size, smell, and color. Having started in the manufacturing end, where every good leaf man must be trained, he knows the effect of the machines and the driers on any given leaf. Tobacco is subject to all the usual hazards of farming, to pests, failing soils, and unfavorable weather; but having passed through these successfully, there is yet the hazard of curing which the farmer must undertake himself. Even after the tobacco is purchased, it will remain on Mr. Reynolds's hands for two years. It must be kept in warehouses of proper temperature and humidity; it must sweat regularly, spring and fall; it must be guarded against spontaneous combustion, which is apt to occur in the hot season. As minutely as anyone else, W. N. Reynolds knows these things and the precious Camel formula and the limit to which the tobacco can be heated in the drying machines.

Mr. Reynolds became president in 1918, a year before his brother's death; he became chairman of the board in 1924, when Bowman Gray was raised to the presidency. As Mr. Reynolds knows leaf, Mr. Gray knows sales. He was employed in the Wachovia National Bank at a salary of $1,000 a year. Perhaps with some premonition of fabulous destiny, he decided to shift to tobacco for a monthly wage of $25. They sent him out on the road, where he sold plug so successfully that when the new northeastern division was opened up, they put him in charge of the headquarters in Baltimore. Since then he has had a rather free rein with his own policies, which he evolves behind an ample desk with an expression of gravity. He always appears somewhat larger than he is, being actually short and thickset. A great asset to the business is his remarkable memory, which takes him back accurately to faces, names, and incidents of his selling days, twenty, thirty years gone. A terrific worker, he will now and then lay down his tools for an European trip, and by way of importing European culture, he and Mrs. Gray have removed whole rooms from Touraine chateaux across the Atlantic for their enormous new house outside of Winston-Salem, just across the highway from "Reynolda." This house is talked about throughout the Carolinas, has a private telephone system extending into every room with up to fifty outlets. Mr. Gray's brother, James, came to Reynolds as a banker from the Wachovia Bank & Trust Co. and is another important stockholder. And all the other executives, who are known to each other as the Reynolds associates, are substantial stockholders, playing their directorate rôles in the peculiar coöperative unit that is Reynolds.

So much for the empire founded by a great merchant. The question now arises as to its future—a question which the journalist approaches with some hesitancy. In 1930, there was an aggregate increase of .49 per cent in cigarette production, representing the smallest advance since the depression year 1920. At the same time Lucky Strike has been making a startling advance—American Tobacco Co. claims 42,000,000,000 for Lucky Strike in 1930, a gain of 6,000,000,000 over 1929. It is evident that Lucky has gained substantially on Camel, just as Chesterfield gained on both brands several years ago. Camel gain for 1930 was probably less than 1,000,000,000. But this conclusion is a precipice from which he who ventures farther leaps at his peril. There have been surveys to prove that Luckies have passed Camels; there have been other surveys to prove that they have emphatically not. That Camel has been feeling the pinch of competition is indicated in its recent introduction of the "humidor" representing installation costs of over a million dollars, a $50,000 prize contest, and a change in its advertising policy. There is no telling what the result of this able move will be, but before it was made it was estimated, after some painful research, that Camels were not producing more than 38,000,000,000, Luckies not less.

But even so. The question of the actual, and perhaps temporary production figure does not seem to be fundamental. For a cigarette is not merely a cigarette, it is—by virtue of the nation's peculiar inability to tell one blend from another—a name and a policy. By contrast to these two fundamental aspects, the frantic race for production takes on the character of a mere game. With the oldest of the popular-priced blends, with the most efficient manufacturing unit, with the shrewdest buyers in the tobacco world, with Reynolds's advertising ante limited to $15,000,000 against American Tobacco's $20,000,000, with a trade-mark written down to $1.00 but otherwise nearly priceless, with a physical and economic concentration rarely found in industry, the question of whether Camels are holding their own in the race for cigarette popularity loses something of its force. For should anyone pass Camels this year, at least one valid answer seems to be: what of it? In dealing with such enormous merchandizing forces as we are here considering, judgments can be passed only with regard to long periods of time. The whole intricate and intangible question of the trade-mark opens up—a question which is as difficult to handle as anything in industry, since it is based upon psychology rather than upon fact and is as a result never susceptible of measurement. Whether for the color of the package, the simplicity of the name, the aroma of the blend, or the belief that Camel puts more money into its tobacco and less in advertising than other brands do, there are millions of smokers who will have nothing else.

One thing is certain. Price-cutting will never solve major problems in the cigarette industry. The possible cuts are too slight and too costly, and except in periods of depression, when pennies mount in importance, the male sex prefers round dimes and nickels. The major campaigns of this industry must be fought out on the nation's billboards and in the nation's periodicals. Here lies the crux of the future, no matter what the present production figures are; and by way of closing this discussion it will be well to take a look at the advertising that is being done.

Camels appeared on the national battlefield under the

slogan "The Camels are coming"; a picture of the desert was shown in which R. J. Reynolds's animal motif was made more and more prominent as the cigarette was marketed. It was a new idea and cleverly presented. In days when popular-priced domestic cigarettes were unblended with Turkish tobacco, it carried with it a proper connotation of the Orient. Furthermore, it was constantly backed by the statement that money which other manufacturers spent in premiums and coupons was being used by Camel for the purchase of the best tobaccos—a statement that Reynolds has made billions of times on the backs of the Camel packages. But the point to be noted here is the gradual disappearance of the animal motif from Camel advertising. Now it is all handsome youths, girls (always conservative as to legs and never actually smoking a cigarette), the sea, and some catchy phrase. The ship of the desert has quite vanished into the haze of billboard history, has been replaced by more sophisticated appeals. Recently it has been "research" to the fore, with charts showing the advantage of the new cellophane package in retaining the moisture content of the cigarette. Indeed, it would even seem that the word Camel is all but a liability in this modern world of sunny swimming beaches and young ladies in Parisian attire; Lucky Strike is perhaps less incongruous; Chesterfield most of all at home.

Advertising tastes, like glaciers, move; and no matter how deeply rooted a trade-mark may be it must bow in the direction of the wind. George Washington Hill's spectacular Lucky Strike is four years younger than Camel. It too is based on the blending of Carolina leaf with Turkish and Burley. With the exception of a violet ray bath, it receives a treatment practically identical to that of Camel, in that hot center of discussion and conjecture, the toaster. Now in the first place it must be pointed out that the toaster, known elsewhere as the drier, is universal to the manufacture of cigarettes; in the second place, that the fumes of any tobacco drier, whether Camel, Chesterfield, Old Gold, or Lucky Strike, are maddening to the eyes, choking to the lungs, and painful to the head—proving, as George Washington Hill has constantly asserted, that irritants are released from the tobacco leaf by heat; in the third place, while Camel claims to heat tobacco in the drier to the uttermost limit and not burn it, Lucky Strike is equipped with machines to carry the heat considerably higher. That the Lucky Strike heat removes more irritants than the Camel heat would seem to depend on whether Mr. Hill has discovered some way of running his tobacco through his drier at a higher temperature than anyone else believes it will bear; but in any case, the difference of effect must always remain a quantitative rather than a qualitative one, and the most fundamental difference between the Lucky Strike and the Camel, besides unknown differences in the blends, is that of the flavoring matter applied to the tobacco before heating it. The Burley leaf of the Lucky Strike is soaked in a dark brown liquid of delicious aroma, containing among other things maple sugar. After this soaked leaf has been mixed in with the Carolina and Turkish and all three of them cooked (i.e., dried) the Lucky Strike flavor emerges as absolutely distinctive, such that Lucky is the easiest cigarette to distinguish in a blindfold test, and, on the whole, is described by the word "toasted" with clarity and justice.

Granting, therefore, that the Camel and the Lucky Strike processes are essentially the same, it would seem that Mr. Hill's advertising has been somewhat more astute in giving it a name. Lucky Strike is especially popular with women and has benefited more than Camel from the increase in feminine consumption. The toasted idea must have played a part in this, being much more understandable to feminine minds than the abstract Camel emphasis on quality. The difference between the Hill advertising and the Reynolds advertising can really be summed up in one sentence. Reynolds has until recently relied on attractive and clever ideas which emphasize a quality product, without undertaking to discuss tobacco manufacture; Mr. Hill has reached into the cigarette itself for his advertising arguments. The famous "I'd walk a mile for a Camel," and "Graduate to Camels" are examples of clever Camel campaigns about as far removed from tobacco fields as the average citizen of the nation is. Contrasted to this Mr. Hill's insistent "It's Toasted" is a simple fact taken from the tobacco factory; while the more conglomerate and intricate arguments recently built up around irritants and the violet ray machine attempt the same appeal somewhat less substantially. With the violet ray, Mr. Hill has not so much drawn an argument out of his cigarette as he has put something new into it. Just how substantial this innovation is, is a question open to extraordinary discussion; at least Mr. Hill's testimonial advertising has not proved any fundamental scientific advance. Most of the celebrities who testify for him know no more about the violet ray and tobacco than a celebrity is in the habit of knowing. Some of them, even, are not smokers. One feels that if the Lucky Strike process as a whole constitutes a simple and lucid scientific advance, better advertising capital could be made of it. The greatest step so far is the collecting of the toaster fumes into several barrels a week of insecticide by-product; though the layman still wonders whether this could not be accomplished by a mere drier. Nevertheless the interesting fact is that Mr. Hill is doing something with a cigarette that the Reynolds company had never tried—placing tobacco advertising on a new, perhaps scientific, ground.

Meanwhile, it is also necessary to note the strength of Chesterfield, issuing forth in their white cartons from the Liggett & Myers plant, which is just across the way from the American Tobacco Co.'s plant in Durham. Chesterfields are not only unlighted by the violet ray; they are not so much as dipped or seasoned with flavoring matter and are in this regard less "manufactured" than either Lucky Strike or Camel. The Chesterfield appeal is to simplicity. Though Liggett & Myers have not exploited this, they have in it a tremendous weapon to use in a sophisticated world over which the idea of simplicity must always exert its attraction. It is presumed that Chesterfield is producing some 26,000,000,000 cigarettes a year, and it is known that some years ago it was the most spectacular performer. The advertising is not unlike that of Camel, though where Camel has emphasized the abstract notion of "quality," Chesterfield has used the more sensuous "mild, yet they satisfy" and the recent appeals to "taste" and "individuality." Both these appeals are justified, since Chesterfield seeks to satisfy with the taste of tobacco alone and without flavors, and it remains for conservative Liggett & Myers to exploit this.

In short, the whole tobacco industry, dependent as it is on great advertising, would seem to be marking advertising time. Mr. Hill has been in the front of the stage with an interesting scientific exhibit; Old Gold's effort ("not a cough in a carload") while undeniably successful, is now worn out; Chesterfield's "individuality girl" is distinctive, but not new; Camel had been at a disadvantage in sophisticated circles because there had been no radical step taken in its advertising since pre-War days. Indeed, Camel had never felt the need for such a step, having so consistently led an industry with fabulous powers of expansion. But given some sort of a limit to the nation's consumption of cigarettes—a limit which the 1930 figures indicate to have been reached temporarily—then cigarette manufacturers will dig hard, perhaps more profoundly, for an advertising idea. And it is certain that he who finds the idea will make new history.

CHEMICAL GIANT

The Mysterious Allied Chemical and Dye. Its President, the Able, Autocratic Mr. Orlando Weber. Reticence as a fine and Profitable Art. Fixation of Nitrogen at Hopewell, Virginia. No Admissions and No Admittance. And the Answer to Two Potent Threats

ALLIED CHEMICAL AND DYE CORPORATION

〰️

I DEALLY, perhaps, an A. Conan Doyle, an E. Phillips Oppenheim, or an R. Austin Freeman should be the author of a story concerning the Allied Chemical & Dye Corp. and Orlando Franklin Weber, its powerful but uncommunicative president. For heavily about this corporation and its corporate head hangs mystery, and nearly all its activities are seen and reported as through a denial, darkly. It is true that chemical companies generally exhibit a logical reticence about processes, and obviously one should not expect them to publish their formulas even though the so-called secret processes are seldom as vital as they appear in popular imagination. Yet the two other great American chemical companies—E. I. du Pont de Nemours and Union Carbide & Carbon—are not so sensitively reticent. The du Ponts went into motors, politics, and prohibition and have become a familiar portion of the industrial scene. Union Carbide, although with less diverse interests, is upon occasion most reasonably informative concerning even so technical a question as its contribution to alloy steels. But from Allied (and Mr. Weber) comes only an annual statement—and that of so fragmentary a nature as to leave the condition of the company (aside from its evident prosperity) considerably in question.

Thus, for example, Allied's extremely liquid assets include some $93,000,000 in U. S. Government bonds and other investments, in the form of sound and basic common stocks. In which industries Allied has chosen to take a position and what has been the result of these investments, neither the stockholders nor the Stock Exchange itself can discover. Allied points to the gratifying increase in the size of this fund ($10,000,000 in 1929) and considers it has done enough. It may be assumed that whatever profits Allied realized from the use of this money were carried to surplus, were not included in its $25,000,000 net for 1930. A stockholder who once objected to the lengthy intervals between announcements from this company was politely informed that it was essential for him to have confidence in his corporation's management. In fairness, however, it should be added that such confidence has never been misplaced.

In fairness, also, a distinction must be noted between Allied and such a company as the open-hearted Ford Motor Co. While Mr. Ford himself inaugurated mass production of the cheap car and may still be said to be the leader in his field, Allied joined the industrial race a long time after the starting-gun had been fired. Mr. Ford has created his competitors, but Allied found itself, in 1920, in immediate and intense competition with Europe and all that Europe meant in the way of a long-established chemical dominance, highly developed processes, and cheap labor. Allied's problem was to make a product as good or better than the German product, with higher labor costs, at a cheaper price. Such a great competitor as the I. G. Farbenindustrie badly underestimated Allied's potentialities, and Allied had nothing to gain by correcting the estimate. The size of its plants, the nature of its machinery, and the number of its employees, therefore, were not made matters of public concern.

This is still true. No one outside the company, and very few inside it, know the current production of the great, new nitrogen fixation plant at Hopewell, Virginia, or what variation of the Haber-Bosch process is used there, or how much man power it requires. Mr. Weber himself has never been at Hopewell, nor has any director of the company; and it is said that only five men at the central office can fully interpret the reports which come each month from Hopewell to Mr. Weber's desk at 61 Broadway. Again, Hopewell is not like Dearborn. Hopewell is a vast undertaking, a promise; Dearborn is a fact.

Thus Allied has gone its way with no accompanying trumpets. Mr. Weber has never given an interview nor made a speech, and under only one document does he sign his name—the annual reports of the company. He has a philosophy of business no less interesting than that of Mr. Ford (whom he greatly admires), but it reposes upon no bookseller's shelves. It is no more public property than the Hopewell accounts. This impenetrable reticence has irritated a good many people. Allied dislikes cartels and is unimpressed by associations for the furtherance of this or that. Accordingly, when that notable crusader, Mr. Francis P. Garvan, urged Allied to join a group of chemical companies to protect the American industry against Germany, Allied replied in effect that two protectors were perhaps better than one and that while Mr. Garvan's group was protecting America in one way, Allied would protect it in another. This aroused Mr. Garvan to such a pitch of irritation and suspicion that he even harbored thoughts that Allied was on the German side of the fence. Later he accidentally discovered that the precise reverse was true, and he is now a staunch friend. Dr. Carl Bosch, the genius of I. G. Farbenindustrie, has not been converted. He invited Mr. Weber to inspect the vast nitrogen plant at Leunawerk, and while Mr. Weber did go to Leunawerk, he observed that war-time monument from the outside. This proceeded neither from modesty nor from a lack of grace, but from an unwillingness to accept a courtesy he could not return. The world knew about Leunawerk; it did not know about Hopewell.

Allied's success in its ten-year lifetime has been phenomenal. Whether or not the reticence policy is to be commended in theory, there can be no doubt but that it has been profitable in fact. As a result of attending strictly to its own business and encouraging a similar policy in others, it has been free to bring that business to a pitch of efficiency which is outstanding in an efficient age. To a brief consideration of that efficiency, it is now useful to turn.

The Allied Chemical & Dye Corp. is a normal artificial person, incorporated in New York, with the usual complement of officers and directors. In form, it scarcely differs from any large manufacturing company, with seventy-two plants spread over the country, each with its superintendent, each reporting to the headquarters in New York. The only extraordinary thing observable by an outsider is the absence of any obvious banking connection. Allied has had no funded debt or bank loans since 1923, and has never sold any stock to the public. Bankers have not been necessary to its expansion, hence it has escaped the usual branding as a Morgan (Kuhn, Loeb; Bonbright; etc.) company.

In the final analysis, it is Orlando F. Weber who runs the Allied show. When the merger had been completed, he was asked to head the new company, and with some reluctance agreed. The decision once made, however, Mr. Weber's hesitancy disappeared. He faced the facts of 1921 with a vigor which always astounded and occasionally angered the older men of the merging companies. Inventories were big, selling prices were high, and business was bad. Out of the situation itself arose policies of drastic reorganization. Personnel was carefully combed, and many a boom executive found himself—together with his fellows in other industries—fighting for his job. A rigid system of monthly reports was instituted. Sales and costs figures underwent cold scrutiny. Executives were taught to look upon accounts, not as necessary bookkeeping, but as vital photographs of the companies.

With such directness did Mr. Weber apply his technique of operation to the new company, and with precisely the same directness is that technique applied today. Allied is now a company where man power is the all-important source of wealth; it is a company with a vast confidence in youth, and a willingness to back that confidence with a considerable investment. Promotion is swift, responsibility heavy. When youth fails, it is instantly replaced. But in ten years, it is said that Allied has made only seven such mistakes. Such a policy naturally provides both an operating staff and an executive reserve. Upon that reserve Allied expects to draw in the years to come, and it is possible to consider it Mr. Weber's answer to the question of what Allied will do when he retires.

For the question is both natural and frequent, and early in 1931 it became immediate when Mr. Weber took a leave of absence and Clinton Stephen Lutkins, a former Allied officer, returned as executive vice-president. But after a few months' absence, Mr. Weber returned, Mr. Lutkins left. Mr. Weber is the complete autocrat, a dictator as absolute as Mr. Ford, and rather less approachable. Away from his office, he is social, genial, wise, past fifty, a student of James and Emerson, a thoughtful and intelligent father of two small children. But in his office, he rules without fear and without compromise.

This, then, is the machine which Mr. Weber began to build in the shadows of the panic of 1921. It has created a great company and has largely helped create a great American industry. It is currently said that (a) the U. S. chemical industry has a production equal (in dollar value) to the production of the iron and steel industry and (b) that Allied is the greatest chemical company in the world. Both statements have a basis of fact, but both are subject to severe qualification. As long ago as 1925 the United States Government, in its census of manufactures, estimated the value of chemical products at $6,400,000,000. This total was reached, however, by assembling nearly every industrial process involving chemical reactions, and was weirdly inaccurate from the standpoint of products turned out by strictly chemical companies. It included, for instance, the manufacture of gas and the refining of petroleum. It also threw in glue, paint, varnish, and soap. If only chemical noses, in the stricter sense of the term, were counted, the products of chemical corporations would have been figured at about $813,000,000, or approximately the output of the tobacco or the rubber businesses. Also a flatly superlative description of Allied as "greatest" must divorce the du Pont company entirely from its motor interests; must ignore the fact that du Pont, aside from its motor income, makes as much as Allied; that Union Carbide has a greater net income; and that, from an international standpoint, it would be very difficult to convince an Englishman that Allied was greater than Imperial Chemical Industries or a German that it was greater than I. G. Farbenindustrie. Allied is, of course, the outstanding American example of a manufacturing company dealing in such diverse things as acids, alkali, coal-tar products, dyes, and sodium nitrate. An analogy could be created by supposing the existence of an American Metals Co., owning and *operating* the U. S. Steel Corp., Anaconda, and the Aluminum Company. No one of Allied's companies is more than theoretically familiar with the methods of any other.

Considering this distinction, it is undeniable that Allied, largest producer of alkali, coal-tar products, nitrogen, etc., is the major factor in that wide industrial field so loosely labeled *chemicals*. Even aside from its automobiles, the du Pont company deals largely with nitrocellulose in peace and war, while Union Carbide centers around oxygen, calcium carbide and its associates. For a strictly chemical company and for a company which sells almost exclusively to other manufacturers and hardly at all to the general public, Allied has built up an extremely large business on an extremely unspectacular foundation. Furthermore, it is currently beginning to specialize in at least one field—the production of synthetic ammonia—in which it has far outstripped its American competitors. And certainly its financial statements bristle with large, round figures indicative of profound solvency. With no funded debt, net working capital of $143,000,000 (du Pont's is $113,-000,000) and current assets of $155,000,000 (du Pont's are $124,000,000), Allied is in a position of great strength. It has no fear of scrapping old for new. When the experimental plant was built at Syracuse, Allied put $5,000,000 into the venture and knew it must abandon it inside a decade. Each one of Allied's plants is subject to the same ruthless treatment. Its properties have been written off by over half of their original cost.

In this last fact lies yet another key to the mystery which appears to surround the Allied Chemical & Dye Corp., enveloping alike the National Aniline plant at Buffalo, the Solvay Process plants at Syracuse, Detroit, and Hutchinson, Kansas, the Atmospheric Nitrogen plant at Hopewell, Virginia (an un-gardened city near Richmond), or any of the numerous plants operated by the Barrett Company or the Semet-Solvay Company. What makes these walls so forbidding, these offices so private, these grasses so kept off of? Partly a policy, but even more a remoteness. For (with very rare exceptions) the Allied companies make nothing that goes into the hands of the general public, nothing that the consumer touches or recognizes or is conscious of in more than the vaguest academic sense. Allied is essentially a middleman company, taking raw materials, putting them through various stages of manufacture, then selling them to some other industrialist through whom (usually in a thoroughly disguised and often unsuspected form) they ultimately become consumer items. There is one conspicuous exception to this statement, however, for the Barrett Company (largest Allied unit) does approach the consumer by way of the Barrett roofs over his head and by the Tarvia roads under his auto wheels and sometimes by the Barrett Queen Bee Coke in his furnace. But most, even of the Barrett products, mean little to the consumer's mind. The dyer buys naphthalene and benzol, the tanner buys Barretan tanning extract, the builder buys creosote to preserve wood, and Dr. Baekeland's Bakelite Corp. may buy phenol to make Bakelite. Thus most of the Barrett products are intermediates subject to further processing or incorporated in some further product before reaching what is to the consumer a real and a tangible world.

And so it is with other Allied products. We do not see in window glass the soda ash which has gone into its construction; we do not realize that our soap is fat plus caustic soda; we therefore fail to appreciate what the Solvay Process Company is doing for us. If the dyes in our clothing do not remain fast, we complain to the clothing store and the clothing store complains to the clothing manufacturer and perhaps the clothing manufacturer complains to National Aniline, but by that time we have received our money back and lost interest in the sequence. As for General Chemical Co., its basic product is sulphuric acid, but unless we need to purify some petroleum, to "pickle" (remove the scale of iron oxide) some steel, to mix sulphuric acid with ammonia and get fertilizer or with nitric acid and glycerine and get dynamite, we are familiar with sulphuric acid largely through the adjective *vitriolic* and through those fortunately rare occasions on which angry persons go about throwing sulphuric acid (or oil of vitriol) in faces. There is no great mystery about most of what Allied does —caustic soda and sulphuric acid, for example, are thoroughly standardized products though their processing may vary from company to company and country to country. Indeed the whole function of (for instance) sulphuric acid of a given concentration depends upon its being precisely like every other equal concentration of sulphuric that ever has been made or ever will be made by any manufacturer whatsoever. But because nearly all Allied products are aloof from the outsider and not especially thrilling to him, he drapes Allied thickly in the majesty of his own ignorance and then gasps at its progress and profits.

One Allied division, however, the Atmospheric Nitrogen Company, is of more general interest, partly because of nitrogen's war-time importance in explosives and peace-time importance in fertilizers and partly because nitrogen fixation is a recent and current development and properly regarded as one of man's most successful and most fundamental experiences in overcoming the stinginess of nature. Nitrogen is an essential of explosives and also of plant food. It is a very common element (the earth's atmosphere weighs roughly some 5,333 million-million tons and three-fourths is nitrogen), but for practical purposes nitrogen needs to be combined with some other element (i.e., to be fixed) in order to be usable. In pre-War days, nitrogen suitable for fertilizer was found chiefly in nitrogenous waste material from birds (guano deposits) and beasts (manure) and natural deposits of sodium nitrate in Chile. There was also beginning the development of ammonium sulphate (which contains nitrogen), a development which is still of the first importance and in which the Semet-Solvay Company participates. High explosives, however, were made largely from sodium nitrate so that Chile had practically a monopoly on explosive raw material. Two processes, the Arc and the Cyanamide, had been devised for forcing nitrogen to combine with other elements (oxygen and calcium carbide respectively), but both were extremely expensive. Then, just before the War, the German Badische-Anilin-und-Soda-Fabrik (now part of I. G. Farbenindustrie) introduced the Haber-Bosch ammonia process by which most of the world's nitrogen fixation (including Allied's) is now carried on. The Haber-Bosch process does not (of course) manufacture nitrogen, but it does manufacture a solution of ammonia, which is one part nitrogen to three parts hydrogen. These gases do not unite at ordinary conditions, but the Haber-Bosch process subjects them to very extraordinary conditions indeed. In one variation of the process, they are heated to a temperature of from 500 to 600 centigrade (five to six times the heat at which water boils) and put under a pressure of 200 atmospheres (or about 3,000 pounds to the square inch), and under these conditions and in the presence of a catalyst (iron to which small amounts of aluminum and potassium oxides have been added) they do unite to form ammonia. From ammonia it is simple to make nitric acid for war use or either sulphate of ammonia or sodium nitrate for fertilizing use. Results of the Haber-Bosch process are best seen in the collapse of the Chile nitrate monopoly. Chilean producers, after a losing effort at fighting the synthetic competition (an effort resulting in the price collapse of 1926–27), finally conceded the superiority of art over nature and made a price-fixing agreement with the German producers. In 1929 Germany produced 800,000 metric tons of fixed nitrogen; America produced 248,000 tons and Chile 490,000 tons of the natural product. Now, under the stimulus of competition and the guidance of the Guggenheims the Chilean government has revamped its nitrate industry by consolidating it all into one company (the Cosach), abandoning the export tax and substituting for it a profit-sharing interest, and thereby hopes that its nitrates may compete with, and possibly undersell, both I. G. Farbenindustrie and Hopewell.

Allied's fixation plant at Hopewell, which went into production in 1928, is reported to have a capacity of 350 tons a day. With the entire building program completed, an annual capacity of from 350,000 to 400,000 tons of nitrogen is possible. This compares with the German capacity of 800,000 tons. But technology moves fast and the German plants are probably already out of date. It is inconceivable that Allied, staking so large an investment in Hopewell, regards itself as unable to meet both the Chilean threat and the potential competition of the large German capacity. The issue, after all, will depend upon production costs. Certainly I. G. Farbenindustrie no longer disregards Allied products in the world market. And it must be said that if the United States *does* take over an industry as firmly entrenched across the water as the production of synthetic nitrogen, Allied will have offered a notable service to the country.

Thus far our personal approach to the Allied Chemical & Dye Corp. has been solely through its reticent president.

There are, of course, other familiar faces in the Allied scene. Since even chemical companies do not combine without some merging mind acting as a catalytic agent and since Allied came into existence as a merger of five large chemical companies, the next step in the process of untangling Allied's personalities must deal with its origin. From one point of view, the Allied birth is simply enough described. The late Dr. William H. Nichols, who in 1920 headed the General Chemical Co., is usually credited with having inspired the merging of General Chemical, National Aniline & Chemical, Barrett, Solvay Process, and Semet-Solvay companies into a well-rounded American chemical organization dominating the strictly chemical field and making American chemistry shock-proof against foreign competition. (Atmospheric Nitrogen was later created by the group.) Certainly the revered Dr. Nichols must have played a large part in the formation of Allied, since he was Allied's chairman from the formation of the company to his death in 1930.

Thus Dr. Nichols, but the merger also brought into the new American company a personality—or rather set of personalities—which may be crystallized out of the Allied solution. To reach them it is necessary to travel across the Atlantic, for although they are a cosmopolitan and world-wandering family, the Solvays are native to Belgium. And their connection with Allied becomes sufficiently obvious upon remembering that the Solvay Process and the Semet-Solvay companies are two vital links in the Allied chain.

The Solvay family (which is an old family with a great many members) has a household wealth of possibly a quarter of a billion dollars, large for Europe. The foundation of the fortune was laid in 1863 when Ernest Solvay and Alfred Solvay worked out the Solvay process. Not to be technical, the Solvay process is a method of manufacturing soda ash from salt, ammonia, and limestone and is far superior to the Le Blanc process previously used. As soda ash and the caustic soda, which is made from it, are basic chemicals in many industries (especially glass and soap making) the Solvays rapidly spread their process throughout the world. One of their first associates in it was the Brunner, Mond & Company, Ltd. (now controlled by Imperial Chemical Industries) of England. In 1881, Mr. W. B. Cogswell, with the help of the ancient Rhode Island family of Hazzards, proceeded to form the American Solvay Process Co., and the European Solvays held therein approximately a half interest. When the Solvay Process Co. went into Allied, the family received in return a block of about 350,000 shares of Allied stock. Brunner, Mond sold its block of 100,000 shares to the Solvay American Investment Co. at the low price of $220 a share. It may be noted in passing that the half interest in the Solvay Process Co., which in 1920 was worth (in Allied shares, at $40 a share) $14,000,000, after a decade of Allied management is now worth about $50,000,000. The Semet-Solvay Company, a later Solvay development (the Solvays were pioneers in the recovery of coal and coke by-products), came into the Allied group along with its older brother. In addition to their holdings in Allied, the Solvay interests were long represented by the late Armand Solvay, who was an Allied director, in much the same manner that Ernest Solvay II is a director in Imperial Chemical Industries. Another active member of the contemporary Solvay group is said to be

Baron Jannssen, who is a Solvay only by marriage. It is impossible to say how much either of the native Solvay companies makes, because, like Allied, they do not wear their hearts upon their sleeves and also because, as limited liability companies, they need divulge hardly anything about their operations. Because of their extensive French, German, and British affiliations the Solvays occupy a key position in any movement toward a general European chemical cartel, a position which they strengthened in 1927 by promoting the formation of the Union Chimique Belge, an association of Belgian chemical companies, dominated by the Solvay influence. It should be pointed out that Allied and the Solvays are in no sense subsidiaries of each other and that while they are affiliates across the sea, each moves its own way in its own sphere of influence.

SOCONY IN THE ORIENT

Money + Time + Men = Mei Foo

STANDARD OIL COMPANY
OF NEW YORK

THE great *potential* market for oil, as for everything else, lies not in Europe and not in South America but in Asia, where half the population of the globe goes about its business on a pre-industrial scale of living. Being without electricity, the Orient buys much kerosene, and being without automobiles, it buys very little gasoline. Now Massachusetts is well electrified, uses kerosene mostly for heating. Yet were each Chinaman to use as much kerosene as each Bay Stater uses, China's present 4,000,000-barrel consumption of kerosene would shoot up to 80,000,000 overnight. It is important to realize that several European countries consume more dollars' worth of oil than does all China or all India. But it is also important to realize that even the smallest step upward in the scale of living is important when it is taken by 800,000,000 people.

When people, including on occasion U. S. government officials, want to know things about the Orient, they are likely to go to the Standard Oil Company of New York for information. This is one of many recognitions of Socony's position in the Far East. Much the greatest of Socony's markets, of course, is that unromantic but thickly settled region known as "Soconyland," which comprises all New England plus New York State. The old Standard used to do about 85 per cent of the business in that area, but the invasion of competitors has cut down Socony's share to 30 per cent—still a good slice. Socony's position in the Orient is comparably strong. Though Texas Corp. has been spending money developing its Far Eastern markets, Socony is by far the dominant American company. Grizzle-bearded Charles F. Meyer, president of Socony, knows the oriental market. He knows that gasoline prospects may improve in Indo-China because of the fine roads the French are building there; that Japan has so much cheap hydroelectric power that the poorest houses use electric lights, whence declining kerosene sales, and that the roads are being improved, whence an increase in gasoline sales that more than counterbalances; that cheap silver and not civil war is the cause of the drastic decline in Chinese kerosene consumption. And he knows equally well what he doesn't know: the future of oil in the Orient. Mr. Meyer's knowledge reflects credit primarily on the organization his company has built up in the Orient. Let us consider this most remarkable and effective instrument which Socony has created for an export trade.

There is more to the creation of an export business than spending money. As everyone knows, General Motors flung men and dollars abroad in a lavish way a half dozen years after the War. Came the world depression, and General Motors withdrew many of its men. The dollars, however, remained. Such has been the fate of many another venture in exporting undertaken in the haste of boom times and repented in the leisure of depression. It is only U. S. Steel, General Electric, Singer Sewing Machine, and such old hands at the export game that are still playing with any enthusiasm today. To them must be added the three big Standard exporters: New Jersey, Vacuum, and New York. The rains of depression have descended on the house Socony has built in the Orient, and the floods of civil war and low silver prices have come, but the house still stands, as secure today as it was at the beginning of the century.

The cornerstone of Socony's house is its "contract system." Socony does not sell kerosene wholesale; it sells it direct to the ultimate native consumer. Now it is out of the question for the company to hire platoons of young Americans and send them through the length and breadth of India selling cupfuls of kerosene to native housewives. Some native storekeeper in each village must act as Socony agent on a commission basis. But India's back country is as complex as it is vast, natives are shrewd bargainers, and there is no Bradstreet to rate their financial standing. How to guard against loss from unscrupulous agents? Socony protects itself by a system which no other company has been able to use. To become an agent, a native must deposit with the company cash or collateral to the value of the oil he receives. So successful is this that Socony's losses from bad debts are considerably less in the Orient than they are in New England. On their deposits, the natives get $4\frac{1}{2}$ per cent interest, which seems a normal rate and would be so, perhaps, were it not that they can get up to 12 per cent for their money in the bazaars. Other companies cannot get the natives to deposit cash guarantees with them. It is the confidence that Socony inspires in the natives that permits the system to work. Even more, it is the fact that when Kwen Lu, of Siping in Honan province, gets the

Socony agency, his credit is at once established everywhere in China. He becomes a big man in Siping, one whose prestige continues despite bandits, famine, and falling silver prices. What is more, Kwen Lu is *exclusive* agent for Siping and vicinity, which gives him a decided edge over Ho Shan Lo, who is only one of several Shell dealers. This granting of exclusive agencies, by the way, is another solid stone in Socony's house of trade.

The money Kwen Lu deposits with Socony (and refuses to deposit with other companies) is a tribute to the unique place of the company in the life of the East. Travelers report that Socony seems to have more power in China than the government itself. Certainly Socony's trade empire, dating back to 1900, is considerably older than the Nationalist Government—and, perhaps, in the eyes of Kwen Lu and his brother agents, considerably stronger. "Mei Foo," which is a Chinese nickname for "Standard Oil," is a household word in China. For up country in the remotest provinces are to be found the five-gallon Socony cans serving as water jars, cook pots, roofs, walls, stove lids, even as the raw material for dolls and jewelry. Ancient, all-inclusive is Mei Foo's empire. But we have yet to reach its roots, which are the same as are the roots of other export empires: young men.

Every year about twenty young men go out to the Orient from the cliff-like Standard Oil Building at 26 Broadway. They are all of them college men, few of them rich men's sons, and they are the survivors of a group perhaps ten times as large that entered Socony's training course some six months earlier. At $2,500 a year they go out to the Orient, there to begin another and more arduous education. Their most important lessons are in dealing with the natives. Soon they are shouldering responsibilities such as back in the states are met by men twice their age. In India, for instance, the Socony personnel consists of eighty white men and a clerical force of 750 natives, which means roughly that each American must think for ten natives. If they go to China, they find themselves part of the most important American group in the country, missionaries aside. Normally there are about 10,000 Americans in China, but of late this number has shrunk to 8,000, of which about 4,750 are missionaries (and wives) and about 500 Socony men (and wives). Into this group go the young men from 26 Broadway, most of them scattered up country so widely that travelers say there are always three white men to be found in the inland towns of China: the missionary, the British-American Tobacco man, and the Standard Oil man. Wherever they are, they form the main props of the house that Socony has built in the Orient. For it is they whom the natives like and trust. To build up the feeling that Kwen Lu and his fellows have for Socony takes time, money, and good men.

The results are measurable. Plying back and forth on China's long Yangtze-kiang are many river steamers, some run by Chinese, most by the foreign devils. As they plough their way up river against the rushing stream, these steamers constantly meet frail sampans loaded to the gunwales with silk from the back country. Unless the steamer slows down, her backwash gives the sampan a good rocking, sometimes capsizes it. But slowing down is a lot of trouble for the captain and engineer, so they pay no attention to the sampans beyond a few curses if one gets in their way. This may have something to do with the bullet holes that pepper the superstructures of these Yangtze-kiang steamers. Or it may be merely the bandits. Now Socony runs a shallow-draft steamer up the Yangtze-kiang, 500 miles up river, with a load of kerosene for Chinese lamps and perhaps a little gasoline for a stray European motor car. On her funnel is painted the big Standard "S." Her skipper is a jovial Italian from Brooklyn, and he makes a point of slowing down whenever he meets a sampan. His boat has never been fired on in all its trips up the river.

Smart Yankee merchandising also plays a part in the battle for the Orient's markets. When Socony tried to break into the Chinese kerosene market, it found itself handicapped by the very excellence of its product. The poorer kerosene of its competitors actually burned better than did its own in the primitive, chimneyless lamps used by the Chinese. Classic is the tale of how Socony (Standard in those days) developed a lamp whose chimney was just wide enough to burn its own superior kerosene and to set up an unholy stench and smoke when its competitors' products were used. And how Standard sold millions of these lamps at low prices to the Chinese, thus establishing an outlet for its kerosene. One of the smart Yankees who built Socony's house of trade in the East is Charles F. Meyer, now president of the company. Sent out to Bombay in 1893, his greatest and most constant job was to persuade the native agents to deposit money with the company at 4 per cent. He remembers his ignorance about geography and how he "blew up" the company's manager in the Dutch East Indies for not inspecting his territory twice a year. The manager said nothing, returned the next day with an itinerary of a trip around the islands, with stops at the important towns. Time: two years. Wherefore Mr. Meyer has been sceptical about the complete adequacy of a college education and a prime mover in the establishment of his company's training school for the oriental service.

Having gone over Socony's house, let us glance at that of Royal Dutch-Shell. There are other companies in the Orient, notably Texas Corp., but none of them has achieved a position approaching those of the two main antagonists. Shell has been in the Orient as long as Socony, perhaps longer. Indeed, this is the original home of the Royal Dutch Co., and here Sir Henri Deterding, like Mr. Meyer, served his apprenticeship. Yet Socony regards Shell as something of an interloper, claims that Shell has consistently sold its oil at lower prices than its own. Nor does Shell seem to have won the natives' confidence as fully as Socony. Its strength is not in its position as a marketer so much as in its sources of supply. To market oil in the Far East, it has formed Asiatic Petroleum Co., Ltd., which represents a potent combination of Shell, with heavy production in the Dutch East Indies; Burmah Oil Co., with some production in Burma; and Anglo-Persian, which controls the Persian fields. These near-by sources of production give Asiatic Petroleum a decided advantage over Socony, most of whose oil comes from its California fields.

The great Shell-Socony battle for the Indian market centered around this vital advantage of Shell in its sources of production. No other sales battle between Shell and an American company rivals it in scope and intensity. The immediate *casus belli* was a $25,000,000 contract which Socony closed in 1927 with the Soviet Naphtha Syndicate.

The contract called for the delivery to Socony over a period of five years of 7,000,000 barrels of refined products. Obvious, painfully obvious, to Sir Henri Deterding was the effect of this contract on the Indian situation: it meant that Russia's Baku fields, almost as close as Persia, could be substituted for distant California as Socony's source of supply. Thus Shell was in great danger of losing its main advantage in the Indian market.

In this crisis, Sir Henri acted with characteristic aggressiveness. Two days before the first shipment of Soviet oil was due in Bombay, Asiatic drastically cut its prices throughout India. Willy-nilly Socony followed suit. And from New York came a cablegram signed "Meyer": "Buy locations for gasoline plants at once." Which meant that Socony, which had limited itself hitherto to kerosene in India, was striking into gasoline as well—a projection which has by now become a reality. As the price war raged in India, Sir Henri laid down a barrage of high-powered newspaper statements. Choosing a high moral line, he berated Socony for dealing with a government which had never compensated the oil companies for their nationalized properties. He spoke of "gasoline which is in the hands of unprincipled cutthroats whose hands are stained with the blood of their victims." To all of which Socony replied not a word until six months later, when it issued a long, sedate, and detailed statement which in the most polite manner called attention to several awkward facts: that Sir Henri had bought much Russian oil prior to 1926, that his Asiatic Petroleum Co., Ltd., had imported over 20,000,000 gallons of the abominable stuff from 1923 to 1925, and that (this by implication) Sir Henri's moral indignation was especially keen because he himself had failed in an attempt to negotiate with the Soviet a monopoly on its oil exports.

The din of battle has long since died down in India, but the usual scars of war remain. There are Socony gasoline plants in India now. Shell pumps have marched into Soconyland in an invasion of Socony's home market which would seem to be retaliatory. Less tangible, more far-reaching is the strain upon the companies' relations. There have been rumors of some sort of an agreement, perhaps even a merger, soon to be announced between Shell and one of the Standards, usually New Jersey and more recently New York. Leaving aside the matter of strained relations, it is not likely that a Shell-Socony union will soon be seen. Certainly no stranger pair of bedfellows could be conceived than Shell, with its close tie-up with British trade and its standing as most potent competitor of U. S. business abroad, and Socony, a leading unit of the typically American Standard Oil group.

(NOTE:—Since the writing of this article, Standard Oil Company of New York has merged with Vacuum Oil Company. The new company is called Socony-Vacuum Corporation.)

THE TIMES AND THE TIMES

A Comparison of the Two Greatest Newspapers of the World's Two Greatest Cities, Showing That While the Times *of London May Never Net $5,000,000 in a Single Year, the* Times *of New York Will Never Be Granted a Coat of Arms*

THE NEW YORK TIMES
COMPANY

◦⌇◦

THERE was a thunderstorm in the valleys west of Verona at four o'clock in the afternoon of the twenty-fourth of June, 1859. The heat of the sun had been very great, and the wounded in the houses of Castiglione lay with their faces toward the darkened doors and the rain. From the church tower where Louis Napoleon had stood all day the rise of ground toward Solferino was hidden. The sound of the guns was dulled by the soft sound of the water. It was said in the town that the Austrians had withdrawn.

In the door of a house, writing on a pad, was an American named Raymond, a small, brisk man with a ruffle of whiskers round his chin. Somewhere, unseen by him but continuously present in his thought, was an Englishman, the correspondent of the *Times* of London, also writing. What the correspondent of the *Times* of London was writing was The Truth About the Battle. Until it was published in London and sold in New York and Berlin and Madrid, there would have been no battle. The correspondent of the *Times* was as essential to the authenticity of the occasion as Louis Napoleon or Francis Joseph or Victor Emmanuel or the dead French Guards on the rise of ground beyond the shadow of the rain. And all this Raymond knew. And

was about to change. Raymond was himself the correspondent (and the editor) of the *Times*—the New York
Times—previously the New York Daily *Times*, eight
years old that year. And it was his purpose to publish in the
New York *Times* an account of that day's engagement
which should appear in New York before the *Times* of
London appeared there and which should, as accurately
and as movingly as the *Times* itself, report the Truth. He
succeeded. The military messenger who carried Louis
Napoleon's victorious dispatches and the solemn utterance
and judgment of the *Times* in one pocket carried Mr. Raymond's impertinence in the other. Mrs. Raymond received
it in her Paris hotel and delivered it to the mail boat out of
Liverpool with her own hands. It arrived in New York on
July twelfth and had been printed, read, and forgotten
before the corresponding copy of the *Times* of London
had reached New York.

What Mr. Raymond had accomplished was certainly an
impertinence. The *Times* of London was not only a great
newspaper in 1859; it was *the* great newspaper. It was then
seventy-four years old. Its circulation was well above that
of all its London competitors combined. It had sent the
first of war correspondents, the great Henry Crabb Robinson, to Germany and the Peninsula and had brought his
dispatches into England by private cutters, French fishermen, and paid smugglers in spite of Pitt and the devil. It
had attacked the Slave Trade, supported the Reform Bill,
and exposed, at its own very considerable expense, the
most spectacular of schemes of international forgery, win-
ning thereby the everlasting gratitude of the merchants of
London and an imposing commemorative tablet. It had

published the Crimean dispatches of its correspondent, William Howard Russell, and those dispatches, with their vivid and convincing description of the hardships of the campaign, the stupidity of authority in the field, and the smug, patriotic impotence of the Government at home, had drawn Florence Nightingale to Scutari and shaken the stones of the War Office. The *Times* of London was already an institution and an independent power in the world. No one knew beforehand what it would say except that "it would be something well-informed and definite." No one knew, or was supposed to know, who wrote for it. Correspondents who had breakfasted together passed each other without recognition in its halls. It was as anonymous as the Church, as grave as Virtue, and as right as Jove. It was called the "Thunderer."

And the New York *Times* was nothing. It was a beginning. Its great journalistic triumph prior to 1859 had been its appropriation of the *Herald's* account of the *Arctic* disaster, and its influence in public affairs had been limited to the repair of the local streets. It had a long way to go before it would have anything but its name in common with the *Times* of London. But once set upon the way by Raymond, it traveled fast. In 1870 the exposure of the Tweed Ring brought it enormous prestige and at last a mounting circulation. It began to make money and to pay dividends up to 90 per cent or 100 per cent on its $100,000 capitalization. And had it not been for the unfortunate combination of a new building, a shift to a new political party (the *Times* retired from the Republican Party and assumed an independent Democratic position in 1884), and a panic, it might have reached a position comparable to that of the

Times of London by the end of the century. As it was Mr. Adolph Simon Ochs, owner and editor of the Chattanooga *Times*, bought it for $75,000 in 1896. At the time of the purchase the New York *Times* had a circulation of 19,000 copies, half of which were usually returned, and a daily deficit of $1,000. It was under the control of Mr. Ochs that the upper reaches occupied by the *Times* of London were eventually attained. A great newsgathering fabric was built up. Prestige was accumulated. And the New York *Times* became in its turn an institution. But an institution, even yet, with a difference. Less an organ of expression than an organization for the sale of news. In the first twenty-five years following the purchase of the *Times* by Mr. Ochs its circulation rose to 350,000 and its annual receipts to $15,000,000 (of which only 3 per cent was paid out in dividends). It took on a corporate importance. Its individual writers were absorbed into the general solidarity. But if the weight and anonymity of the *Times* of London seemed to invest it, they invested it for different reasons. The anonymity of the New York *Times* was not a device to hide the personalities and powers of its writers, most of whom were anonymous in their own right and none of whom were men of great personal influence or noticeable literary attainments. And the ponderosity it displayed was not the effect of its political responsibilities, but the natural and common result of business success and size.

In the meantime, however, the *Times* of London was itself changing. John Thadeus Delane, who had been made editor at the age of twenty-three, had fought the Stamp Act and the tax on paper and with their repeal had brought the price of his journal down from 5d to 4d to 3d, and his circulation (in 1864) up to 66,000. Thomas Chenery, professor of Arabic at Oxford, who succeeded him, had employed the great Henri George Opper de Blowitz, of Blovice, Bohemia, most melodramatic and mustachioed of special correspondents, whose abstraction of the unsigned text of the Treaty of Berlin from under Bismarck's nose was a European wonder, and whose publication of a communication privately received from the French Minister of Foreign Affairs is said to have prevented a second Franco-Prussian war. George Earle Buckle, Fellow of All Souls College, Oxford, had succeeded Chenery. John Walter III, son of John Walter II, son of John Walter I, coal merchant, underwriter, printer, and founder of the *Times*, had in his turn died to be succeeded as proprietor by Arthur Fraser Walter, his son. And in the year 1908 the whole, ancient fabric had, after the failure of various undignified devices for the inflation of circulation, such as the circulating Book Club, fallen flat. Lord Northcliffe bought the pieces where they lay for £320,000 ($1,552,000) cash. From that time until the death of Northcliffe in 1922 the *Times* was a kind of monster, an amalgam of unrelated limbs. Part of it jigged like Northcliffe's two-time *Daily Mail*. Part of it paced like Chenery's Victorian columns. Editors changed. Buckle was invited to devote his attentions exclusively to the *Life of Benjamin Disraeli*. His successor, Geoffrey Dawson, also a Fellow of All Souls, invited Northcliffe to find another editor. H. Wickham Steed followed upon Dawson. In 1922 it was only too evident to all right-thinking persons that a similar hurly-burly must never be allowed. The controlling interest was therefore purchased from the Northcliffe estate for £1,350,000 ($6,547,500) by the Honorable John Jacob Astor and John Walter IV. Shares owned by Sir John Ellerman were bought for another £200,000 ($970,000). And a committee was established to see to it that the present owners of the shares should never part with them at any sacrifice of "the best traditions and political independence of the *Times*" or of the national interests, and to eliminate from such transfers, "so far as reasonably possible, questions of personal ambition or personal profit." The members of the committee were to be, ex-officio, the Lord Chief Justice of England, the Warden of All Souls College, Oxford, the president of the Royal (Scientific) Society, the president of the Institute of Chartered Accountants, and the governor of the Bank of England. That the present incumbents of these offices accepted the rather curious responsibility of seeing to it that Major Astor and Mr. John Walter or their heirs and assigns should sell their shares only to public-spirited gentlemen like themselves, is a most forthright and conclusive witness to the institutional and public character of the *Times*. One would say that nothing remained but to bestow a coat of arms. On December 23, 1929, this was done, and the *Times* was granted the first coat of arms ever bestowed upon a newspaper.

These committees and the adornment of a coat of arms are not without their pertinence to a comparison of the corporate qualities of the London and the New York *Times*. It is not solely because the United States Government supports no College of Arms that the New York *Times* will never have a coat. The United States is familiar with the uses of committees. But it is inconceivable that the Chief Justice, the governor of the Federal Reserve Bank of New York, the president of the American Academy of Arts and Sciences, the dean of Harvard College, and the president of the U. S. Chamber of Commerce should agree to serve upon a committee to prevent Mr. Adolph S. Ochs, his son-in-law, Mr. Arthur H. Sulzberger, and the members of his family holding stock in the corporations, from selling their shares to persons of less public interest than themselves for motives of private profit.

The New York *Times* is called the most valuable newspaper property in the world. The Chicago *Tribune* calls itself the "World's Greatest Newspaper." Neither description is just, although, reversed, each would be more nearly appropriate than it is. The Chicago *Tribune* makes more money, at present, than any other newspaper in the world— made probably not less than $6,000,000 in 1929. And the New York *Times* is certainly the world's greatest business exclusively devoted to the collection and sale of *news*. But the measure of a great newspaper is not so simply taken.

The gross income of the New York *Times* in 1929 was probably close to $40,000,000, including some 32,000,000 lines of advertising at about $1.00 per line—there being fourteen "agate" lines to the inch. In 1930, the advertising dropped to some 26,000,000 lines while the gross income was probably under $34,000,000. (In this discussion we omit entirely any consideration of the company's revenue from valuable real estate or from such other sources as its large interest in the Spruce Falls Power & Paper Company.) While normally a 10 per cent profit in such a competitive market as New York, would be close to the limit, it is probable that in 1929 the New York *Times*' net profit was as much as $5,000,000. By general pre-stock market crash standards, the *Times* might have been valued at fifteen times earnings, which would have made it worth the resounding and magnificent sum of seventy-five million dollars. Even if the Chicago *Tribune* made more than $6,000,000 (as some local enthusiasts imply) it would not necessarily be deemed worth more than seventy-five million—unless the future of the *Tribune* is greater than that of the *Times*.

All this, of course, is in sharp contrast to the ideas of only a few years ago. Then, few people would have dreamed of paying more than five times earnings for such a queer business as a newspaper.

With more recent ideas deflated, good estimators, if they do not revert to the five-times formula, will still be reluctant to value any "industrial" at more than ten times average earnings. The ten-times formula would, with 1930 earnings at about $4,000,000, possibly value the New York *Times* at $40,000,000. On the one hand Mr. Ochs might—one would suppose he would—refuse that price. But, *per contra*, it would be a bold soul who would pay that price with the implied boast that his genius could more than justify the price over the period of a generation.

The *Times*, in short, is perhaps the classic example of the unpurchasable. Money cannot buy it because, in money, it is worth so much: the great paradox of our age. But aside from the colossal nerve which would be involved in buying (and hence placing a value on the *Times*) there is grave reason to suppose that, like some other industrials (such as Fleischmann's Yeast which already goes to dealers covering 95 per cent of the United States), the *Times* may have nearly exhausted its possibilities for growth. The average number of pages in a daily issue in 1930 was 50.38. Sixty-four pages is now thought to be the limit—of course, sixteen was once considered maximum. Nor is any maximum assured. During 1930, the *Times* coined 20 per cent or about $6,000,000 less advertising than in 1929. Being in a position where it *can* lose much more than it is likely to gain, any such sum as $75,000,000 is fantastic—although, aside from sentiment, Mr. Ochs might still refuse $40,000,000.

In comparison with such sums the *Times* of London is, of course, nowhere. Its profits for the year ending in June, 1930, were £236,372 ($1,150,000), for the preceding year £331,592 ($1,600,000), for the year before that £272,274 ($1,320,000), and for the year before that £225,855 ($1,100,-000). It carried 7,676,000 lines of advertising in 1929—between a quarter and a fifth of that carried by the New York *Times*, and its average daily circulation in 1930 was 187,000 as against 155,000 in 1913, an increase of 20 per cent (which is almost the percentage of increase in the circulation of the New York *Times* in the same period). Even granted that it has not yet reached the dangerous bulk of the New York *Times* (it averages twenty-four to thirty-two pages) it is yet doubtful whether its possibilities of future expansion are very much greater than those of the New York paper. For the *Times* of London, even more than the New York *Times*, has a limited public, the public of rentiers and professional men and landowners, which is not increasing in either numbers or power in present-day England. Nevertheless, the dividend and profit record of the *Times* is impressive. In 1922 when the present owners purchased it for £1,550,000 ($7,517,500), it was paying dividends on its preferred shares only (£320,000 [$1,552,000], out of the £1,000,000 [$4,850,000] authorized shares) and its net profits were only £1,339 ($6,494). Since that time it has paid from 6 per cent to better than 8 per cent on its preferred shares and up to 15 per cent on its common shares. Conceivably, therefore, a purchaser would be willing to pay ten times present earnings for the property, i.e., about £3,500,000 ($16,975,000). But even so the superiority in value of the New York *Times* is striking enough.

The financial success of the New York *Times* is the great proof of the adage that virtue is its own (but not its only) reward. Mr. Adolph Simon Ochs came to New York from Chattanooga with an idea and $75,000 worth of credit. With the credit he purchased the then almost defunct New York *Times* and with the idea he built a great journal. The idea was, in the phrase of the late Melville Stone, that decency means dollars. "If a sincere desire," said Mr. Ochs in his statement of policy, "to conduct a high-standard newspaper, clean, dignified, and trustworthy, requires honesty, watchfulness, earnestness, industry, and practical knowledge applied with common sense, I entertain the hope that I can succeed in maintaining the high estimate that thoughtful, pure-minded people have ever had of the New York *Times*." This was in 1896. In 1896 Mr. Pulitzer's *World* and Mr. Hearst's *Journal* were "yellows" with enormous circulations, screaming headlines, and a content which, if it would not make a modern newspaper reader wince, was enough to shock most of the decent citizens of the nineties. Mr. Ochs' manifesto was directed against these journals and his motto "All the News That's Fit to Print" was meant to stand as a daily condemnation of their methods. Also it was applied in practice. Mr. Bryan was never again, after Mr. Ochs' purchase, referred to as the "gifted blatherskite from Nebraska" in the columns of the *Times*.

But it was much more than a victory over yellow journalism that Mr. Ochs was preparing. The Lord was on his side, and a future that Mr. Ochs never foresaw was waiting to bless his labors. He was right, as the event proved, in supposing that a considerable proportion of the people of New York would prefer a decent statement of fact to a routine of prurient scenarios. What Mr. Ochs did not foresee in gambling on the news as against mere journalistic liveliness was that, with the 20th century, there would "break" a series of great news stories of such importance and interest and excitement that the paper which was prepared to handle them would easily leave its other-minded competitors in the dust. And a second thing which Mr. Ochs could hardly have foreseen was the great 20th century American appetite for Instruction, the appetite which has called forth the Book Clubs and the Chautauquas and the Current Events Clubs and the Little Theaters, and the biographies and the biographical novels and the anthologies, and the Outlines of Science and the Outlines of Philosophy and the Outlines of History and the Outlines of Outlines and the whole overwhelming mass of informative information. To such a public the serious and decent newspaper is almost sacred. And to such a public the *Times* appeals. When, for example, as during the Naval Conference and the Byrd Expedition, the *Times* forces upon its readers news (and hardly news) of the least possible interest, they are grateful. They realize that it is done for their own good. And they receive it chastened and with thanks.

There is such an element of chance or of heavenly intercession in the lives of all successful men. But in the life of Mr. Ochs and his *Times* it lifts so large that Editor Dr. John H. Finley's jocular intimacy with the Lord and cozy ease in His presence, which are manifest in his composition of a versified "Grace Before Meat" for the *Times'* table, seem somehow quite appropriate and just.

> "O Lord, the Giver of All Good
> In whose just Hands are all our Times,
> We thank Thee for our daily Food
> Gathered (as News) from many Climes.
> Bless All of Us around this Board
> And All beneath this ample Roof:—
> What we find fit to print, O Lord,
> Is, after all, the Pudding's Proof."

Mr. Och's conception of decency and editorial honor led him to other disciplines than those of news and to other rewards. He refused to print deceptive or improper or untrue advertising. It was a great and radical step and one that seemed bound to lead to bankruptcy. Even the best English papers, even the *Times* of London has published medical advertisements of doubtful merit. But Mr. Ochs felt himself under obligation in his advertising as in his news columns not to deceive his readers, and he acted accordingly. Nothing is more to his credit than his refusal, on occasions when he could hardly have afforded to refuse, of advertising patronage of which he disapproved. And if he has profited by his courage, if the effect has been to make an advertisement in the *Times* to some degree a guaranty of honesty and therefore more valuable to the advertiser, he deserves the reward. The *Times* itself, in its *History*, is as frank as the most carping of its critics could be: "In this matter, too . . . the conductors of the paper have always felt that good business and good morals were identical. If it is morally dishonest to permit advertisers to dictate the policies of the paper, it is likewise commercially ruinous in the long run . . ."

The *Times*, which is to say Mr. Ochs, is therefore chiefly responsible for one of the greatest and most honorable changes in modern journalism. The advertiser who still believes that he can, or should be allowed to, dictate in any measure the policy of a paper is as ignorant and short-sighted as he is coarse. Only by maintaining its independence and its virtue can a paper make effective the notices it publishes. In 1901, when the circulation of the *Times* was only 100,000 and its advertising less than 5,000,000 lines, Mr. Ochs wrote to a meddlesome advertiser a letter which deserves to be set forth in full:

"You must excuse me from discussing with you the policy of the New York *Times*. It is a subject we do not care to discuss with an advertiser. We consider it a privilege to anyone to be permitted to make an announcement in the columns of the *Times*, aside from the fact that our rates for advertising space are far from commensurate with the service rendered. If the New York *Times* as it appears every day is not a sufficient recommendation for the use of its columns by advertisers (such as we will accept), assurance otherwise would be of little or no value.

"We do not want to sail under false colors. The New

York *Times* is not published solely for the purpose of attracting advertisers. We hope, however, to attract by the number and the class of our readers. We are seeking to secure the good-will and confidence of intelligent, discriminating newspaper readers. The advertiser is a secondary consideration. We take great pride in the knowledge of the fact that we have succeeded in impressing the honesty of our efforts upon the largest number of the best citizens of this city, representing both readers and advertisers. Of course, there are some exceptions. Among the latter class a conspicuous example is yourself. You seem to wish that the New York *Times* should go about as a mendicant, begging for advertising patronage. We will never do anything of the kind and are happy to say there is no occasion for our doing so.

"This all leads to the statement that if your advertisement remains out of the New York *Times* until you have some assurance other than the paper as it appears every day, as to the policy of the publisher, the *Times*, as long as it is under its present management, will endeavor to get along without your business."

With increasing size and wealth the freedom of a newspaper obviously becomes greater. The *Times* in 1930 rejected over $500,000 worth of advertising it considered improper. Its means are such today that no corporation or business could hope to influence it. And it should be, with its position and its ideals of news, as unbiased a publication as any reader could desire. But the means of independence are themselves a restraint. As the *Times* has grown rich it has taken on (it always had the inclination) a rich man's mentality. Its more radical (and perhaps most prejudiced) critics believe this mentality to have affected even the high neutrality of its front page. During the Communist Revolution in Russia, for example, the *Times* reported, according to Mr. Oswald Garrison Villard, "that Petrograd had fallen six times, been on the verge of capture three times more, been burned to the ground twice, been in absolute panic twice, and in revolt against the Bolsheviks on six different occasions—all without the slightest foundation in fact." To which Mr. Villard adds, "Only in the columns of Hearst could one find a record to equal this." Since then Mr. Walter Duranty, the best of its correspondents and much the best of its writers, has sent considerably more accurate news from Russia. But the social complexion of the *Times* has scarcely changed: it still gives undue space to the nightmares of the witch-burners and the discovery of propaganda plots, and it still shies like an oat-fed horse at a red banner.

Also it has taken to the ex-cathedra manner so frequently observed among persons of power and great influence. And not in the editorials alone. Mr. Edwin L. James, when head of the *Times* European bureau and its Paris correspondent—a man whose amazing power of penetrating the intentions of the French Foreign Office was equaled only by his capacity for assimilating its publicity—reported the London Naval Conference with such Bismarckian asides as, "How much simpler, how much easier, and how much more effective was it to let the others blow off steam and rest with dignity on our claim for parity with the greatest other navy." And "As we did today we shall listen sympathetically and in readiness to give our advice. And when they are ready to reduce we will talk business." As the excellent and subtle newspaper critic of the *New Yorker* neatly observed, "There really was no need to have sent anybody but Mr. James to London."

It is the richness, material and verbal, of the *Times*, and the saying that the *Times* is merely the manifolded shadow of Mr. Adolph Simon Ochs, that leads people like Upton Sinclair to depict Mr. Ochs as the archreactionary. In practice he is no such thing. He has taken more business chances than most men; and two of them, his gamble on the appeal of sober news, and his gamble on the value of clean advertising, were radical enough in their day. The truth of the matter would seem to be that Mr. Ochs is a constructive and practical man whose purpose was to build up a great business (devoted to the sale of news); who succeeded magnificently; who has, as a result, a very great stake in the existing order. And also that the business is now more important than its creator, and weightily unresponsive to his personal views. Mr. Ochs set out to create an institution, and he created one. It is hard to believe that the shadow does not now fall in the other sense—from the Times Building across the shoulders of Adolph Simon Ochs.

It certainly falls across the shoulders of his subordinates. Only one or two of them are visible beneath. Rollo Ogden, editor-in-chief, is a mild and kindly gentleman who refuses to betray his presence by so much as a gesture of his own. He is a graduate of Union Theological Seminary, a former Presbyterian minister and missionary (to the Mexicans), and the ex-editor of the New York *Evening Post*. He claims to feel radically on only two subjects, reformed spelling and experiment with the rules of golf, to both of which he is opposed. The *Times* editorial page is said to be less camphorated under Mr. Ogden than in the days of Charles R. Miller, but the difference, if it exists, is faint. Carr V. Van Anda, the managing editor, who is, however, no longer very active, has a great reputation among newspapermen and is credited with the organization of the newsgathering service for which the paper is chiefly famous. Arthur H. Sulzberger, vice president, husband of Mr. Ochs' only daughter and his probable successor, is a young man of parts and presence, who does not, as yet, permit himself to talk about the *Times*. Julius Ochs Adler, nephew of the owner and vice president and treasurer of the corporation, is a military man with an honorable record and patriotic views. The *Times* is greater than them all. But not than Louis Wiley.

Louis Wiley has been the business manager of the paper for thirty-five years. If any man in America has a monument he has one. And he is sixty, an age when monuments are frequently in mind. But Mr. Wiley is too busy about a great number of very exciting and entertaining and absorbing things even to think of the subject. He is probably more engaged in living than any man of his years in New York or out of it, and he hasn't come to the end yet. Dancing is his great love, but when there is no dancing to be done he will dine out or sit in a theatre or even attend a reception. He goes out every night in the month but one, and that one he has the world in to dinner. He is very small, a Jew, and strong and energetic as many small Jews are. He talks well. He knows everyone. A hall in his Park Avenue bachelor apartment is lined with signed photographs of the great, and framed awards of his own degrees and orders, and the names of persons of importance are always in his mouth. And yet he never gives the impression of toadyism and valetdom that such practices usually carry. He is simply interested in great men and great names. He prefers people to objects and famous people to others. "What I really like best," he observes with a well-practiced look, "are attractive young women."

He came to the *Times* from Rochester. His father was a clothing merchant in Hornell, New York, and Mount Sterling, Kentucky, in which latter town Louis Wiley began newspaper work. "Mount Sterling," says Mr. Wiley, "had and still has a population of two thousand. I prefer to point to New York as an example of what a newspaper man can do for his community." Rochester offered a better opportunity. But even Rochester was smaller than New York, and Louis Wiley got a job with the New York *Sun* under Dana. A few weeks later, he left the *Sun* and joined the *Times*, which Mr. Ochs had just taken over, and since that first year of the new régime he has supported the policies and purpose of his employer. The first object to meet the eye in Mr. Wiley's apartment is a large desk and on it, alone, a picture of Adolph Simon Ochs.

Mr. Wiley is not a man to let business routine destroy him. He makes a game of it. Much of his thinking he does impulsively from step to step, scattering his home and his office with pencil jottings on a multitude of subjects. He walks, every decent morning, from Seventy-first Street to Forty-third Street with his secretary beside him, so marshalling his advance as never to be halted by the traffic lights, dictating occasional observations as he goes. He has two offices, one in the midst of his duties, the other high up in the Times Tower, where he can sit on a high cushion in a revolving chair, with his feet on an elevated hassock, his photographs around him, and play his rôle. He travels much, frequently abroad, and always among people of importance. He has the continuous, and, to him, the necessary and gratifying sense of being in touch with the world's life. And he has never lost his own. Mr. Ochs in 1921 described Mr. Wiley as "of unusual ability, alert, indefatigable, and agreeable . . . One of my most useful and valuable assistants." He is much more than that. He is the only man whose personality has survived the *Times*. The rest of them are elements of value in the richest news-dispensing business in the world.

Let the New York *Times* have its Wealth and the journals of Mr. Hearst (of the Hearst-while London *Daily Mail*) their Personality. What the *Times* of London has is its Character. Sometimes it has had nothing but its character. Sometimes its character has been all bustles, bangles, and Paisley shawls. But the *Times* has never lost it. If it did, like any kitchen maid or clergyman or prime minister, it would never get another place.

Those with characters to maintain are careful where they live. The *Times* occupies premises in Playhouse-Yard and Printing House Square, Blackfriars, in "the City." The site is respectable. The deeds run back through the King's Printing House, the Blackfriars Playhouses, one William Shakespeare, and a Dominican monastery. The conveniences are honorably few: Fleet Street, the news center of London, is far away; so is the Stock Exchange; so are the offices of Government. The composing rooms are dark and crowded. The two machine rooms are cramped and inconveniently located with reference both to the foundry and to the dispatching room. Many of the offices are in a building which was from 1784 until quite recently, the private house of the Walter family. But the *Times* will never move. When, some years ago, it was suggested that it might find better quarters elsewhere, the whole body of its workmen and a large number of its readers protested. And the upshot of the matter was an appropriation of 50,000 or 75,000 pounds sterling ($242,500 or $363,750) per year for reconstruction of the plant in some undefined future. In the meantime the present plant, enlarged since its Hoe & Goss presses were installed under Northcliffe in 1908, succeeds in putting out more than 180,000 copies per day of the most beautifully printed and most skillfully edited of newspapers. And it is the boast of the *Times* that "from the year 1784 until the present day all the chief improvements in the printing of newspapers have been either invented or first tried and fostered in what is now the office of the Times."

But a respectable address is not enough. There is also the question of opinion. There is no more certain way of losing an excellent character than the expression of unworthy opinions. The opinions of the *Times* are impeccable. "The *Times*," according to a statement generally supposed to have been written by Geoffrey Dawson, who returned to the editorial chair under the Astor-Walker régime, "claims to be national, independent, and complete . . . It is committed to no political party, but supports whatever party, whether in or out of power, it believes to be acting in the national interest." It has always, as a matter of fact, believed the Conservative Party to be "acting in the national interest."

And its independence consists in occasional criticisms of Conservative conduct which are all the more delightful to read because they are fatherly. But it would be a mistake to suppose that there is anything venal about the opinions of the *Times*. Not even Northcliffe could change their shape. They are imbedded in the presses of the plant.

As for its news, its practice of its profession, the *Times* deserves all the good that is said of it. Its news is true not only in its facts but in its presentation the event described has not only happened, but it has happened in the crisp daylight of accurate and intelligible English. The correspondents and editors of the *Times* are so far masters of their tongue that they can be just without being general, and not only plausible but precise. In this its style differs marvelously from the lucid and reasonable insipidity which the New York *Times* seems to require of its correspondents and which many of them are able to supply. Whether the dearth of newspaper writers capable of living speech is responsible for the style of the New York *Times* or whether the style of the New York *Times* is responsible for its lack of writers is a question for those who care to ask. But if the situation is fortunate in that it permits the New York *Times* to find an abundance of reporters at $60 to $100 a week, it is also not without its dangers. An editorial by Mr. Lippmann or a column by Mr. Heywood Broun or a sports story by Mr. McGeehan might wreck the sheet.

In bulk, the news published by the *Times* of London is less than that published by the New York *Times*. The *Times* of London scraps 45 per cent of its cabled news and calls the process selectiveness. The New York *Times* scraps 5 per cent and calls it waste. The New York *Times* covers an important story from four or five angles. The *Times* assigns it to one man and makes him responsible for the whole. Not long ago, the opening of an Egyptian tomb alleged to contain the mummy of a queen was witnessed by the correspondent of the *Times*. There was also present, on a tip from the *Times* of London, a representative of the New York *Times*. The tomb was opened. The London office of the New York *Times* received a wire from its representative stating that the tomb was empty. And the London office of the New York *Times* offered the story, such as it was, to the *Times*. It was politely but definitely refused. And the next day the *Times* published (from its "own correspondent") the identical story. He had rooted about in the tomb until he was assured, and was able to record for all time, that that tomb was EMPTY.

So far as domestic news is concerned, the *Times* makes no effort to compete with the scooping activities of its London competitors. It will frequently publish a story of murder or scandal one or even several days after the penny press has reported it. It views itself as the historical record of current events and cannot afford to regale its readers at the risk of misinforming posterity. In the words of "a correspondent," "There is printed every morning a certain number of copies called the Royal Edition, on paper specially made to resist the decay caused by time, and having a life of several hundreds of years. Two copies of this edition are sent to the King every morning wherever he is in residence, the farther from his capital the swifter the means of transport."

And in addition to its opinions and its news the *Times* has its departments. Its reports of law cases are so accurate and so neatly summarized that they are admitted as authority in the British courts and are cited for advance cases in American briefs.

Its society notices are indispensable to a society that has already read the *Daily Express* and the *Daily Mail* for the gossip.

Its agony columns are better reading than most best sellers and made up of about the same material. "LITTLE PAL—Remembrance sometimes makes us sad, yet shall we not seek the happiness which may be ours? Nous verrons! S.B.M...S...E." "YOUNG LADY desires PURCHASE good, slightly worn CLOTHES; small figure. Write Box V. 1992." "PORTRAITS of the late 18TH CENTURY ENGLISH SCHOOL WANTED by advertiser buying for American collectors; very high prices paid for beautiful women and children. Write Box M. 1331." "CAN ANY—ONE OFFER POSITION with permanent prospects ex-officer (War period wounded), aged 35, single, good birth and education, now disengaged and in desperate circumstances? . . ."

Its correspondence column is superb and is frequently a source of news. The gentleman who writes a letter to the *Times* may be anyone. He may be Lord Birkenhead writing about the perfidy of the Attorney-General; Robert Bridges protesting against a proposed aërodrome near hallowed Oxford; Horace Plunkett on agricultural policy; A. P. Herbert, the humorist, seriously proposing a water bus upon the Thames; Lord Cushendun explaining his differences with Beaverbrook as regards the Empire trade platform; "A Naval Wife" on her husband's pay; the Aga Khan on British policy in India; Bernard Shaw on the stupidity of film censors; Lord Robert Cecil on the felicities of the League of Nations Union; Balfour, Lloyd George, and Smuts "as members of the War Cabinet responsible for the Balfour Declaration twelve years ago"; whimsical Mr. A. A. Milne on musical censorship.

And its supplements, the Literary Supplement, the Educational Supplement, and the Trade & Engineering Supplement are excellent. The Literary Supplement appears Thursdays, sells at 3d and has a circulation of 30,000. The corresponding section of the New York *Times*, its Book Review Section, goes out with the Sunday paper and has, consequently, a circulation of 775,000. The two offer a contrast which is characteristic of the two papers as a whole. The Literary Supplement carries its advertising upon its literary prestige, which is certainly greater than that of any other literary supplement; the Book Review Section of the New York *Times* supports its literary prestige upon its advertising, which exceeds the book advertising of any other paper in the world. Where the first is read for what it has to say, the second is read for what it has to sell. The book reviews of the New York *Times* are, for the most part, dull, its reviewers without authority, and its reputation among writers (as distinguished from Literary business men) nil. The reputation of the *Times* Literary Supplement on the contrary is high, its matter interesting, and its contributors important. It would be difficult to name a contemporary English writer of distinction whom the *Times*' rule of anonymity has not covered (and made known). Among its contributors in the generation now coming to power are, or have been, T. S. Eliot, Herbert Read, Richard Aldington, Robert Graves, and as many more as one cares to take the space to name. That there is some relation between excellence and profits is indicated by the fact that whereas the New York *Times* Book Review charges $1,300 a page for a circulation of 775,000, the Literary Supplement of the *Times* of London is paid £100 ($485) a page for a circulation of 30,000, or about ten times as much per subscriber. The same thing is true of advertising in the two papers themselves.

Between the editorial pages of the *Times* of London and the New York *Times* no such easy comparison is possible. They differ in kind rather than in degree. The editorials of the New York *Times* are comments or expressions of opinion or occasional essays embroidering some bit of homely news with rather unnecessary drafts upon Bartlett's *Familiar Quotations*, or making sly, waggish fun of some young painter or poet whose manner resembles nothing the editors of the New York *Times* have ever seen. The leading articles of the *Times* of London, on the contrary (though they may bloom sometimes with very similar flowers), contain a considerable increment of news. They are frequently devoted to full and exhaustive discussions of problems which have appeared piecemeal in the daily dispatches. And they are read by people to whom pronouncements of editorial opinion in general are about as important as the *Congressional Record*.

The editor of the *Times* of London must consequently be a different kind of man from the editor of the New York *Times*. Mr. Geoffrey Dawson (born Robinson: changed his name to Dawson by Royal Licence in 1917 for reasons said to revolve about a legacy) is a graduate of Magdalen College, Oxford, and a Fellow of All Souls. He was trained in the Colonial Office for three years, and in Lord Milner's school for bright young men in Africa for four. For five years he edited the Johannesburg *Star*. He has had experience of the Empire and of the British Isles. Also he "belongs." He believes in the majesty of the *Times* and the "best people." He is not always approachable (but when approached agreeable and human), and he is given to corresponding distantly with his various departments. He can be counted on (with the *Times*) not to be aware of things it would be embarrassing to notice. But he is capable of emotion, e.g., his break with Northcliffe, leading to his resignation as editor in 1919. Although he is not one of the great editors of the *Times*, he is clearly in the great tradition for he belongs to the (once) ruling class, he has himself been employed in the government of the Empire, and he possesses the *kind* of education which has produced the *kind* of tradition which the *Times* preserves. The *Times* was once described as a newspaper written by gentlemen for gentlemen. And the first part of that dubious description remains true.

Few newspaper proprietors could say, even if they cared to, that their journals were the *property* of their readers. The *Times* of London can say just that. The carefully preserved and protected character of the *Times* is not its own to change. If Northcliffe had changed it, he would not only have destroyed the *Times* but he would have done thousands of foreign-living Englishmen an irremediable harm: he would have robbed them of their goods. Should the Weekly Edition with its news, its special articles, its leaders, letters, illustrations, crossword puzzles, and chess problems selected from the six daily numbers of the *Times* and further enlivened with bridge hints for the garrison club-houses and the officers' wives, change in its form or substance, the sweltering porches of the consulate at Bushire would know it, and Indragiri and Pukapuka and Griffin Cove would be, by that much, farther off from London. "From Iceland in the frozen north . . ." begins the prospectus which recites the merits of this weekly. And so it is. There is no considerable settlement of the British Empire and no Colonial town to which the weekly does not go. And its power is immeasurable. What the Scotch prospector at Forty-Mile wants is not news of Glasgow. Anyone can give him that in time. He wants the look of something British and the familiar, human sameness of a thing he knows. In a world in which all other newspapers owe their profits to their ability to change, the *Times* remains unaltered. It cannot change. It has a character to keep.

THE MASTERS
OF LIGHT

Halfway Between the Atom and the Star is Man. With His Telescope, His Microscope He Examines Both. And Thus He Conquers Disease, Analyzes Metals, Makes War, and Steers Ships. This Because Light Can Be Bent, With Infinite Pains, but With Considerable Profit. The Story of Both Pains and Profit is the Story of Bausch & Lomb

BAUSCH AND LOMB
OPTICAL COMPANY

$\backsim\!\!\!\sim\!\!\!\sim$

On the banks of the Genesee River in Rochester, New York, there flourishes a concern that is not so well known as it will be. Not that Bausch & Lomb is obscure, but that it has in its possession one of the keys with which the future of American industry must be unlocked. This is the optic lens, a most talented prima donna, whose virtuosity is able to disclose the quality of steel, temporarily immortalize the faces of movie actresses, measure the accuracy of tools to within 1/100,000 of an inch, plague the microbes, analyze metals more accurately than a chemist, and determine the constitution of stars millions of light-years away. She alone makes the talkies possible, by converting sound to light and reconverting light to sound. She alone has gazed on *Amphipleura Pellucida*, whose precise structure is the utmost test of human vision. She alone can direct the guns of a modern army, steer ships across the sea, construct bridges, assist the geologist to find oil.

Offhand it might be supposed that this prima donna and her greatest American impresario would be known more widely than the average $10,000,000 business. But the reverse is true. The manufacturer of the optic lens is involved in too many industries to achieve a popular renown; he is too diversified; a moderate advertising bill is far too quickly dissipated among dozens of trade magazines and scientific journals. Perhaps it is not worth while for him to try to explain 17,000 specialized products, most technical in their nature, to the public.

The importance of Bausch & Lomb lies in the fact that it is master of light, and the only one in America. Competitors it has in one field or another—the American Optical Co. makes more spectacles, the Spencer Lens Co. makes microscopes, and Eastman Kodak Co. now grinds its own lenses. But not a pound of scientific precision glass is made in America commercially outside the Bausch & Lomb factory; nor does any other American company attempt to meet the combined optical requirements of ophthalmology, science, and industry.

The evolution of the business to its present $10,000,000 dimensions is a story to warm the heart of the most ardent nationalist. For although the Italians were the first to use spectacles in Western civilization and though Galileo was the first to apply the optic lens to science, the Germans soon became the real masters of light. Their patient love of detail fitted them preëminently for the construction of instruments whose business is to bend and otherwise manipulate waves no larger than 3/100,000 of an inch. To do this successfully with high-powered compound instruments, they learned how to work glass to plus or minus 1/1,000,-000 of an inch. This workmanship and the complicated mass of theory underlying it received their greatest development after 1868 in the shops of Carl Zeiss of Jena, whose name became international and whose scientific methods converted the optical instrument from a serious plaything to a precise tool. Every nation in the world paid tribute to Zeiss. Not an army or a navy but was dependent on Zeiss range finders, binoculars, periscopes. The Zeiss microscopes revolutionized bacteriology, opened new worlds in biology, mineralogy, crystallography. Zeiss spectroscopes analyzed the stars, Zeiss camera lenses broke new ground in photography, and the knowledge that Zeiss acquired of the science of bending light enabled the manufacturers of large astronomical telescopes to drag the great nebulæ several thousand light-years closer to the earth.

In order to understand the difficulty of breaking into this near-monopoly that Zeiss held, consider for a moment the nature of light. Swiftest and most intangible of all cosmic phenomena, we have had to invent the ether for it to travel in, while an analysis of its bewildering atomic sources leads us astray into the revolutionary quantum theory. So ignorant are we of its nature that, after 300 years of believing it to consist of waves, the old corpuscular theory that Newton suggested has been revived with some scientific enthusiasm.

For the present purposes, however, it is well enough to conceive of light as waves traveling through the ether at 186,000 miles a second. There are a great number of waves. They range from the largest electromagnetic wireless waves, about twenty miles from crest to crest, to the shortest known pulsations, called cosmic rays, whose wave length is some 8/1,000,000,000,000,000 of an inch. Presumably it would be possible to "see" by any of these waves, the ones that we call "light" being not inherently different from the infra-red waves that we call "heat." Photographs have been taken by means of heat waves, which are too large for our eyes, and also by means of ultra-violet and x-rays, which are too small.

The point about light waves which is important to grasp in connection with the optical industry, however, is that to bask in a flood of light is not necessarily to "see." As it comes to us from the sun, light is infinitely reflected, dispersed, absorbed, and scrambled—first by the air, then by the objects around us. Until it is organized or bent into a focus, no animal can see where he is going or what is approaching him—he is conscious only of a vague brightness and darkness. This was Nature's profound discovery when she developed the eye, and the optical business is merely one that is based upon the technique of bending light more than the eye is able to bend it. The photomicrographic microscope intercepts the very few rays reflected from *Amphipleura Pellucida* (a fresh water alga as small as the point of a needle, with a skeleton of siliceous substance) and spreads them into an image as large as a good-sized trout.

Light can travel at full speed only in a vacuum—it is slowed up by air, and even more by water, glass, or crystal. In passing at an angle from a fast medium to a slower one, light will bend, the action being very similar to that of an automobile when the brakes on one side grip more tightly than those on the other. This phenomenon is called refraction, and its laws—involving chromatic and spherical aberration, spherical zones, sine condition, and focal lengths—are affairs for able mathematicians. Until the discoveries of Ernst Abbe of the Zeiss Works, opticians had fumbled into these mysteries by trial and error. They had fumbled with different kinds of glass, radiuses of curvature, lens separations, different thicknesses. They were never able to tell what would happen to their combinations until the whole instrument had been constructed; and since the complications of light-bending increase with the power of the lens, they were never able to make instruments of sufficient power and accuracy for science. Carl Zeiss and Professor Ernst Abbe, the latter an optical genius, were the first to realize that light is the world's greatest logician; that one had but to formulate its laws in order to predict exactly what paths it would follow through any given medium or combination of mediums. Not a glass, not a radius of curvature should go into their instruments until their effects had been foretold. The instrument must in reality exist before any grinding was begun.

While these lofty principles were being evolved and erected into a scientific empire, a humbler drama was enacted in Rochester, New York, where a German immigrant who had lost two fingers in a buzz saw was peddling spectacles from house to house, explaining their virtues with great difficulty. There was a tradition in the Bausch clan that the family was unlucky, and penniless John J. Bausch was no apparent exception. For reasons that had more to do with friendship than economics, Henry Lomb, another immigrant, had become his partner. During the Civil War, the "business" was held together chiefly by Lomb's pay as a captain under Grant. In 1871, John J.'s son, Edward, who has ever since demonstrated a similar sure-footedness, decided to go to Cornell, graduated in 1875, and began the study of microscopes under a German expert. This was Bausch & Lomb's first venture into the scientific market, and those early microscopes were made and sold by Edward Bausch himself. The year 1890 found the family jinx quite shattered: John J. was the head of something worthy of being called a business, and Edward (now president) was making valuable contacts with the Zeiss Works at Jena.

What it is about the American scene that so stimulates applied rather than theoretical science would make an interesting sociological study. Transplanted as they were from the soil out of which Carl Zeiss had grown, these men nevertheless carried the matter of machine production of lenses further than Zeiss. The most precise grinding operations were performed mechanically, leaving only the final polishing to be done by hand. Since the early nineties, Zeiss had granted them licenses to manufacture under the Zeiss patents. Now with the increasing importance of Bausch & Lomb, a selling agreement was reached whereby Zeiss sales in America were not pressed, leaving the licensees a clear field for expansion; and at the same time, the Germans put all their wealth of theory at the disposal of the Americans in order to expedite this manufacturing. Under this arrangement, the American optical business flourished, and Zeiss bought one-fifth of the Bausch & Lomb stock; but since Zeiss had by then become a perpetual foundation (1888), the Americans could not reciprocate.

The independent development of the American optical industry might very well have stopped there, for the arrangement was profitable to both concerns, Zeiss receiving the patent royalties, the Americans acquiring a priceless education from the scientific staff at Jena. Then quite unexpectedly the War in Europe was driven between them like a wedge. The Allies, formerly dependent upon Zeiss, now turned frantically to Bausch & Lomb. So dire was England's need for field glasses that the government sought to purchase them from private citizens who had Zeiss glasses in their possession. Barely a generation removed from German soil and with some 1,000 German workmen in his factory, Edward Bausch, who had taken over the active management, had a chance to display his characteristic sure-footedness. Backed by his father, who was then living, and by other members of the family, who were major stockholders, he filled the Allied orders. As a stockholder, Zeiss protested. The determined Rochesterians filled more orders. Finally, before America entered the War, they were forced to repurchase their own stock from Zeiss.

Not only did this action help to create confidence in Bausch & Lomb when America entered the War (many of the employees becoming technically enemy aliens), but it set the company up as a world figure in its own right, in full competition with Zeiss. In a single hurried year, William Bausch, youngest son of the founder, worked out a process for the manufacture of scientific precision glass—a stupendous achievement, considering that no one had been able to produce it commercially in this country before or has so much as tried it since. (Glass for spectacles is, of course, made by many American concerns, notably Pittsburgh Plate Glass Co., Corning Glass works, and American Optical Co.) Bausch & Lomb at once became, and has remained, the government's right hand for optical equipment of all sorts, much of it secret. Government engineers now maintain headquarters on the premises. The War also bequeathed to the company that research-consciousness which is so characteristic of successful modern industry. The present large research staff includes Dr. Max Poser, one of the leading microscopists of the country, who had formerly built up the Zeiss sales in England and who had been sent to America just before the War to coöperate with Bausch & Lomb. Mild and eloquent, with a mind embracing a dozen different sciences, Dr. Poser is the Bausch & Lomb contact with universities and scientific institutions throughout the land, carrying on research into non-optical sciences with no uncertain air. Most closely linked into the Bausch & Lomb research activities is the Optical Institute of the University of Rochester, and also the Mechanics Institute, whose graduates frequently enter the company shops.

Many and surprising are the turns of American industry, but on many counts this business in Rochester can claim to be unique. Optical glass had never been ground in America until John J. Bausch began grinding spectacles in his meager shop. It will be recalled, too, that Pasteur did not announce his conclusion that fermentation is the result of minute organisms until 1857. Hence the life of Bausch & Lomb embraces the whole optical industry as we know it, and all the amazing expansion of science that has taken place around the microscope and allied instruments. But besides this, those two careful German immigrants were largely responsible for the placing of microscopes in high schools and smaller colleges—it was with that intention that they undertook their manufacture in 1874, and it was with that intention that they developed the machine processes that enabled them to offer their instruments at remarkably low prices. In two generations, they not only succeeded in this, but made themselves indispensable to the army, the navy, the educators, the health directors, and the scientists of their adopted country.

However, the old Bausch & Lomb adage that the family is unlucky will never be entirely dispelled. Bausch & Lomb is a glittering success, financially, intellectually; to the founders and to their sons, the fates granted long and ample lives; but beyond this destiny would not go, for to J. J. Bausch and Captain Henry Lomb there will remain no direct male heir. Mr. Bausch died in 1926, aged ninety-five, and left four children. Edward, the seventy-six-year-old president, was the eldest son and has become, with George Eastman, a first citizen of Rochester. But he and his brother William are childless. Also childless was Carrie. Henry (who died in 1909) had a daughter Elsa (Mrs. M. H. Eisenhart); Annie (who married Treasurer William A. E. Drescher) has two daughters and a son, Theodore. Captain Lomb's son, Adolph, is a director but otherwise inactive, and has no children. Under Edward Bausch's leadership, therefore, the management of the business is passing quietly and efficiently to the grandsons-in-law: to M. H. Eisenhart, general manager; to J. F. Taylor, assistant treasurer, who married Hilda Drescher; to Gordon Baird of the sales department, who married Clara Drescher; to Theodore Drescher, factory manager. These are the chief owners of the $4,000,000 Bausch & Lomb common stock, which does not go outside the family. (The $2,000,000 preferred is offered to employees.) Their brains are augmented by the presence on the board of Cousin Carl L. Bausch, in charge of research, and Carl S. Hallauer, high-pressure Rochesterian. And from the Bausch & Lomb standpoint, all this is very well, for it has brought new blood into the business, new brains, new ideas.

It has brought General Manager Eisenhart, graduate of Princeton and of M. I. T., who had a meteoric rise with the Eastman Kodak Co. before his marriage to Edward Bausch's niece, Elsa. He is a keen and modern executive in his late forties. He is not, perhaps, to be envied the strictly executive problems in the business of bending light. The ophthalmic aspect of the business is the least difficult, although even here the constant shift of style in spectacle frames (as in automobile lines) and the pressing competition of the American Optical Co. and the Shur-On Standard Optical Co. offer normal industrial problems.

Ever since 1874, however, the Bausch & Lomb shift has been toward science. The spectacle business has enjoyed a normal growth, but whereas it used to represent 70 or 80 per cent of the total, it is now only 50 per cent. Catering more and more to scientists, the management has become surrounded by specialists and temperaments of all sorts. Normally, the firm has about 16,000 different orders on hand, many of these for instruments of which they sell some half-dozen a year. Some instruments with the least turnover have taken two or three years to develop. Inventory under these conditions becomes somewhat staggering. Frequently a single scientist will demand a new instrument to accomplish his own particular research, and rather than build one only, the company will make several. These may sell easily, or they may be inventoried for years, and the prediction of how they will sell requires a minute study of the science in which they are to be used.

But the special problems do not end here—far more than

the average industry, this one is dependent on labor. It is not everyone who can machine glass to plus or minus 6/1,000,000 of an inch, yet Bausch & Lomb must attain this accuracy in actual production. The Germans are the only people who have so far shown themselves capable of such work day in and day out, and consequently a large percentage of the 4,000 employees have been imported. The resulting pay roll is anything but elastic. There are, moreover, some 500 workers at Rochester who can scarcely be duplicated anywhere, and the problem of replacing these men is one of lifetimes, even of generations. Bausch & Lomb foresight has backed the Mechanics Institute, where many new workers are trained; has kept American citizenship to the fore; has paid salaries that can be had nowhere else in the optical world. In their labor, they have this unique advantage over the usual manufacturer: that the very difficulty of obtaining skilled workmanship has barred competition in their more advanced lines. And when something like the talking movie comes along, requiring skilled optical workmanship, Bausch & Lomb gets the whole national business.

And it is extraordinary labor—more minute than the work of ants and as painstaking. For test purposes, these workmen can grind glass to plus or minus 2/1,000,000 of an inch (about one-tenth of a wave length of light). In doing this, they pass the limits of measurement, and may have made surfaces of much higher accuracy without being able to detect the fact. They pass also the limits of ordinary mechanics and step into the world of miracle: for two pieces of glass so accurately ground, when placed one on top of the other, will adhere by molecular attraction, and human power cannot draw them apart. If broken with a hammer, they often will not crack at the fusion. Two flat pieces of Bausch & Lomb glass, as they are worked in actual production (plus or minus half a wave length of light), will adhere by vacuum—in lifting the top piece you will lift the bottom one also. The right angles of prisms are machined to within one second of an arc: that is to say, were the sides of the prism to be extended, the error from the right angle would be less than one foot at a distance of forty-three miles. The sides of these prisms are only about an inch long.

The Bausch & Lomb scientific specialty is the microscope, and they sell about 15,000 of these a year. The average medical microscope has 300 parts, to manufacture which 3,250 distinct catalogued operations are required. But such operations! The avowed purpose of a telescope is to gather light, and hence its lens must be made as large as possible. But since the sole aim and significance of a microscope is to magnify, its first lens is no larger than a pinhead. This lens is indeed so small that one would scarcely see through it at all were not a flood of light focused upon it by a concentrating lens system at the base of the instrument. Yet the barely visible speck of glass must be machined to an accuracy surpassing anything in the metal industry. A watchmaker thinks well of a watch machined to within 1/10,000 of an inch: the tiniest of microscope lenses must be accurate to within 6/1,000,000. Behind it are placed six or eight other lenses, the largest about the size of a dime. They are all just as accurate and must be perfectly centered and held in place by the diamond-machined metal nosepiece. The price of these instruments ranges from $70 (this model being inadequate for ultra-scientific work) to about

$900. The popular seller, used largely in college laboratory work, goes for $120. It is reported that Henry Ford said that he did not see how it was profitable to sell this microscope at this price.

It is not generally realized that from the atom to the star, speaking in terms of size, man is about halfway between, being somewhat closer to the atom than to the star. This thought is overpowering, so well have the astronomers impressed us with the size of the stars; but as far as the optical industry is concerned, it lends a certain grandeur that no other industry can boast. For it is by the optical lens alone that we can so much as approach these vast extremities of the cosmic horizon. It is probable that no lens will ever enable us to see the limits in either direction. The telescope cannot magnify the remote stars, but only make them brighter; the microscope can by no means reach the atom, which is many thousands of times smaller than a wave of light. Yet of the two, the microscope is the more valuable to civilization, because, between us and the atom, there exists a wonderland worthy of Alice herself, a world in which the survival of this race is now being fought out by silent armies of whose existence we have only been aware for some seventy years.

Naturally the first microscopists were elated by the power of their instruments to show the existence of this world of sporilla, bacteria, blood cells, and minute organisms by the million. But now that is considered child's play, and the aim of the scientist is to study the actual structure of these invisible beings. Thus Bausch & Lomb microscopes have shown that certain bacteria are multicellular, by resolving not only their outlines, but the actual cells. Thus too, our friend *Amphipleura Pellucida* has been "resolved" and his structure found to be a skeleton of siliceous material. With the micro-manipulator, these infinitesimals can be moved around, picked up, turned over, while the microscopist watches through the eye-piece. The metalloscope, an allied instrument, is used by the U. S. Steel Corp., Bethlehem, Canadian Pacific Railways, General Motors, to mention only the largest, to determine the crystalline structure of their steels, and whether or not the carbon has been dissolved. The nature of steel depends as much on its physical structure as on its chemical formula. Old-timers in the steel industry know how to produce the right physical structure by their methods of heating, but it is now possible for the eye to see whether they have done their work well. This metalloscope, together with the industrial spectroscope, can analyze metals more accurately than chemistry; can, for instance, find traces of manganese in steel that would have eluded the chemist entirely.

Then there is the contour measuring projector, by which the outlines of tools, dies, gear teeth, screw threads, and any number of other items can be thrown on a screen and their accuracy checked to within 1/10,000 of an inch. Contour projectors are used by all large automobile concerns, by American Can to determine the accuracy of the sealing mechanism, by Western Electric to make telephone plugs fit neatly, by Henry Ford, A. C. Spark Plug, and a hundred others. If we are to have airplanes traveling 300 miles per hour, the motors must be precisely machined, the metal must be of a certain known quality, the pilot must be able to fly without seeing where he is going. All three of these factors are dependent on optics. In tool shops, for instance, the limit of the accuracy of a micrometer measuring a three-inch piece of metal is plus or minus some 2/10,000 of an inch. Bausch & Lomb's optical thickness comparator is twenty times as accurate.

And then there is the matter of reflectors. Bausch & Lomb has equipped almost every movie studio in America with these instruments, all the airfields, all the battleships, all the coast-defense system. They make about half of the nation's movie projection lenses, a quarter of the nation's camera lenses, all the optical mechanisms for the talkies. Their balopticons have entered nearly every high school and college in the land. Their analytical instruments are invading the textile, ceramic, and food industries; drugs are being analyzed by indexes of refraction in special Bausch & Lomb refractometers; Bausch & Lomb saccharimeters are used by the government and by importers of sugar to determine the amount of sugar in a given imported solution; Bausch & Lomb microscopes cater to jewelers and the manufacturers of ball bearings. And so on across the length and breadth of the Union.

The prediction, therefore, that this concern on the banks of the Genesee is not so well known as it will be is by no means a dangerous one to make. It is worth while observing that neither Bausch & Lomb nor Zeiss has made the largest telescopes in the world. Zeiss has gone very much farther in this regard than the Americans, having installed many large observatory telescopes ranging up to a sixty-inch aperture—enormous instruments capable of searching the remote fixed stars and spiral nebulæ. The Zeiss line of terrestrial telescopes is also exceptionally fine. Bausch & Lomb's largest astronomical instrument has only a six-inch lens, though larger ones can be constructed on demand; and to Bausch & Lomb goes the distinction of equipping the Empire State Building, Manhattan.

But the real strides in the optical industry have been made by the microscope and its cousins, and the reason for this is that the microscope and the spectroscope are essential to all scientific research, and are rapidly becoming essential to modern high-speed industry. While Zeiss was the first to grasp this important fact, Bausch & Lomb now equals its former stockholder in the matter of catering to industry with specialized products. Indeed, the Rochesterians claim to manufacture a more diversified list, to carry more different items on their books than any optical manufacturer in the world. Nor could anything be more congenial to the American scene than their profound interest in the applications of science to industry—a passion that has never gone unrewarded in this industrial land.

EXHIBIT "A" OF SUPERPOWER

Strong Link in the Strong Chain of Eastern Utilities, Niagara Hudson has Incomparable Raw Material, a Great Market, Great Names. If Superpower is Desirable, Niagara Hudson is a Notable Public Servant; if Dangerous, an Outstanding Menace

NIAGARA HUDSON POWER
CORPORATION

In the peerage of American business, Niagara Hudson has certain sharp distinctions.

It is the largest power company in the U. S., keystone of a combination of two companies which will produce and sell 10,000,000,000 kilowatt hours of electrical energy in 1931—twice the output of their nearest rival.

It is a holding company of rock-bottom strength and rapidly enlarging girth in which Morgan money, Mellon money, Brady money, money from a dozen of the greatest fortunes in America is pooled with money willingly invested by 95,000 humble Joneses.

It is a young and restless giant among power companies, the most actively expanding unit in a great group of units covering the eastern third of the U. S., and touching with its finger tips the Insull system in the Middle West.

There are various distinctions which give this company a position of unquestioned leadership in the power industry of the U. S. It is the largest producer of electric power in the country. It is incomparably the largest producer of hydroelectric power. It commands the richest industrial market in the U. S. It is a pioneer, as we shall see, in its attitude toward certain much-vexed questions in the field of politics. It is admirably equipped with sources of cheap power, blessed with the good fortune of an alliance with the House of Morgan. It has at its head, in Floyd L. Carlisle, an executive who combines a canny sense of what his business needs with a canny sense of what the public expects it to deliver.

Here, in short, is Example I of the modern public utility in the form in which it is widely advertised and endlessly debated: a strong unit in an alliance of strong units, possessing all of the physical advantages which flow from an exchange of power and all of the responsibilities which are bound to follow from any circumstances so highly providential.

These advantages and responsibilities Niagara Hudson sums up in its own experience. We have here a test case of all that we mean by modern superpower.

Of the creation of Niagara Hudson, it may be said that the conception of this plan was no more one man's idea than the law of gravity was one man's idea. As naturally as apples fall or comets bump, a number of independent or quasi-independent operating companies found themselves drawn into closer association in the territory which Niagara Hudson came at a later day to occupy.

This territory, as the name of Niagara Hudson itself reveals, was the corridor of intensively industrialized territory lying between Buffalo on the west and the Hudson Valley on the east: a corridor approximately 250 miles in length and sixty miles in width, strategically placed for access to large markets at both ends. In this corridor, the mighty General Electric manufactures some third of a billion dollars' worth of electrical equipment every year.

George Eastman makes all but a handful of the cameras produced in the U. S. Here the Aluminum Company of America has three plants: American Cyanimid, American Locomotive, American Radiator, Union Carbide, Vanadium, and Bethlehem Steel all employ an army of workmen.

Three power companies catered to the bulk of this rich area as late as 1928: as late as 1928 because the evolution of Niagara Hudson is an event so recent that it post-dates the Hoover-Smith campaign, the appearance of the "power issue," the Gann-Longworth controversy, and the Wickersham Commission. These were the three, in order of their size:

I.—*Buffalo, Niagara & Eastern:* operating in the western quarter of New York; controlled by the Schoellkopf family, whose fortune was founded in the years from 1850 to 1880 by Jacob Schoellkopf, German immigrant, tanner, miller, amateur hydroelectric engineer, experimenter with Edward Dean Adams in the first development of power at Niagara Falls. By 1928, Buffalo, Niagara & Eastern had grown from the unpretentious power company which Jacob Schoellkopf founded on the banks of the Niagara River to a vast corporation, controlling through one subsidiary the 452,000-horsepower hydroelectric plant installed on the American side of Niagara Falls; controlling through another subsidiary the 125,000-horsepower plant installed on the Canadian side; controlling through a third subsidiary the electric-light and power system which feeds Buffalo; manufacturing and distributing through these subsidiaries and others 4,400,000,000 kilowatt hours of electrical energy in 1928, the largest output of power marketed by any public utility in the U. S.

II.—*Mohawk Hudson:* organized as a holding company in 1925 by United Gas Improvement and General Electric (General Electric sold its stock in 1928); functioning chiefly in the industrial area around Schenectady; numbering among its directors in 1928 Owen D. Young and Nicholas F. Brady (son of the Anthony N. Brady who laid the cornerstone of the Brady fortune in the public utility business of Albany, Utica, and Cohoes); controlling as its subsidiaries in 1928 Utica Gas & Electric, Syracuse Lighting, and a string of smaller companies; marketing in this same year 1,100,000,000 kilowatt hours of electricity, at which point, among producers of power in the U. S., it stood sixteenth.

III.—*Northeastern Power:* controlled by the St. Regis Paper Company, with Floyd L. Carlisle as president; controlling in turn Power Corporation of New York and Northern New York Utilities; operating for the most part in the rugged, sparsely settled panhandle north of Utica between the St. Lawrence and the Mohawk Valley; standing thirty-seventh on the list of American utilities in point of power output with a production of 630,000,000 kilowatt hours.

In the eyes of the law, these three companies were still independent entities in 1928. Yet the same force of gravity which pulls apples from a tree, masked here as a common interest in low-cost sources of production, had already begun to pull them from their independent orbits into closer union. At certain times, Northeastern and Mohawk Hudson purchased Niagara power from their neighbor on the west, finding it cheaper than power generated in their own stations, and tapping the trunk lines of Buffalo,

Niagara & Eastern for this purpose with their transmission lines. At other times, when circumstances gave Mohawk Hudson and Northeastern an advantage in the matter of low costs, Buffalo, Niagara & Eastern willingly returned the compliment.

It is the first step in understanding the Niagara Hudson merger, as it is the first step in understanding all recent power mergers, to realize that the kilowatt hour is not a curio, not a collector's item, not a Chinese dollar good only in the province of its manufacture. It is, on the contrary, the most highly standardized and easily exchangeable of all products in the modern world: an invisible bit of energy easily transported from station to station over hundreds of miles and equally serviceable in Buffalo, Rochester, Syracuse, Schenectady, and Albany—or Honolulu, for that matter.

Well in advance of an actual merger, the power industry in the Niagara Hudson corridor had already arrived at a state bordering upon interlocking control, because a gradual drift in the direction of interlocking control is the inevitable drift in an industry which manufactures electrical energy.

What the corridor lacked in 1928 was not the rudiments of interlocking control but the benefits of unified command and an exchange of brains as well as of horsepower.

There is a myth, current to this day in certain newspaper offices and brokerage houses in New York City, that the negotiations which created one dominant company in place of three in the Niagara Hudson corridor were difficult negotiations, stubborn, long-drawn-out, and consummated in the end only by a Napoleonic effort. As a matter of fact, the negotiations preceding the organization of the new company were relatively swift and on the whole untroubled, requiring less than a month from start to finish, and for this ease and swiftness three factors are primarily responsible:

First, as we have already noted, the drift of affairs in the power industry was logically and inevitably in the direction of a closer union between three companies doing parallel business in contiguous territory. In the long run, it would actually have taken more effort and ingenuity to have prevented this merger than it took to achieve it.

Second, precisely at the time when the movement in the direction of a merger needed leadership and vision, it found large quantities of both in a banking house which was ready to act as *entrepreneur* in a month's swift negotiations. This banking house was J. P. Morgan & Co., which had entered the public utility field for the first time in its broad experience through the agency of United Corporation, incorporated as a holding company a few months before this time. United Corporation owned large blocks of Mohawk Hudson stock. Mohawk Hudson was one of the three component units in a merger.

Third, Northeastern Power, another of the three units, had at its head in 1928 a man with more than average drive and far more than average clairvoyance with respect to power opportunities and power mergers. This man was Floyd L. Carlisle, forty-seven years old in 1928, a product of Watertown, New York, a lawyer who turned banker and a banker who organized a syndicate in 1916 for the purpose of purchasing the great St. Regis Paper Company, which later became chief owner of Northeastern Power stock.

It is a fact of some importance in the present story, the story of a power merger, that Mr. Carlisle had been merging corporations all his life, from the time he started merging two small banks in Watertown, but it is a fact of more importance that he was able to foresee, from the start of his experience in the power industry, the advantages of interconnection and long-distance transportation.

The thin, steep rivers of the Adirondacks were regarded primarily as "logging streams" when Mr. Carlisle came into the power business via St. Regis—"logging streams" which offered good enough sites on which to erect paper mills, because pulpwood could be floated down to them in the spring months and power enough flowed over the waterfalls to operate the grinders. But this was all. The Adirondacks made no bid for distant power markets. Mr. Carlisle proposed to make a bid. In 1921, he proposed to build a new transmission line from the Adirondacks south to Utica. Bankers shook their heads. They told him he would sell no power. They likewise told him he would soon go broke. He did not go broke. He sold his power— so much power that in 1928, after almost a decade of Carlisle management, the power companies in the Adirondack area increased their output from 50,000,000 kilowatt hours of electrical energy to 600,000,000—a gain in ten years' time of approximately 1,100 per cent, fair enough, as percentages go, even in the glamorous annals of the power industry.

Given a man of Mr. Carlisle's faith in the development of power, at the head of one of the three pivotal companies in a prospective merger; given the influence of J. P. Morgan & Co., exerted through a second of the three pivotal companies; given a logical drift within the industry itself in favor of expanding ownership and unified control—and the result is inevitable.

An incident in the summer of 1929 supplied the necessary impetus to action. This incident was a cash bid for the purchase of Buffalo, Niagara & Eastern made by a company outside the Niagara Hudson corridor, reported at the time to be the Associated Gas & Electric System. There were important men who had long been talking merger in all three companies within the corridor. Mr. Carlisle found them ready to talk in concrete terms. He found the House of Morgan a willing ally in the proposal for a merger and an expert counsel in the art of blending diverse interests.

So persuasive was the argument for early action that negotiations shortly simmered down to a question of the value to be placed upon the outstanding stock of the three existing companies. This question was solved (J. P. Morgan & Co. has large experience in finding a least common multiple for companies about to merge) by the decision to exchange four shares of the new company for each share of Buffalo, Niagara & Eastern stock, three and one-half shares for each share of Mohawk Hudson stock, and two and two-thirds shares for each share of Northeastern Power stock—with warrants for additional purchases in proportion. On these terms, more than 95 per cent of the outstanding stock of the old companies having been willingly deposited by its owners, the merger was declared effective.

Not, however, without a flurry in the headlines on the part of Demos. No real doubt of the legality of this merger existed, or could exist, in view of the fact that New York State had given its consent to mergers involving no less than 253 utility companies within the previous five years. Nevertheless, in the case of a merger of the present size and interest, the proprieties of the occasion required a *pro forma* gesture.

Accordingly, on the twenty-ninth of June, Governor Franklin D. Roosevelt wrote to State Attorney-General Ward, requesting his opinion on the legality of this affair— an inquiry to which Attorney-General Ward, being of a political party opposite to that of Governor Roosevelt and therefore mindful of his *p's* and *q's*, replied at the end of two weeks' deliberation that if the Governor really wished to know, he would be very glad to tell him.

The answer being "Yes," Mr. Ward affirmed in a second communication, dated the twenty-ninth of July, that he found the merger legal. Thereupon Governor Roosevelt ordered his own investigation of the merger, an investigation of which nothing more was heard.

Meantime the new company created by the merger had named itself Niagara Hudson Power Corporation and announced the terms of its financial set-up. A capital issue of 45,000,000 shares of stock was authorized, with a par value of $10 a share. Of this amount, 22,625,612 shares were issued in exchange for the shares of the older companies whose properties had been acquired. An additional 2,000,-000 shares, with warrants to buy common stock in future, was sold for $50,000,000 cash, of which $20,000,000 was allocated to capital and $30,000,000 to surplus.

No senior securities were issued, no debt created. The partners in the enterprise emerged from the negotiations with unaltered status, except that they now held slips of paper representing ownership in one new company instead of in three old ones. Since more than 95 per cent of the stock of the old companies had been exchanged, the great bulk of the ownership of the new company remained in the hands of the original investors in the power industry of the Niagara Hudson corridor.

These investors included 31,200 individuals and corporate organizations (the number is now 95,000) scattered throughout all forty-eight states and showing, as might be expected, a wide variety in the value of their holdings.

On the lower level stood a large number of small investors who had held stock in the old companies for years and a large number of small speculators who had bought it in a hurry on the rumor of a merger—an extremely profitable engagement in midsummer of 1929 if it was rightly timed; for these were still bull-market days, the best of all bull-market days, and under the spur of the inevitable talk of great things coming. Northeastern Power rose from 40 on the thirtieth of March to 73 on the twenty-first of August (the day when slips of paper were exchanged); Mohawk Hudson from 38 to 102; Buffalo, Niagara & Eastern from $61\frac{1}{8}$ to 120—an average gain of approximately 100 per cent in a period of twenty weeks.

Meantime, at the opposite extreme from marginal stock in the hands of small speculators, there were certain large blocks of stock securely held in hands where they were meant to stay. Eleven individuals or companies owned as much as 50,000 shares of Niagara Hudson stock when the company filed its first report. These eleven, in order of importance, were:

	Stock	Per Cent of Stock Outstanding
St. Regis Paper Company (*largest owner of Northeastern Power stock before the merger*)	4,240,370	16.5
Niagara Share Corporation (*the Schoellkopf interests*)	3,500,000	13.6
Aluminum Company of America (*owned stock in Buffalo, Niagara & Eastern, and also in Mohawk Hudson*)	2,500,000	9.7
United Gas Improvement (*stockholder in Mohawk Hudson*)	1,880,732	7.3
United Corporation (*stockholder in Mohawk Hudson*)......................	1,659,249	6.5
American Superpower (*allied with United Corporation*)	301,889	1.2
H. S. Lewis, Beaver Falls, New York (*Carlisle associate*)	236,666	0.9
M. J. Warner, Pine Orchard, Connecticut (*Mohawk Hudson*)....................	148,662	0.6
M. S. Warner, Watertown, New York (*Carlisle associate*)	145,873	0.6
F. M. Tait, Dayton, Ohio (*Brady associate; Mohawk Hudson*)	75,000	0.3
J. P. Morgan & Co..................	72,000	0.3

One fact which will be noted from this list of names is that no name is followed by a large enough block of shares to permit one stockholder or a group of two or three stockholders to command majority control. The board of directors chosen to manage the affairs of the new company was accordingly not a board representing a dominant clique, with a scattering of outsiders, but a board catholic enough in its personnel to represent all of the major interests allied in this new venture.

Floyd L. Carlisle was chairman of this board. His associates included three members of the Schoellkopf family, active in the management of the great property founded by the first Jacob Schoellkopf at the western end of the Niagara Hudson corridor—Alfred H., Paul A., and Jacob F. Jr.; and these representatives of large stockholders in Niagara Hudson: Harold Stanley (Morgan), George H. Howard (United Corporation), Arthur V. Davis (Aluminum), John E. Zimmermann (United Gas Improvement), George Roberts (Bonbright), and Landon Thorne (Bonbright and United Corporation).

Three circumstances are arresting in the make-up of this board:

First, its youth. The average age of these directors was fifty in 1929. (Compare this figure with sixty-two for U. S. Steel, fifty-eight for National City Bank, and sixty-one for New York Central.) Fifty is a low average for a corporation large enough to command assets of $750,000,000—an appropriately low average if that corporation is engaged in the young and still experimental business of transmitting superpower.

Second, its wide connections. Through United Corporation, American Superpower, Bonbright, and United Gas Improvement, this board is linked to the whole network of utilities which spans the eastern seaboard from Massachusetts to the Gulf of Mexico.

Third, its emphasis on engineering brains and experience in management as well as experience in banking—an interesting and significant fact in the case of a corporation with the many-sided business of Niagara Hudson.

This business includes the sale each year of 8,500,000,000

cubic feet of gas, manufactured in nine cities in the Niagara Hudson corridor. It includes the sale of by-products of this manufacture: upwards of 500,000 tons of coke a year, 1,000,000 gallons of benzol, 10,000,000 gallons of coal tar. It includes the planting of approximately 5,000,000 trees a year, on property belonging to Niagara Hudson in upstate New York, for the purpose of converting wasteland into timber and conserving water. It includes the operation of a system of 101 stores, selling to a wide market anything and everything that feeds on kilowatts: radios, waffle irons, washing machines, sewing machines, flatirons, toasters, egg cookers, corn poppers, fans, and coffee percolators.

All this, however, is mere side show. The main business of Niagara Hudson, the business which it was organized to carry on, the business in which the experience of its directors counts to best advantage, and the business in which it enjoys preëminence among all corporations in America, is the production and transmission of electric power.

Power in the modern world is the product of compressed steam or falling water. Steam is the commoner source in the case of most utilities, for the reason that great waterfalls are usually too far removed from great industrial markets to serve effectively as sources of electric power. Niagara Hudson, however, differs from the average utility at this point, as at others. Seven-eighths of the power it generated last year came not from steam, but from falling water. Whatever the comparative merits of the two sources, steam and water—on this point engineers will quarrel—the fact remains that 87.4 per cent of all Niagara Hudson's 1929 power came from water, that this is more than one-seventh of all the hydroelectric energy developed in the U. S., and that Niagara Hudson is incomparably the most important factor in the controversy over water power.

A map of New York State is a sufficient explanation of this situation. Rich markets in New York lie in exceptional proximity to power sources. At the west end of the Niagara Hudson corridor is the Niagara River, with an unbroken flow of 210,000 cubic feet of water a second and 6,000,000 horsepower in its rapids, falls, and gorge. In the center and at the east end of the corridor are steep rivers like the Salmon, Raquette, Black, Beaver, and upper Hudson, descending from the Adirondacks in swift torrents. On these rivers, Niagara Hudson has a battery of ninety-three electric generating stations, and the battery of ninety-three is constantly increasing in number and in power.

As evidence of this increase, consider the case history of the great Schoellkopf Station, named in honor of the first experimenter with hydroelectric power at Niagara Falls.

Twenty years ago, the old generating units of 1,200 horsepower at this station were replaced by modern units of 10,000 horsepower. Thirteen of these units came in the course of time to squat in a row in Schoellkopf Station, black toadstools capable of producing a total of 130,000 horsepower. This was a good deal of power, but not enough for the expanding business of the Niagara Hudson corridor.

Three more toadstools came to join the family, still larger toadstools, adding 110,000 horsepower to the Schoellkopf Station. This brought the total to 240,000. It was still too small. New factories were coming to the corridor, attracted largely by the availability of cheap power. New industries, such as the manufacture of aluminum, were developing new uses for electrical energy. Once more the battery at Schoellkopf Station was expanded. The latest installation consists of three gigantic units of 70,000 horsepower, bringing the total installation to 450,000 horsepower. At this point Schoellkopf Station is not only the largest single hydroelectric station in Niagara Hudson's battery of ninety-three. It is the largest single hydroelectric station in the U. S.

Oddly enough, seventeen miles from Schoellkopf sits the largest single steam-electric plant in the Niagara Hudson system, the Huntley Station on the north side of Buffalo. It is, apparently, an odd coincidence. Why should the largest coal-burning plant in the Niagara Hudson system be built on the very banks of the river which supplies the largest hydroelectric plant, actually using for steam condensation the same torrential water that passes later through the penstocks and the turbines of the great Schoellkopf Station?

For a variety of reasons. First, because Huntley Station was originally built as an ace-in-the-hole, to supplement the hydroelectric output of Schoellkopf in periods of great demand; second, because no additional water from Niagara Falls has been available for hydroelectric development in recent years, due to the failure of the Senate of the U. S. to ratify a pending treaty with the government of Canada; third, because industry in the Niagara Hudson corridor has continued to expand, Senate or no Senate, and to clamor for more power.

Huntley Station has today an installed capacity of 308,000 horsepower developed entirely by steam, as against Schoellkopf's 450,000 horsepower developed entirely by water, but like the rest of the Niagara Hudson system, Huntley is growing larger. Recently three new steam turbogenerators with powdered fuel boilers (of a type Niagara Hudson engineers have been pioneers in developing) were installed. These three generators, with an aggregate capacity of 314,-000 horsepower, brought the total installation at Huntley to 622,000 horsepower. At this point, it outmatched even Schoellkopf in the power it is capable of producing.

By midsummer of 1931, these new turbines were operating at capacity, supplementing the hydroelectric output of Schoellkopf with power made by steam. Whether they will continue to operate at full capacity will depend upon a variety of factors, including the Senate's second thoughts about the Niagara River treaty and the continued expansion of business in the territory of Niagara Hudson.

We begin, then, with a great chain of ninety-three hydroelectric stations, including the largest hydroelectric station in the U. S.—Schoellkopf Station at Niagara. We find these ninety-three stations producing 87.4 per cent of the total power output of the Niagara Hudson system. We find the remaining 12.6 per cent produced by steam: chiefly at Huntley Station, but also at five lesser stations in Albany, Amsterdam, Lyons, Utica, and Deferiet. We find the grand total of power produced by steam and water sufficient to generate 6,000,000,000 kilowatt hours a year—at which point Niagara Hudson becomes the greatest producer of power and the greatest merchant of electrical energy in the U. S.

The medium through which it serves as merchant is a superpower system of transmission lines, symbolized for the average man by the tall steel towers that loom up suddenly with a shoulderful of wires on a quiet country road. This superpower system is amazingly complete. Every one of the ninety-nine steam and hydroelectric plants which develop power for Niagara Hudson is interconnected with every one of the ninety-eight others by transmission lines owned by the company itself.

From Buffalo on the west, these lines lead east across the state to Syracuse, at some points three abreast, at some points four, at others five. At Syracuse, they branch: one line swinging north to tie in hydro stations on the west slope of the Adirondacks; the other continuing east to Albany, then turning south, as if to cast a loving eye in the direction of still larger markets, for a distance of thirty miles along the Hudson. Scattered throughout the system are switching stations which serve as its nerve centers, receiving power from the main trunk lines, reducing it in voltage, and sending it out again along minor distribution lines to the 648,679 patrons of Niagara Hudson who are its ultimate consumers.

It is, on the whole, a comparatively new system, built for the most part within the last ten years, and constantly becoming newer as fresh strands are woven into it. For an electrical transmission system is one of the instruments of modern industry which is never more than half completed. New markets develop the need for additional facilities. New experiments devise safer and more economical means of carrying power at high voltages. Aluminum is now replacing copper on many of the more important circuits of Niagara Hudson. Twenty-one million dollars was allotted for 1931's expenditures on new trunk lines and substations. One section of the main line east of Albany (between the villages of Thomson and Greenbush) has been "lightning-proofed" by a new arrangement of porcelain insulators and more widely spaced ground wires, worked out by engineers who play light-heartedly with lightning in the laboratories of General Electric.

Most interesting, however, of all new additions to the transmission system of Niagara Hudson is the construction of a new transmission line from Greenbush (east of Albany) as far south along the Hudson River as Peekskill. For this new line, pushing well beyond the most southern outpost of the older lines, is intended to prepare the way for a dramatic step in the history of Niagara Hudson: an interconnection between its own upstate power plants and the greatest of all power markets—New York City.

Such interconnection between upstate power and downstate demand was logical from the first in theory and became inevitable in fact, once Niagara Hudson had consolidated the upstate power companies into an alliance capable of delivering power to New York City under unified control.

Picture for a moment the geography of the state. East and west across the upstate counties runs the Niagara Hudson corridor, containing the great industrial cities of Buffalo, Rochester, Syracuse, Utica, Schenectady, Albany, and Troy. This is Niagara Hudson territory.

South of this territory lies a tier of rural counties with the sleeping towns of Binghamton, Oswego, and Elmira its chief cities. This tier of rural counties is not served by Niagara Hudson but by Associated Gas & Electric, with a system of transmission lines that pricks the Niagara Hudson corridor only at one point—Rochester. On the map, Associated Gas & Electric looks like a Chinese Wall between the upstate corridor and New York City. But Associated Gas & Electric does not serve the great upstate industrial centers. It has no power sources comparable with Niagara Hudson's in the Adirondacks. Once Niagara Hudson had consolidated the existing power companies in the corridor, once it had linked Niagara River with the Hudson, it was inevitable that it should turn south, pierce the Chinese Wall as if it were a piece of cardboard, and round out a single interconnected system feeding both the upstate and the downstate markets of industrial New York.

A series of events beginning approximately eight months after the organization of Niagara Hudson foreshadowed this conclusion. First United Corporation (holder, as we have seen, of a large block of Niagara Hudson stock) acquired an interest in the stock of Consolidated Gas, which in turn controls New York Edison.

Next Floyd L. Carlisle, chairman of the board of Niagara Hudson, was elected a trustee of Consolidated Gas, a director of New York Edison, and a director of United Corporation. Then, in February, 1931, Mr. Carlisle, still retaining his chairmanship of Niagara Hudson, was elected chairman of New York Edison. Finally, in March, came definite announcement of the plan to link both systems through the construction of new trunk lines which will meet at Peekskill. These trunk lines will be built through territory south along the Hudson River, served by Central Hudson Gas & Electric Co., with which Niagara Hudson stands on friendly terms and in which it owns a minority interest.

Actual interconnection between Niagara Hudson and New York Edison was to be effected before the end of 1931.

Both companies will benefit from an exchange of power. For New York Edison, which now generates all of its power at steam plants in its great tidewater stations, will find in the hydroelectric power of Niagara Hudson insurance against a future increase in the cost of coal; and Niagara Hudson, with an excess of hydroelectric power at certain seasons of the year, will have at hand a mighty market for its surplus.

How much power will actually be exchanged between the two systems will depend upon the comparative cost of steam and hydro development, upon the possible construction of new hydro stations in the Adirondacks, and upon the question of what future use is made of the vast power that still lies undeveloped in the extreme northeastern corner of the state—the much-discussed and much-debated power now running to waste on the St. Lawrence.

This question of St. Lawrence power brings us to a new type of question which confronts Niagara Hudson. If kilowatts were overshoes or razor blades and Niagara Hudson were engaged, like nine corporations out of ten, in the manufacture and distribution of some such modest but worthwhile utensil, it might be enough at this point to suggest that the feat of linking New York City to the Adirondacks is an accurate index of the energy and vision of a young company which has still to celebrate its second birthday. The story of Niagara Hudson is, however, in no way the story of an average corporation. Fate made Niagara Hudson not in the form of a manufacturer of overshoes or razor blades, but in the form of a public utility corporation, equipped with special problems belonging to no other industry. One of the largest of these problems, in the case of Niagara Hudson, is the St. Lawrence.

For Niagara Hudson finds itself at the present moment functioning as a privately owned utility in a state in which "public ownership of St. Lawrence power" has become one of the most insistent slogans of the Democratic party, and Niagara Hudson is not remote from this controversy over St. Lawrence power. It is squarely in the middle of it. For in September, 1929, in the second month of its existence, Niagara Hudson acquired, in return for 317,000 shares of its own stock, the property of the Frontier Corporation.

What was the Frontier Corporation? A landholding company organized in 1914 by the Mellon interests, General Electric, and du Pont. The Frontier Corporation owned some pastures. It also owned some cows. It owned very little else. But the important fact about its ownership was this: its pastures lay along six miles of water front on the St. Lawrence River, precisely at the point where the rapids of this river are capable of developing 2,000,000 horsepower—four times the power now installed at Schoellkopf Station on Niagara. The farsighted Mellon interests had acquired the major portion of these water-front pastures a quarter of a century earlier. Frontier Corporation claimed, and Niagara Hudson reasserts the claim, that under Anglo-Saxon law the right to the use of water for power purposes resides in the owner of the banks, and dares any three lawyers in the country to say them nay. The cows are unimportant.

Niagara Hudson, therefore, is precisely in the storm center of a controversy which has been a turbulent factor in New York politics ever since Alfred E. Smith was first elected Governor in 1918. The traditional attitude of the power companies toward this controversy has consisted of opposing any and all proposals for the development of St. Lawrence power through a public agency. Niagara Hudson broke with this tradition. The new company was less than a month old when the chairman of its board announced to the press on September 17, 1929, that Niagara Hudson was ready to coöperate with the State of New York in any development of the St. Lawrence which promised to bring 2,000,000 latent horsepower into operation with the least delay.

This offer he has repeated on five occasions subsequently, going so far as to declare specifically in the first annual report of Niagara Hudson to its stockholders that "while your company would itself undertake development of St. Lawrence power upon fair and generous terms, yet it will consider any and all other plans, particularly that of having the development made by a state-owned corporation, the power to be marketed under contract by our operating companies." "Any and all other plans," of course, as Mr. Carlisle has made clear, must provide adequately for the vested interests Niagara Hudson enjoys in its six miles of cow pasture and the ancient Anglo-Saxon doctrine of riparian rights.

Niagara Hudson, nevertheless, declares its responsibility in this question to be not the settlement on its own terms of a vexed question in state politics, but the distribution on fair terms to itself, to New York State, and to its own consumers of cheap power from whatever source it comes and by whatever agency it is manufactured.

The question of St. Lawrence power is the stormiest of the various politico-economic questions which have confronted Niagara Hudson in its first two years. It is not the only question. There is criticism of the utilities on the score of the complex financial structure which results from the merging of companies created by mergers of still other companies. There is more criticism of utilities (read the records of state legislatures) on the part of spokesmen for rural districts who insist that the average utility is interested solely in catering to the manufacturer and the city men, and that it skimps its service to the farmer. There is the brisk dispute which is now in progress (in New York, as in other states) over the desirability or the undesirability of financing public utility operations through the new medium of holding companies. There is the large question of rates and regulations.

If Niagara Hudson were asked to write its ticket on each of these widely and somewhat bitterly debated points, the result would be somewhat as follows:

I.—*Re mergers:* It is the policy of Niagara Hudson to eliminate intermediary holding companies from its system and to concentrate responsibility in three operating companies which are already functioning logically along geographical lines, in total disregard of the boundaries of previously existing companies. On this point, the 1931 report of the corporation to its stockholders asserts that "the confusion which has prevailed in the security markets has delayed progress in the plan for simplifying your system's financial structure." (Among other things, such simplification involves refinancing; 1930, with its depressed and confused security markets, was a very poor year to finance anything.) The corporation stated, however, that it expected at a later date to be able to carry out this program.

II.—*Re farmers:* It is the stated aim of Niagara Hudson "to bring electricity to every farm within its territory which it is economical to serve." This, the directors of the company would insist, is not mere theory. Niagara Hudson has developed a plan (the "Adirondack Plan," first formulated by one of its subsidiaries) whereby farmers are not required to contribute to the cost of constructing transmission lines to serve them (the usual practice in the case of small utilities), but are merely asked to guarantee a monthly use of service sufficient to make the extension yield a fair return.

Under this plan, Niagara Hudson is steadily reaching out beyond the suburbs. In 1930 the company built 860 miles of rural lines. It added 3,764 farmers to its clientele. It sold so much electric light and power on 20,000 upstate farms that in a year when its total sales decreased by 6 per cent (result of the business depression of 1930), its sales to farmers increased by 35 per cent.

III.—*Re holding companies:* The directors of Niagara Hudson are not living in an ivory tower and are not unaware of current criticism of this comparatively modern innovation in the field of public utility finance. A commission created in 1929 by the New York Legislature has recently recommended that the state public service law be extended to cover holding companies. A minority of this commission characterized holding companies as mere instruments for inflating capitalization and declared that in the case of Niagara Hudson, the actual inflation amounted to $145,000,000.

Vigorously combatting this criticism, the directors of Niagara Hudson volubly assert their faith in the merit of holding companies and frankly state their policies.

It is the position of these directors that the holding company is the only effective means of providing the immense amounts of capital annually required for the expansion of utilities; that unless this instrument had been developed, many smaller communities and thinly populated areas would be without electric service; that in the case of Niagara Hudson, the fair value of the properties involved far and away exceeds the increased value at which they were recapitalized following the mergers; and that the holding company is too useful an institution to be hampered by legislation regulating its securities and thereby limiting the free flow of capital into the utilities. Niagara Hudson, however, unlike most holding companies, has ruled out management, engineering, or similar fees as a source of income from their subsidiaries, and has canceled the charge of 5 per cent on gross income which Buffalo, Niagara & Eastern had previously levied on its subsidiaries.

It is along these lines that the debate over holding companies has progressed; along these lines, it will certainly continue.

IV.—Finally, *re rates and regulation:* It is the announced policy of Niagara Hudson to *lower* the cost of electrical energy to a point commensurate with a "fair return" on the "value" of its property. This, of course, remains in the realm of theory until "fair return" and "value" are determined. It insists that the calculation of a fair return must take account of reproduction cost as an element in determining rates. In its balance sheets, however, it continues to base the value of its properties on the par value of the stock issued in exchange for the securities of the acquired companies—about $77,000,000 more than their previously stated value.

Rates at the present time vary with the amount of power used. Niagara Hudson served an average of 640,542 customers in 1930. The main groups of these customers, the amount of power sold to them, the revenue received, and average rate paid by each group follows:

	Average Number Customers	Kilowatt Hours Sold	Revenue	Average Rate per Kilowatt Hour
FARMERS	22,079	15,272,211	$1,033,060.04	6.76 cents
CITY HOMES	525,171	330,212,374	15,874,991.89	4.81
OFFICE BUILDINGS, STORES, ETC.	88,576	469,790,127	14,465,820.70	3.08
MANUFACTURERS	3,806	4,408,309,234	25,908,557.43	.58
ALL OTHERS (*including other power companies*)	919	908,095,299	9,865,074.61	1.09
TOTAL	640,551	6,131,679,245	$67,147,504.67	1.09 cents

It will be noted from this table that while people using electricity to light city homes form the vast majority of Niagara Hudson's clientele (525.171 customers out of a grand total of 640,551), these people use only a small part of the total power output—330,000,000 kilowatt hours, less than 6 per cent. The great bulk of Niagara Hudson's power goes from its giant turbines into manufacturing.

It will also be noted that the manufacturer who uses the bulk of Niagara Hudson's power pays a far lower rate for it than the householder pays for the lighting of his home— 5.8 *mills* against 4.8 *cents*. Niagara Hudson justifies this spread by pointing out that it costs less to serve a few large customers than many small ones (less meter-reading, less cost of installation, etc.) and that low rates to large industrial customers are necessary if full use is to be made of the vast equipment of Niagara Hudson, with resulting economies of operation. If power were manufactured solely for small customers who use less than 6 per cent of it, its cost would be prohibitive.

Even at 4.8 cents a kilowatt hour, Niagara Hudson claims, however, that its rates for residential lighting are low: among the lowest rates of any of the larger power companies in the U. S. (the average for the country as a whole is 6.04) and lower by 4 per cent in 1930 than in 1929, as the result of reductions made without duress on the part of any governmental agency.

Moreover, Niagara Hudson points to these two facts: first, that its rate for power of all kinds (commercial as well as residential) is less than half the average rate for the country as a whole (1.09 cents against 2.68) and second, that since the date of its creation, it has never been involved in an important rate case—a record indicating, in its judgment, some measure of satisfaction on the part of its large public.

In the story of Niagara Hudson, we arrive at the point from which we started, the fact that in the peerage of American business this company has certain sharp distinctions. These distinctions we now know to be access to abundant water power, complete interconnections of ninety-nine producing stations, prosperous and varied markets, a hook-up of the greatest hydroelectric system in the country with the greatest steam-electric system, potential exchange of power with other systems ranging along the whole Atlantic seaboard.

The structure of Niagara Hudson is not complete. Its development is still experimental. It is too soon to predict the results of a pooling of power between Niagara Hudson and New York Edison. The question of St. Lawrence power remains a riddle bound up in the even more perplexing riddle of water-power economy vs. steam-power economy. It is impossible to measure the full effect of economies resulting from interconnection (past and future) of great power systems: economies in management and finance, in a greater conservation of resources, in averaging the different "loads" of different communities, and in avoiding duplication of emergency equipment, since the pooling of power makes it possible to reduce reserve facilities.

Of this much, however, we may be certain: that the physical equipment of Niagara Hudson is unmatched anywhere in the U. S.; that its financial position is secure; that it has derived great strength, and will derive more strength in the future, from its alliance with the House of Morgan; and that it has found in Floyd L. Carlisle the boldest pioneer who has appeared in the field of public utility enterprise in many years.

No industry in America is working today with finer tools. Here is every asset needed for a demonstration of the worth of modern superpower.

TO PAUSE AND
BE REFRESHED

... is a Basic Need of the South, a Need
to Which Coca-Cola Lovingly Ministers
With 9,500,000 Drinks a Day. How the
Sugar Goes into Solution, Solving Also
the Problems of Men and Machines—
and Leaving a Thirty-eight-cent Profit
Per Dollar of Sales

THE COCA-COLA COMPANY

⟨∾∾⟩

OFF the lobby of Atlanta's Candler Building (one of the many "largest" office buildings in the South) is located a small store. It would be a drug store if it sold any drugs and a candy store if it sold more candy, but it is mainly a soda fountain surrounded by floor space. The soda fountain is small—soda fountains cost $150 a foot—but it brings in considerably more than half the store's income. The overwhelming sales leader, both in drinks and in dollars, is Coca-Cola. Every month the customers down seven forty-one gallon barrels of Coca-Cola syrup. As there are more than 100 drinks to the gallon, sales run to 28,000 a month, or more than 900 drinks a day. Furthermore, the little Candler Building shop makes about $750 monthly profit on Coca-Cola alone and figures that, no matter what else may happen, Coca-Cola can always be relied upon to pay the rent. The one requirement for Coca-Cola profit is volume, and in Atlanta the steady sale of Coca-Cola is hardly more than a matter of meeting a strong and continuous demand.

Throughout the Southeast, indeed, sufficient Coca-Cola is sold to supply every man, woman, and child with one Coca-Cola a week. In the country as a whole, each male and each female consumes about one Coca-Cola every two weeks. Even this national average is figured from a daily consumption of nearly 10,000,000 Coca-Colas—a consumption which makes Coca-Cola incomparably the largest selling trade-marked beverage in the world. But in the South, Coca-Cola is not so much a drink as an institution. Following the American habit for nicknames, they call it "dope" and "coke" (terms which greatly distressed the late Asa Candler). They offer it to the northern visitor with slightly apologetic enthusiasm. They do not drink it much at meals (except perhaps at lunch), and it is no more evident in the dining room of the Atlanta Biltmore than in the dining room of the Manhattan Biltmore. But they like it; they like it every day and many of them like it several times a day. It is the great between-meals drink of the South. It is also (shades of the mint julep) the great convivial drink (at least between dawn and dusk), and common is the spectacle of a half-dozen southern gentlemen seated at a table in one of the many Nunnally candy stores, discussing the cotton crop while the rounds of Coca-Cola come and go. Nor is such a sign an indication that warm southern blood has congealed. No one can subsist throughout the day on hard liquor, and though the South is by no means bone-dry, a drink that is neither expensive nor intoxicating has obviously much to recommend it as the staple liquid of the business day. Like coffee to the South American, like tea to the Englishman, Coca-Cola is the cup that cheers but does not inebriate. Its advertising slogan, *The pause that refreshes*, has in it much truth. For the Southerner exhibits an inexhaustible capacity for pausing and an equally inexhaustible capacity for being refreshed. To both these basic needs, Coca-Cola lovingly ministers.

It is indeed the psychology of the South (not the climate

of the South) that makes Coca-Cola so typically a southern drink. This is not to say that the empire of Coca-Cola is roughly conterminous with the empire of the boll weevil. Coca-Cola sells nearly as well in Montreal as in New Orleans, is making gratifying progress in seventy-six foreign countries, and winter sales equal about two-thirds the summer volume. Coca-Cola men see nothing sectional in their beverage, and feel that in the course of time, effort, and advertising the per capita consumption in New York and in Boston may at least approach the per capita consumption in Memphis and Mobile. They may be right, and they need to be only a little bit right to increase tremendously the 30,000,000 gallon sales which made 1930 their all-time record year. But although the New South is not much like the Old South, though the Ku Klux Klan has given way to a feeble successor known as the White Legion, there remains a marked difference between the southern and the northern way of life.

Atlanta itself flaunts little of its southern character in its physical appearance. Ponce de Leon Avenue and Peachtree Street are picturesque names for picturesque avenues; and spring comes early in Atlanta, where the pink and the white dogwood blossoms are in flower at a time when the Northerner is still encompassed by drizzle and fog. But Druid Hills (now perhaps Atlanta's choicest residential section) looks much like Walnut Hills in Cincinnati or Chestnut Hill in Philadelphia. The town is dotted with the Atlantic & Pacific Stores, which would be exactly alike on either the Atlantic or the Pacific. There is a Ford plant and a Chevrolet plant and a Sears, Roebuck warehouse. Entertainment in Atlanta, as elsewhere, is recorded chiefly by the Western Electric Co. With the notable exception of the southern feminine voice—a voice which makes the telephone a musical instrument—the visitor to the South has no overpowering physical evidence of being on the underneath side of Mason and Dixon's famous boundary. But when he begins to deal commercially with the Southerner, when he changes from onlooker to participant, he is immediately conscious of a notable difference in what may best be called the tempo of existence.

Not that the Southerner is lazy. On the contrary, he is a galloping enthusiast: an excess of gallop with respect to horses, women, and real estate amounting almost to a regional hazard. But, as far as possible, he adjusts the labors of existence to the amenities of existence. He walks down the street. He meets a friend. He knocks his friend's hat over his friend's eye—Southerners are continually punching each other—and arm in arm they turn to the nearest fountain (which is never distant) and make a small contribution to Coca-Cola's income account. So also with the office day of the Southerner. The custom of a morning and an afternoon recess for office employees is so firmly established that many Southern companies officially concede the privilege, granting each employee two ten-minute periods in which to pause and be refreshed. When one Atlanta corporation withdrew this concession, long and bitter was employee resentment. Indeed, there was finally a compromise whereby the office porter was sent to the lobby fountain at 10:00 A.M. and again at 4:00 P.M., on each occasion returning with enough Coca-Cola to supply each desk with one bottle. Doubtless the Southerner does as much work as the Northerner—it is, after all, a Georgian and Coca-Colan who has provided the astonishing precedent of simultaneously directing two large corporations, situated 600 miles apart. Certainly the southern office-worker, deprived of his innocent tipple, would experience a notable disintegration of morale. Yet whether the northern office-manager will ever be converted to the merit of the refreshment interval is extremely dubious. And it is precisely this interval, and the attitude of mind supporting it, which makes Coca-Cola so profitable in southern office buildings, which supplies Coca-Cola with fertile soil wherein to flourish.

Let us reiterate, however, our previous statement that Coca-Cola has sold, is selling, and will continue to sell in northern communities. It is indeed for sale at all but about a half dozen of the country's 110,000 soda fountains, and is dispensed by 800,000 bottle purveyors—a perfection of distribution which certainly establishes its national status. Yet though it has come out of the South, it is essentially a southern drink; and the Southland will always be its homeland, no matter how far and how flourishing its travels. Arabs of the desert pause for Coca-Cola in the shadow of the Sphinx. East Indians refresh themselves with Coca-Cola, and Coca-Cola effervesces also on Shanghai bars. In western Europe, Coca-Cola lemonade (lemonade is the generic term for the soft drink, but by it is meant what in this country would be called lemon soda) is rapidly developing into a best-seller. But in New Orleans last Mardi gras, thirsty celebrants consumed 500,000 drinks of Coca-Cola in a single twenty-four hours; and on the day after Mardi gras, Coca-Cola bottlers reclaimed 17,000 cases of Coca-Cola "empties." It will take many a year and many a billboard before the Northerner or the foreigner deposits such offerings at the Coca-Cola shrine.

Coca-Cola was born in 1886, fathered by Dr. J. S. Pemberton, Atlanta patent-medicine maker. The soft drink in general has somewhat a proprietary remedy background; Moxie (a drink older than Coca-Cola, though not so flourishing) was first sold as a "nerve food," and carbonated water itself was for some generations a medicine before it became chiefly a soda. It is hard to say what influenced Dr. Pemberton to turn from medicine to refreshment. The first ice cream soda had been made in 1874 when a Philadelphia druggist, accidentally dropping ice cream into soda, discovered that the combination was an improvement, but not until 1876 did the Centennial Exposition make the ice cream soda famous. Bottled soda was widely dispensed (it was called "pop" because the cork of its bottle, when knocked in by the imbiber, made a loud "pop"), but it was notably synthetic and grudgingly accepted. The bottling business, too, was something of a back-yard affair with much to be desired in the way of capital investment and operating cleanliness. But Dr. Pemberton patiently experimented with extracts, oils, and essences, and patiently took the results of his labors to Venable's soda fountain where customers sampled the beverage and freely suggested alterations and improvements. At length the doctor achieved a blend of which he and friends approved; a business associate, one F. M. Robinson, christened the concoction Coca-Cola, and the manufacture of Coca-Cola, on a small and tentative scale, was begun.

It consisted (and consists) chiefly of sugar and water,

plus an assortment of fruit flavors so thoroughly blended that no trace remained of any individual component and the resulting taste belonged to Coca-Cola alone. Even the syrup from which Coca-Cola is made consists of up to 99 per cent sugar and water. As one ounce of this syrup is diluted with five ounces of carbonated water for the finished drink, it will be seen that the customer swallows some 599 parts of sugar and water to one part of essential ingredients.

Yet Coca-Cola was at one period regarded as harmful and habit-forming, the late Dr. Harvey Wiley even prodding the U. S. Government into a Pure Food suit against it, for in addition to caramel, fruit flavors and phosphoric acid, Coca-Cola also contained caffeine, derived partly from tea, coffee, or chocolate, and partly from a mysterious ingredient known as "Merchandise No. 5," which constitutes the "secret" portion of Coca-Cola's "secret formula." "Merchandise No. 5" consists of about three parts coca leaves (decocanized) to one part cola nuts. Innumerable analyses have demonstrated that the beverage is free from questionable drugs. The government's attack centering upon caffeine as an allegedly harmful and allegedly added ingredient. Coca-Cola makers cheerfully concede the caffeine content, admit that in a glass of Coca-Cola there is from one-fourth to one-third as much caffeine as in a cup of coffee. But caffeine is an essential, not an added ingredient; has always been an integral portion of the beverage; belongs in Coca-Cola just as it belongs in, for example, coffee, tea, cocoa and chocolate. Thus the prosecution failed and in the course of fighting the suit Coca-Cola took its case through the U. S. Supreme Court and established many basic precedents for trade-mark laws as they now exist. There remains some popular prejudice (so that, as one Coca-Cola official regretfully conceded: "A child probably enters the Coca-Cola market about five years after entering the soft drink market"), but on the whole the tempest in the coffeepot has pretty well subsided.

Meanwhile, let us return to Dr. Pemberton. Only twenty-five gallons of Coca-Cola were sold in 1886. In 1887, the doctor, no good business man, sold a two-thirds interest in his drink for the sum of $283.29. The purchasers, however, were equally guiltless of a prophetic strain, and for some years the rights to Coca-Cola were carelessly hawked about Atlanta. Creditors settled bills with an interest in the company; wholesale and retail druggists took Coca-Cola stock in return for supplies furnished; soon there were many Coca-Cola stockholders, but few with enthusiasm concerning their investment. In 1889, Dr. Pemberton died, orphaned his beverage. Meanwhile, however, one Asa Griggs Candler, of Walker & Candler, Atlanta druggists, had secured an interest in Coca-Cola. Here was one man who realized the possibilities of the beverage. Collecting, without much difficulty, the various scattered Coca-Cola holdings, he became first the majority-interest and finally, in 1892, the sole owner.

For the next twenty-seven years, Coca-Cola was strictly a Candler enterprise, and under Mr. Candler it throve mightily. One Samuel Candler Dobbs, nephew of Mr. Candler, supplied the selling and advertising genius, and to Mr. Dobbs the major credit for Coca-Cola expansion is usually given. It was he who plastered the countryside with Coca-Cola billboards and painted walls (the company is today one of the world's largest paint-users); who developed Coca-Cola cut-outs, fountain decorations, signs, and other "point of purchase" advertising. Coca-Cola sales neared $500,000 in 1898; approached $1,000,000 in 1902. By 1907, they had risen to $3,300,000, and during the next ten years to $15,700,000. By this time, however, War restrictions on sugar were beginning to be reflected, and though sales subsequently skyrocketed in 1919, profit lagged tardily behind volume.

The company was suffering from ingrowing executives. The owner was Asa Candler. The president was Son Charles Howard Candler. The vice president was Nephew Samuel Dobbs. The secretary and treasurer was Son William Candler. In 1919, the home office staff, including stenographers, janitor, and executives, totaled exactly thirty-three persons, though during this year Coca-Cola, already nationally distributed, took in nearly $25,000,000. At executive conferences old Asa Candler, able but conservative, would listen to some proposed change, some suggested expansion, and then, with his eyes gleaming behind steel-rimmed spectacles, and his thin, narrow mouth thinner and narrower than ever, remark, "I vote 479 shares (out of 500 shares outstanding) against that." Since Mr. Candler thus voted more than 90 per cent of the outstanding stock, his remarks concluded all discussions. The company also lacked a sales organization in the modern sense of the word. Between Sales Manager Dobbs and a salesman in, for instance, Seattle, there was hardly anything except large stretches of geography. If the Seattle man concentrated on decorating hotel lobbies, it took a long while for his dereliction to show in sales and for his replacement with another man who might easily repeat the same process.

Furthermore, Mr. Candler founded no dynasty. Son Asa Candler Jr. was never connected with Coca-Cola. Son Walter also avoided the paternal factory, devoted himself chiefly to trotting horses, of which he had (and has) a notable assortment. Sons William and Charles Howard were, as we have seen, Coca-Cola executives by inheritance.

In September, 1919, this situation resulted in the sale of Coca-Cola to a group of Georgia capitalists, aided somewhat by Manhattan capital. Dominant in the purchasing group was Ernest Woodruff, then and now as the world knows, an outstanding financier of the South; Atlanta banks and street railways; the Atlanta Ice & Coal Corp. (one of the largest ice and coal companies in the world); the Continental Gin Co. (cotton); Atlantic Steel Co.,—these and many other southern businesses were developed with Mr. Woodruff's energetic assistance. Associated with him in the Coca-Cola purchase was William Clark Bradley, of Columbus, Georgia, and Georgia-born Eugene William Stetson, of Manhattan's Guaranty Trust. Mr. Candler received $10,000,000 in cash and $15,000,000 in preferred stock (since retired), the $25,000,000 purchase representing the most notable transaction in strictly southern history. Mr. Candler then withdrew from Coca-Cola, devoting himself to charitable and personal enterprises which, however interesting, have little place in the present discussion. In 1929, Mr. Candler died in a hospital founded by his Coca-Cola money, and in a room overlooking the campus of a college (Emory University) which was also chiefly the result of his philanthropy.

Following the transition from Candler to Woodruff control (for although the new proprietors made public stock distribution, the Woodruff family is still the majority interest), there came an intermediate period during which old executives carried on. Mr. Dobbs and Mr. Howard Candler, first presidents under the new ownership, are still Coca-Cola directors. They were succeeded, in April 1923, by Robert Winship Woodruff, son of Ernest Woodruff and also vice president of White Motors. With the arrival of the younger Mr. Woodruff, management and ownership were at last united, and beginning with 1924 every Coca-Cola year has established a new record of sales and of profits. In 1930, sales totaled $34,580,493, with a net profit of $13,088,616. These figures are remarkable in that they represent about a 5 per cent increase over the boom year of 1929. They are even more remarkable, however, in that the percentage of profit to sales reached the astounding ratio of 38 per cent. Even with an advertising bill of about $5,000,000, Coca-Cola saved as profit about 38 cents on every dollar of gross sales. Thus before further discussion of Coca-Cola's present management, it is desirable to examine briefly its virtually unique position in the manufacturing world.

It would be impossible to overstate the simplicity of Coca-Cola production. There exists no labor problem. At the Atlanta plant, which makes about 25 per cent of Coca-Cola's annual 30,000,000 gallons of syrup, there are less than seventy-five laborers. Most of these men make not syrup but barrels to contain it, the lack of good barrel-making facilities in Atlanta forcing the company reluctantly into the barrel business. With the exception of a few chemists who analyze syrup samples to see that they remain uniform, Coca-Cola labor is totally unskilled. Should every Coca-Cola workman walk out tomorrow morning, Mr. Woodruff need only stand on his front steps, whistle, and have a complete force operating in the afternoon.

Nor is there any major investment in machinery to consume power and to depreciate. Sugar arrives in bags, is dumped into 2,500 gallon tanks of city water, and thereupon, in accordance with the inscrutable laws of Nature, goes into solution. When the sugar is dissolved, the vital ingredients are added in the proper proportions and mixed, the resulting syrup is poured into barrels, kegs, and gallon containers, and the freight cars in Coca-Cola's back yard start the beverage toward its various destinations. The Atlanta Coca-Cola plant, located in a residential district (a few doors from the Georgia Tech buildings), looks much more like an engineering school or a university than like a factory. It has no noise; it has no dirt. It sweats not, neither does it roar. Waiting for the sugar to go into solution is the major operation in the Coca-Cola plant.

Neither is fluctuation in the price of sugar now a potential menace. Current low-priced sugar adds to the company's profit; bulging are the sugar stocks stored at the Atlanta plant alone. But low commodity prices are not always a manufacturing boon, as woolen, tire, and shoe manufacturers will eloquently testify. The standard selling price of five cents per glass (or bottle) is the decisive factor in freeing Coca-Cola from inventory worries. Shoes and clothes and tires may be unsold or sold at "bargain" prices that leave no profit. But Coca-Cola knows that its 900,000 distributors are almost certain to sell in the neighborhood of 30,000,000 gallons of syrup per year, and that their

9,500,000 drinks per day will be dispensed at the guaranteed price of five cents. A nickel for Coca-Cola is so logical that it is inevitable. No retailer (except a few concessionaires) charges more; and it is doubtful whether there would be more sales at four cents than at five. Barring the rise of a major competitor in its own field (and the company has seen more than 1,100 trade-marked soft drinks come and go) Coca-Cola's outlet control is so complete that inventory crises can hardly arise. The price of its syrup is on a sliding scale, varying with the price of sugar. Coca-Cola, world's largest granulated sugar consumer, buys 150,000,000 pounds of sugar a year. But every pound of sugar is disposed of at a certain and a predictable profit.

A further striking illustration of Coca-Cola simplification is seen in the fact that the company does not even do its own bottling. For every nine distributors of Coca-Cola, eight sell the bottle, one sells the glass. The glass-seller (the soda-dispenser in 110,000 U. S. soda fountains) is supplied by the Coca-Cola company (through 2,000 jobbers). But the bottle-seller (who numbers more than 800,000) buys not the syrup but the finished drink, and buys from a bottler who is, in most instances, wholly independent of the Atlanta concern. True, this bottler buys his syrup, directly or indirectly, from Coca-Cola, but he does his own bottling in his own bottles and makes (or loses) his own money on his own investment.

The business of bottling Coca-Cola was begun in 1899 by two Chattanoogans—Mr. Joseph Whitehead and Mr. B. F. Thomas. In addition to being Coca-Cola drinkers, Messrs. Whitehead and Thomas were also baseball addicts, and found their pleasure at the ball park distressingly diminished by the absence of their favorite drink. They went to Mr. Candler, pointed out that bottled Coca-Cola would have many more points of contact with the public than fountain Coca-Cola could ever hope for, and suggested the bottled drink. Mr. Candler therefore gave them a perpetual franchise to sell bottled Coca-Cola throughout the U. S. (except in New England, where an exclusive sales agent had already been appointed), the bottlers to look after all the bottling and Mr. Candler merely to supply the syrup. Later Mr. Whitehead and Mr. Thomas divided the country between them, and in turn franchised a great many sub-bottlers in many cities and every state. The original bottlers (called *parent* bottlers) now have about 1,250 children. There was at one time an independent New England bottler who, however, made no great progress, with the result that the Coca-Cola company purchased his business and is therefore its own bottler in New England. Canadian and other foreign bottling is also in the hands of the Atlanta company, and a subsidiary operates in Utah and California.

Now it can be argued that Mr. Candler made a terrible error in letting the bottling rights get out of his hands. There are Coca-Cola bottling fortunes (notably in the Whitehead, Thomas, and Lupton families) just as there are Coca-Cola syrup fortunes. The Coca-Cola company supplies parent bottlers with syrup at $1.35 cents a gallon. Now let us suppose that a bottler puts up 500,000 gallons a year (which is about the production of the New Orleans bottler). This amount of syrup makes about 2,167,000 cases of Coca-Cola, with twenty-four bottles to the case. The retailer pays 80 cents a case, so the bottler receives $1,730,000 on a syrup investment of $675,000. He must, of course, buy his carbonic gas and maintain his bottling plant, but (provided he gets back his empty bottles to refill) he makes on his business a very fine profit. Indeed, his franchise to bottle Coca-Cola is a privilege upon which he can borrow money at the bank, and which he can sell at from $7 to $12 per gallon bottled per year. In other words, our New Orleans bottler has a franchise worth (at a $10 a gallon median figure) some $5,000,000; and a franchise which any New Orleans bank would accept as good collateral. If Coca-Cola did its own bottling, it would get the bottling profit as well as the syrup profit, and perhaps make another $13,000,000 a year.

The flaw in this otherwise excellent argument is that it interprets the past in terms of the present. Simplicity of manufacture and distribution permitted the original Coca-Cola company to concentrate, with phenomenal success, on sales and advertising. To have developed the bottling business as well would have produced a terrific strain on Candler energy and Candler capital. Then, too, Coca-Cola franchises were not worth much in their early years. It was because the bottler has from Coca-Cola a *perpetual* license —something which made Coca-Cola bottling his business and not the business of some distant corporation—that he was willing to go out and sweat not for the Coca-Cola company but for himself. Consider, for contrast, the relations between the usual automobile dealer and the usual automobile manufacturer. The automobile dealer is usually overloaded with a sales quota of the manufacturer's devising; he goes out of business with disturbing frequency and marked ill-will. It is true that the Coca-Cola company today, with its product universally established and its treasury overflowing, would doubtless be delighted to buy out its bottlers at almost any figure. But if we consider Mr. Candler's decision in the light of conditions existing thirty-three years ago, it may rather be applauded as a master-stroke than deplored as an error.

At any rate, whether for better or for worse, the Coca-Cola company is only mildly in the bottling business, and can still devote its major attention to advertising and promotion. Advertising is, from many standpoints, the most vital element in Coca-Cola effort, but there is no corresponding interest in Coca-Cola's advertising story because other advertisers are now doing much the same thing. It is true that Coca-Cola was one of the earliest of large-scale advertisers. Even Dr. Pemberton, in that first Coca-Cola year during which he sold only twenty-five gallons of syrup, spent $46 (or about 90 per cent of his income) on advertising. His 1887 bill of sale included such items as 1,600 posters, 14 oilcloth signs, 45 tin signs, 500 street car cards, and one stencil plate of Coca-Cola's signature. The oil-cloth sign, attached to drug-store awnings by safety-pins, was indeed one of the earliest attempts at "point of purchase" advertising. Coca-Cola originated also the "festoon" (artificial foliage draped around the rear section, or back-bar of the soda fountain) and pioneered in distributing cut-outs of the soda-dispenser, with his white uniform, his soldier-cap, and his winning smile. During 1930 the name Coca-Cola was brought to the attention of the public five hundred million times in letters varying from 1/16 of an inch to sky-written characters one mile in height. It was written in glass, paint, gold, fibre, cardboard, leather, bone, wood, and flowers. Coca-Cola advertisements were painted on

20,000 walls and 160,000 posters; more than 5,000,000 Coca-Cola glasses were sold (at cost) to U. S. fountains: 400,000,000 magazine and newspaper pages carried the Coca-Cola "message," and a radio campaign, featuring Sportswriter Grantland Rice, was broadcast on fifty-four National Broadcasting Co. stations. Coca-Cola advertising is marked by simplicity (the name itself is, in many instances, the entire advertisement, and some variation of "delicious and refreshing" is always the burden of the song) and by a disposition to make "dealer helps" truly helpful by concentrating the advertising in the dealer's store and pointing it directly toward his benefit. Indeed, Coca-Cola salesmen are known as "service men." They preach the gospel of Cold and of Cleanliness (the two major items in the sale of carbonated beverages); they go behind the soda fountain and show the dispenser how his job should be conducted. Both Western Electric and Eastman Kodak regard a Coca-Cola talking-cinema on fountain operation as a model of the industrial film.

It would be rather tearing a passion to tatters to maintain that the Coca-Cola company is responsible for the growth of the soda fountain. Yet there is no question but that Coca-Cola and the fountain have grown side by side and that it has always been the Coca-Cola policy to work for increased fountain sales, Coca-Cola relying upon its own merit to attract its portion of whatever fountain volume may be built up. Roughly speaking, about six persons out of every ten who enter a store containing a fountain make a fountain purchase, and nearly three of the six get Coca-Colas. In 1898, soda fountain sales totaled $100,000. In 1930 they were safely past the two billion dollar landmark.

Presumably the time will come when the U. S. public will place $3,000,000,000 on the marble tops of many fountains. And of that third billion dollars Coca-Cola will doubtless get its share.

All of which brings us back to Atlanta, Georgia, and to the Coca-Cola company as it is today. The company currently revolves about two individuals—President Robert Winship Woodruff and Executive Vice President Harrison Jones. Mr. Jones (who is no relative of Robert Tyre Jones Jr., nor of Turner Jones, Coca-Cola advertising manager) was an Atlanta lawyer who handled certain legal work associated with the 1919 sale so successfully that he was persuaded to abandon his law practice and move to the Coca-Cola building. He is a very large gentleman who masks a kindly and patient disposition with a slightly ferocious exterior and a vocabulary more graphic than recordable. It is Mr. Jones who listens to the white folks' troubles, and who gets the colored folks out of jail. Yet Mr. Jones who is everybody's friend, is thereby no less everybody's boss. There is something very forthright about Mr. Jones. He condemns with equal clarity and vigor the dash-dash-dashes who persist in raising sixteen-cent cotton to sell at ten cents a pound; the dash-dash-dashes who uneconomically cultivate beet sugar when the supply of cane sugar is adequate for the world's needs, and the dash-dash-dash double dashes who cover wasteful production costs by an exorbitant tariff and provoke world-wide discrimination against U. S. merchandise. Well-read, well-traveled, well-grounded, Mr. Jones is the epitome of the national and international viewpoint now prevailing in Coca-Cola's home.

Very different is Mr. Robert Woodruff, though equally cosmopolitan. Where Mr. Jones forever appears to be about to hit something with an ax (which he never does) Mr. Woodruff forever appears to be about to go to sleep (which he seldom does). He is another large man (though not quite so large as Mr. Jones); slow-spoken (though with no southern drawl and hardly a southern accent). A characteristic photograph would snap him in the act of looking out the window while filling a pipe. Nothing disturbs Mr. Woodruff (except the accusation of being a rich man's son) and nothing is more evident than his ability to stand on his own feet quite aside from the question as to where Father Ernest Woodruff's feet may be located. Atlantans not in the Coca-Cola employ will inform you that the merger which produced in the First National Bank, Atlanta's largest financial institution, was a project which the elder Mr. Woodruff cherished for many years; which the younger Mr. Woodruff put through with a maximum of rapidity and a minimum of friction. Nor was Mr. Woodruff's career with White Motors even remotely connected with the paternal influence. Before joining the White company, Mr. Woodruff was purchasing agent for the Atlanta Ice & Coal Co. (a Woodruff family company) and there exists one tale concerning a difference of opinion between father and son regarding the number of White trucks the younger Mr. Woodruff was purchasing from his good friend Walter White. At any rate, Robert Woodruff exchanged ice and coal for trucks and buses, and in the course of events became White's vice president. When, in 1923, he was called home to take over the enterprise to which a large portion of the family finances had been entrusted, marked was the disturbance in Cleveland and many were the protests. Then, in 1929, came Walter C. White's sudden and tragic death, and Mr. Woodruff's decision to operate White Motors with one hand and Coca-Cola with the other. During the whole depressed year of 1930, Mr. Woodruff functioned in his dual capacity; spent three nights out of four on Pullmans (usually taking the Big Four through Cincinnati and Chattanooga); finally located (in Ashton Bean) a man to whom he felt the White business could be entrusted, and returned to his Coca-Cola presidency as a full-time job, though he is today Chairman of the White board. It should also be noticed that the Coca-Cola company this winter added to its directorate Walter Teagle, White director and president of Standard of New Jersey.

"It wasn't so difficult," said Mr. Woodruff, regarding his dual rôle as transportation and beverage executive. "It was mostly a matter of working all the time. I mean the time you would take for a vacation, you just didn't take. You kept on working, you see. That was all there was to it, really." Mr. Woodruff also subscribes enthusiastically to the standard formula of the modest executive—the argument that finding the proper lieutenants is the captain of industry's major occupation. Said Mr. Woodruff optimistically, "You get yourself a good man and you're all right." Everything was going all right here. And everything will go all right in Cleveland with Mr. Bean there. I don't think we'll have very much trouble from now on."

Having no trouble means for Mr. Woodruff more time to hunt. Avidly interested in sports of all types, a plus-average golfer (i.e. 85 to 90), a director of the Atlanta base-ball club, and close friend of Tyrus Raymond Cobb, hot-tempered Georgian who was perhaps baseball's all-time "greatest," Mr. Woodruff is happiest with a gun in the hand and a bird on the wing. In South Georgia he has a 30,000 acre plantation, called Ichaway (named from the Ichaway Notchaway River, Indian for "where the deer sleep") where, with Walter Teagle and Bill Potter (Guaranty Trust of New York) and a few others he shoots quail and forgets industry. When (as often) he is patronizing the Pullmans, he lunches on sardines and saltines, sleeps through the afternoon, dines adequately, and is then ready to work all night, much to the discomfort of his traveling companions. He is in his early forties, notably good-looking, but a difficult subject either for camera or artist because his personality centers about an animation which disappears in repose.

Some five years ago Mr. Woodruff decided to turn his salesmen into service men, to accent the building up of fountains rather than the taking of orders. So he collected his entire sales force and announced that there were not going to be any more Coca-Cola salesmen and so they did not have any more jobs. He added, however, that there would be established a new department concerning which he would be glad to talk to them on the following day. The salesmen went back to homes or hotels, uneasily awaited developments. On the following morning, Mr. Woodruff explained his idea of a service staff, invited all the salesmen to submit applications for positions on it. Needless to say, the applications were almost universally submitted and accepted, but no service man received the same territory on which he had previously functioned as salesman, and the psychological result of the temporary dismissal was far more potent than a mere announcement of a change in title. A maximum of labor with a minimum of perspiration is perhaps the simplest description of Mr. Woodruff's functioning.

Thus Coca-Cola past and Coca-Cola present; as to Coca-Cola future, the company seems as soundly established and as prosperously busy as well may be. The very absence either of an excessive sweetness or of a single pervasive flavor (such as chocolate, vanilla, cherry or what not) appears to be a major Coca-Cola asset. For while Coca-Cola is certainly nothing that children cry for, it is certainly something of which its consumers seem never to tire. The ordinary soft drink shows sales increases for three years; holds its own for two years; then goes into a decline either gradual or rapid but always uninterrupted. Coca-Cola, in its 46th year, shows no sign of hardened arteries, of fading vogue. "Take five drinks and you'll like it" is Coca-Cola's private slogan, and presumably five million advertising dollars are sufficient to hurdle whatever barrier the first four drinks may establish.

Certainly Coca-Cola's financial statements are adequate testimonials to a national acceptance. Shares priced at $40 in 1919 were quoted at 140 in the low 1931 market, even taking into account a 2-for-1 split up. There has also been a stock dividend of one Class A share worth about $50, and the annual dividend has never been omitted. The man who put $40 into Coca-Cola in 1919 could for all the depression sell out today with about a $400 return on his investment.

INDEX

INDEX